Any Way You Cut It

Rural America

Hal S. Barron
David L. Brown
Kathleen Neils Conzen
Carville Earle
Cornelia Butler Flora
Donald Worster

Series Editors

Any Way You Cut It

Meat Processing and Small-Town America

Edited by

Donald D. Stull

Michael J. Broadway

David Griffith

 University Press of Kansas

© 1995 by the University Press of Kansas

Published by the University Press of Kansas (Lawrence, Kansas 66049),
which was organized by the Kansas Board of Regents and is operated
and funded by Emporia State University, Fort Hays State University,
Kansas State University, Pittsburg State University, the University of
Kansas, and Wichita State University

Library of Congress Cataloging-in-Publication Data

Any way you cut it : meat processing and small-town America / edited
    by Donald D. Stull, Michael J. Broadway, David Griffith.
        p.   cm. — (Rural America)
    Includes bibliographical references and index.
        ISBN 0-7006-0721-8 (alk. paper). — ISBN 0-7006-0722-6 (pbk. :
alk. paper)
    1. Meat industry and trade—United States—Case studies.
2. United States—Rural conditions—Case studies.   3. Rural
development—United States—Case studies.   I. Stull, Donald D.
II. Broadway, Michael J.   III. Griffith, David Craig, 1951–   .
IV. Series: Rural America (Lawrence, Kan.)
HD9415.A68   1995
338.4'76649'00973—dc20   95-259

British Library Cataloguing in Publication Data is available.

Printed in the United States of America

10   9   8   7   6   5   4   3   2   1

The paper used in this publication meets the minimum requirements
of the American National Standard for Permanence of Paper for
Printed Library Materials Z39.48–1984.

Contents

Preface

Until recently, there has been little systematic research into the consequences of the restructuring of the meat-, poultry-, and fish-processing industries. This volume examines the industries' increasing reliance upon workers with diverse ethnic and cultural backgrounds, and their impact upon rural communities. Earlier versions of most of the essays to follow were presented at a conference entitled "New Factory Workers in Old Farming Communities: Costs and Consequences of Relocating Meat Industries," held in Queenstown, Maryland, April 12–14, 1992. Cosponsoring the conference were the Institute for Public Policy and Business Research of the University of Kansas; the Department of Geography, State University of New York at Geneseo; the Department of Anthropology, University of Colorado at Boulder; and the Department of Sociology and Anthropology, University of Nebraska at Omaha.

Twenty-three professionals met to assess what is known about how meat, poultry, and fish processing and their workers are transforming rural America. They represented a wide range of disciplines (anthropology, community and regional planning, economics, geography, health sciences, journalism, policy studies, social welfare, and sociology), and they spoke from differing regional and professional vantage points (research, state and local government, service delivery, the industry, foundations, and agencies). Much of the conference comment underscored the need to assess the current status of knowledge about these industries, their workers, and their host communities, as a prelude to careful consideration of future research as well as public policy options. We hope this collection will extend that dialogue to many others.

We are grateful to the Rural Poverty and Resources Program of the Ford Foundation for funding the conference. We also wish to thank Maureen Kennedy and Julie Marx of the Aspen Institute's Rural Economic Policy Program, who worked closely with us to conceive, plan, and implement the conference.

Many people have contributed to this volume, not the least of whom were the 23 conference participants who provided their keen insights into the modern meat industries. This book would never have been completed without the valuable support of office staff from the editors' respective institutions. Louise Lamphere and Mark Moberg reviewed drafts of this manuscript for the University Press of Kansas and made valuable suggestions for its improvement. *Meat&Poultry* provided many of the photographs. Laura Kriegstrom Poracsky drew the maps.

And when all others failed, Judi Banks came up with the book's title. Her entry fees are forever waived.

Finally, the editors wish to acknowledge our debt to those in the meat industries and host communities who have shared their time and expertise with us over the years.

Contributors

Steve Bjerklie is editor of *Meat&Poultry*, the business journal of the meat and poultry industry in North America. He has written extensively on virtually every issue facing the business, and his hard-hitting editorials are widely quoted in debates ranging from animal welfare to inspection reform to labor management. Bjerklie has interviewed nearly every important leader in the meat and poultry industry in the effort to provide for the readers of *Meat&Poultry* the true pulse of the industry he covers. His interview of IBP chairman Robert Peterson, published in 1990, has been widely cited in the consumer and general business press, and was honored for its excellence by the Western Publishers Association. Under Bjerklie's leadership, *Meat&Poultry* has been recognized with more than a dozen awards for magazine and editorial excellence from a variety of organizations, including the American Business Press, the Western Publishers Association, and the American Meat Institute. "No Way Up?"—his three-part series on the conference that forms the basis for this volume—was named 1992's best series in a trade publication by the Western Publications Association.

Michael J. Broadway is associate professor and chair, Department of Geography, State University of New York at Geneseo. For the past decade he has studied rural industrialization, particularly the impact of the meatpacking industry on small towns in the Midwest. He was a coprincipal investigator of the Ford Foundation's Changing Relations Project in Garden City, Kansas. His findings from Garden City have been published in the *Journal of Cultural Geography, Geography,* and *Urban Anthropology,* and with Donald Stull, he has written two articles in the *Kansas Business Review* and a chapter in *Structuring Diversity,* recently published by the University of Chicago Press. His examination of the impact of Nebraska's Employment and Investment Growth Act appeared in *Great Plains Research,* while his analysis of changes in midwestern communities, where pork-processing plants have reopened using nonunionized labor, was published in *Rural Development Perspectives.*

Lourdes Gouveia is associate professor of sociology at the University of Nebraska-Omaha. For the past several years she has examined the socioeconomic forces and consequences associated with the utilization of Latino workers by IBP, Inc., in Lexington, Nebraska. Her interests are the political economy of development (with emphasis on Latin America), the sociology of food and agriculture, and U.S. Latino/a issues. She coedited *From Columbus to ConAgra: The Globalization of Agriculture and Food*, published in 1994 by the University Press of Kansas.

Mark A. Grey is associate professor of anthropology at the University of Northern Iowa. He received his doctorate in cultural anthropology from the University of Colorado-Boulder. Recently he has conducted research in rural communities of the American Midwest, with a particular interest in the effects of large meatpacking plants. Other research interests include education, ethnic relations, and migration.

David Griffith holds a joint appointment with the Institute for Coastal and Marine Resources and the Department of Sociology and Anthropology at East Carolina University. His research interests lie in low-income populations, fishing communities, labor migration, minorities, and the roles of ethnicity, kinship, and gender in labor control and worker resistance. In recent years he has studied food production processes, including poultry and seafood processing, meatpacking, and agribusiness. He has published on migration, women, labor, minorities, and the expansion of capitalism among peasants and other rural populations in *American Ethnologist, International Migration Review*, and the *Stanford Journal of International Law*. His book about low-wage labor in the seafood- and poultry-processing industries, entitled *Jones's Minimal: Low-Wage Labor in the United States*, was published by the State University of New York Press in 1993. A second book, *Working Poor: Farmworkers in the United States*, was published by Temple University Press in 1994.

Robert A. Hackenberg is professor of anthropology and director of the doctoral program in medical anthropology at the University of Colorado-Boulder. He also serves as faculty associate in the Native American Mental Health Research Center and the health and behavioral science doctoral program of the University of Colorado Health Sciences Center. His recent research is focused on design of delivery systems for providing primary health care to underserved Native American and Hispanic communities in the rural Southwest and Denver metropolitan areas. His previous work in development anthropology includes direction of USAID, World Bank, and Ford Foundation projects ranging from population planning and urban squatter resettlement (Philippines) to agribusiness management and employment generation (Panama). He is past chair of the National Institutes of Health Study Section on Social Science and Population Research and member of the National Research Council Assembly of Behavioral and Social Sciences.

Bob Hall, research director of the Institute for Southern Studies, has conducted a variety of environmental and occupational-health studies over the past 20 years. He joined the institute in 1970, after receiving a master's degree from Columbia University. Mr. Hall is founding editor of the institute's quarterly journal, *Southern Exposure*, which has won many awards and earned a national reputation for its investigative coverage of social concerns and its sensitivity to grassroots movements. The journal's series on the poultry industry's impact on workers, farmers, and consumers won the 1990 National Magazine Award for public-interest reporting. In addition to coauthoring the poultry series, he has had articles in publications ranging from the *New York Times* and the *Columbia Journalism Review* to the *St. Petersburg Times* and the *Nation*. Among the books Mr. Hall has conspired to produce are *Environmental Politics: Lessons from the Grassroots; Working Lives*, a labor history of the South; and the 1991–92 *Green Index*, which analyzes environmental conditions and policies in all 50 states. Hall and the institute have also been deeply involved in a number of community-based projects that address rural workplace conditions, including the Brown Lung Association from the mid-1970s and the Healing Hands Project for poultry workers in central North Carolina. In 1992, Mr. Hall was named a MacArthur Fellow.

Gary Kukulka is associate professor of clinical sciences and rural health research at the West Virginia School of Osteopathic Medicine in Lewisburg. He directs the introduction to family medicine curriculum, and is responsible for establishing and conducting research in rural health and primary care and supporting the medical school's role in community-based programs and medical education. Formerly he served as senior staff associate at the National Rural Health Association, Kansas City, Missouri.

Donald D. Stull is professor and chair of anthropology and research fellow in the Institute for Public Policy and Business Research of the University of Kansas. From 1988 to 1990 he led a team of six social scientists from four universities in a study of ethnic relations in Garden City, Kansas, as part of a national project funded by the Ford Foundation. Many of their findings appeared in a special issue of *Urban Anthropology*, entitled "When the Packers Came to Town" (vol. 19, no. 4, 1990). During the early 1990s, Stull studied rural industrialization and rapid growth in Lexington, Nebraska. Most recently, he has served as an applied workplace ethnographer for a major meatpacking firm.

Any Way You Cut It

1 | Introduction: Making Meat

David Griffith
Michael J. Broadway
Donald D. Stull

IN AUSTIN, MINNESOTA, the Hormel hog-processing plant held the loyalty of its workers for decades. George Hormel and his family lived in Austin and participated in community events alongside women and men who bloodied butchers' aprons in his plant. Hormel's union-negotiated wage rates and incentive programs allowed line workers and bosses alike to live next door to one another in Austin's middle-class neighborhoods. Hormel's executives, supervisors, and line and clerical workers earned salaries within a few thousand dollars of one another; their children played together, learned together, celebrated rites of passage together.

But the Hormel family's community spirit did not last. In late 1985 and early 1986, responding to labor unrest and a drawn-out strike by Chapter P-9 of the United Food and Commercial Workers Union (UFCW), Hormel Meat expanded its recruiting beyond Austin and southern Minnesota into rural communities of northern Iowa. Across the state line, personnel managers hoped to find young men and women, unemployed or dispossessed by the farm crisis, who would work for wages that had been recently reduced from over $15 to under $9 an hour (Hage and Klauda 1988). Equally important, they hoped to find recruits unsympathetic with the collective bargaining positions of Hormel's unionized workers. In and around Austin, too many knew of the wage concessions workers had willingly accepted in the late 1970s to help finance modernization of the plant.

Before the strike, restructuring in the meatpacking industry caused both labor and management to reevaluate their competitive position. Together they decided to modernize, both sides recognizing that meatpacking in the United States was undergoing a profound change. Beginning in the 1960s, new low-cost competitors emerged, building high-tech plants in rural areas close to the supply of beef and pork and using nonunion labor forces. In the wake of this competition, older companies, like Hormel, either closed their plants or sought concessions from their workers. Austin's residents were well aware of the workers' sacrifices. Later, community members remembered management's refusal to honor the earlier terms of modernization, precipitating the strike.

Management's decision to recruit "scabs" from Iowa represented more than a search for a more pliant labor force. Hormel became mired in the transition from one form of corporate involvement in rural communities to another. Today, a few corporations headquartered in metropolitan centers dictate the industry's wages, working conditions, and production schedules. No longer can the larger food-processing plants meet their labor needs solely with workers native to the community. Whether plants relocate to new regions of the country or old plants recruit from beyond the region or even outside the nation's boundaries, today's food-processing plants rarely assume a benign position in relation to a community's demographic profile, housing stock, infrastructure, or health care facilities.

Food Processing Industries and Rural Development

Rural poverty and population decline are endemic to much of rural America. In trying to deal with these problems, economic development strategies focus on adding value to raw agricultural materials by attracting food-processing plants. The U.S. Department of Agriculture (USDA) predicts that meat, poultry, and fish processing will play crucial roles in the economies of many rural communities in the coming years (Brown, Petrulis, and Majchrowicz 1991). The works in this volume, constituting in-depth examinations of food-processing plants and workers in several locations across the rural United States, suggest that communities reassess this strategy in light of the ways food-processing firms influence local institutions, infrastructures, and behaviors. They suggest that community planning is necessary to prepare for and temper firms' positions regarding labor control, political influence, and occupational and environmental health. Over the past three decades, a handful of large corporations such as Cargill, ConAgra, and IBP have emerged to dominate the food-processing industry through horizontal and vertical integration and industrial restructuring. Such companies are difficult to regulate, direct, or influence, especially when they represent major sources of employment.

Food-processing firms depend on a ready supply of willing labor, no less today than when Upton Sinclair shocked the nation with *The Jungle*. Despite increased automation, meat, poultry, and fish processing remain labor-intensive. Today's major food-processing companies still draw their workers from among minorities, new immigrants, refugees, and women. Between 1990 and 1991 there were 2,400 new jobs in meatpacking as well as 12,800 in poultry slaughter and processing (U.S. Bureau of the Census 1993). One out of sixteen new industrial jobs in the United States is in a poultry plant. Almost 50 percent of America's 150,000 poultry workers are women, the majority African-American (Kwik 1991).

The composition of the labor force varies across industries and regions—native African-American women in catfish processing, newcomer Latinos and Southeast Asians in meatpacking, Latino and Haitian immigrants in some poultry plants in the Southeast (Griffith 1989, 1993). These employment patterns reflect targeted recruitment as well as recent changes in the character and enforcement of immigration laws. This confluence of public and corporate policies determines the composition and stability of the labor force, which in turn influence the cultural, ethnic, and linguistic makeup of host communities. Labor-force stability, although affected by governmental policies such as the 1990 Immigration Act, is largely dictated by corporate strategies.

According to the Occupational Safety and Health Administration (OSHA), meat-, poultry-, and fish-processing jobs are among the most hazardous in America. In 1990 the probability of incurring an injury in a meatpacking plant was three times higher than for manufacturing workers as a whole (U.S. Department of Labor 1992). A principal cause of excessive injury is the speed of the disassembly line along which carcasses are processed. Workers make thousands of repetitive motions each day, leading to cumulative trauma disorders, the most common being carpal tunnel syndrome.

As people across the country agonize over rising health care costs and the transfer of health care from the private to the public sector, injury rates in meat, poultry, and seafood processing place an added burden upon host communities. Most workers are uninsured until they have worked at a plant for several months. Thereafter they are eligible for the companies' health insurance, but many cannot afford the premiums or the large deductibles and turn to voluntary organizations for health care. This situation is exacerbated by high rates of turnover, which in some plants approach 100 percent a year. Workers injured on the job before becoming eligible for health insurance are frequently unable to pay for their own health care and resort to governmental and nongovernmental agencies for care.

Rural communities that attract new meat- and fish-processing plants can also expect to be confronted with school overcrowding, homelessness, housing shortages, elevated unemployment, crime, and social disorders (Broadway and Stull 1991). And the many Latin, Asian, and Caribbean laborers upon whom these industries increasingly depend often pose unprecedented linguistic and cultural challenges for schools, law enforcement officials, and the agencies that attempt to serve their needs. Food-processing plants' reliance on governmental agencies and nonprofit organizations to meet a portion of their workers' needs constitutes an added burden on the public, an informal kind of subsidy.

Economic Impacts

Food-processing workers rarely earn a "living wage"—one sufficient for workers to reproduce their households. The income needs for labor-force reproduction approximate federally established poverty levels, the income necessary to feed, clothe, and shelter a family of four. Gross annual incomes from meatpacking jobs usually fall a few thousand dollars above or below these levels; income in poultry processing is less, while in fish processing earnings can fall to half of established poverty levels. These income estimates all assume workers will enjoy full employment, but seasonal slowdowns in demand, occasional plant closings, and occupational injuries reduce time on the job and hence reduce annual earnings.

Without alternative survival mechanisms, food-processing workers are encouraged to employ economic strategies that either increase household income or reduce household consumption. Sometimes this stimulates entrepreneurial behaviors, leading family members to develop small businesses to make ends meet. These businesses thrive on the very ethnic enclaves plants have constructed through their recruitment practices, meeting worker demands for spices, home remedies, clothing, linguistic services, culture brokers, revolving credit, and folk methods of physical therapy and psychological counseling borrowed from natal communities. Other ways of making ends meet are less heartening. Drug dealing and prostitution attract and haunt populations living at the margins of existence. People from foreign cultural and linguistic backgrounds make easy prey for con artists drawn from among those with even slightly superior linguistic and cultural skills. Living in poorly secured housing, the working poor become particularly vulnerable to the lure of burglary and petty theft, at the same time becoming crime's victims.

The working poor also adapt by lowering their consumption thresholds. Typically, they submit to overcrowded, deteriorating housing. They trim food budgets and adopt lower standards for mental and physical health, putting up with sickness and putting off medical attention. Another response to low wages and high rates of occupational injury is migration. Locally, low-wage workers may "migrate" among several food-processing plants or between food-processing jobs and informal economic activities. Migration also occurs at regional and international levels, especially among workers from Mexico who migrate between different agricultural sectors: between agricultural harvest work, fruit and vegetable packing, and meat and poultry processing (Griffith and Kissam 1994).

Yet a far more politically significant way migrant workers deal with poverty and occupational injury is by returning periodically to their sending regions. They become cyclical migrants, moving between their low-wage jobs and regions with lower costs of living. Among Latino workers, cyclical migration generally involves crossing international boundaries and stimulates a variety of problems and opportunities. The most commonly noted effects of cyclical international labor migration involve the reproductive costs of labor: simply, governments and communities of sending countries like Mexico bear the costs of raising workers and providing some training for their entry into the labor force, yet the industries and governments of the receiving, usually richer, countries reap the benefits of their labor and tax revenues. While the sending regions receive migrants' remittances, as well as earnings from returning migrants, these earnings tend to be channeled into the reproductive costs of labor or into "cosmetic" development (Griffith 1985; Reichert 1981; Rhodes 1978). The conspicuous consumption that cyclical migrants, returning home, display encourages more emigration, especially from poorer regions (Massey et al. 1987).

Policy Issues

Rural communities that host food-processing facilities are frequently marginal. They often suffer from decades of environmental deterioration—physically, economically, demographically, and socially. Processing plants, while promising economic development, bring their own environmental costs. Unlike the Hormel family earlier in this century, today's company managers remain largely absentee, answering to stockholders instead of community members. Located far from the plants, they find it convenient to avoid community involvement and deny responsibility for deteriorating conditions.

The problems appear intractable. Yet communities are far from powerless in dealing with major food processors; indeed, industries locate in particular locales because of their special resources, such as water and livestock. These resources allow communities to bargain on favorable terms with potential employers. And research can be an important resource for community leaders as they formulate policies and bargain with industry executives. Regional planning and development strategies offer broader perspectives within which such negotiations may occur.

Governmental agencies divide responsibility for aspects of the problem. Acronyms for official functionaries permeate plant, neighborhood, and community: OSHA, INS, DOL, USDA, FDA, HHS, HCFA.[1] Countless others—public and private; local, state, and federal—are continuously involved. There are also more subtle impacts on local governments, such as increases in policing immigrant neighborhoods due to native xenophobia, pressures to tighten or relax housing codes, and problems arising from general cultural misunderstanding. Yet no single department or office combines the missions required to simultaneously address the policy issues emerging from the interplay of industries, communities, and workers. Industry survival, maintenance of communities, health care, and income support for workers and their families require development of a policy agenda and action program.

Theoretical Issues

Using immigrants, refugees, women, and minority workers in food processing is nothing new. Sinclair's novel *The Jungle* and Steinbeck's *Cannery Row* share the shelves with recent books entitled *Cannery Captives* and newspaper exposés on "The Gripes of Rath." Packers brought blacks to Chicago to break unions during the 1930s and 1940s; today they are bringing Mexican and Southeast Asian immigrants to Iowa. The industry's use of culturally distinct groups of workers against one another still involves shifting the balance of power between labor and capital, as the Hormel struggle so clearly indicates.

Social scientists discuss this well-known practice in the context of split labor-market theory. Bonacich (1972) coined this term in a study of southern African-American migration to northern industries (including meatpacking) where unions were establishing extensive power bases. In split labor markets, new workers, different from current workers in terms of ethnic or social backgrounds, are brought in to undermine organized, established labor by promoting ethnic antagonisms. New workers, like new immigrants, are more susceptible to labor-control mechanisms simply because they haven't had time to interpret the industry's behavior or to calculate the costs of resistance or militancy. Examples include "hillbillies" from Appalachia in the auto industry; women, Chinese, Filipinos, Mexicans, and college students in the salmon canneries of Alaska; and Jewish immigrants in the turpentine farms of northern Florida (Daniel 1972; Gordon, Edwards, and Reich 1982).

Split labor-market theory is one of a family of theoretical positions that criticizes neoclassical economic models of labor by conceiving of labor and labor markets in the context of divisive social and cultural processes that compartmentalize workers. These positions include segmented labor-market theory, the dual labor-market hypothesis, and colonized minority models; they differ from one another in terms of such factors as the nature of the benefits of dividing labor markets, the effects on the quality of labor control (simple, technological, or bureaucratic), and how the costs and benefits of segmenting workers are distributed within the production process. Edwards (1973) has argued that some workers in the production process may benefit from "splitting" or segmenting the labor market, because the savings accumulated from hiring low-wage immigrant or minority workers can be passed on to a more privileged part of the labor force. At the very least, the new workers complement the entire labor process by assuming low-paying, low-status positions in "internal" labor markets or firm hierarchies. Not only does this allow companies to stay in business and remain competitive, but the higher profits derived from extracting greater surplus values from the disadvantaged portion of the labor force may be partially redistributed to the established workers. In short, the presence of the new, disadvantaged workers allows management to give regular pay raises to more established workers. U.S. businesses have used this logic recently to justify the North American Free Trade Agreement (NAFTA) by arguing that relocating a portion of their production in Mexico allows them to preserve jobs for U.S. workers.

The other benefit disadvantaged workers bring to established workers is less material in nature: they offer the psychological benefit of occupying lower positions in internal labor markets. This allows established workers to feel superior within the firm's hierarchy and even empowered, despite weak positions relative to management. Meat-, poultry-, and fish-processing labor forces are often divided into "core" and "marginal" workers. Core workers tend to be longtime, native employees who offer stability to plant labor forces, while marginal workers sustain higher rates of turnover. Within each group, as well as cutting across them, are differences based on gender, race, ethnicity, nationality, and legal status. Recruitment strategies combine "free-market" movements of labor into the plants with practices designed to construct docile, highly productive, vulnerable workforces. Single mothers and foreign-born agricultural workers in Lexington, Nebraska; Southeast Asian refugees in Storm Lake, Iowa, and Garden City, Kansas; Latinos in Gainesville, Georgia, and Oriental, North Carolina—they all occupy cornerstones of plant recruiting strategies. Different groups exhibit different degrees of vulnerability to injury, to plant policies regulating workers' space and time, and to management's ability to control workers' lives beyond the walls of the plant. At the same time, these differences entail degrees of potential empowerment for workers.

Despite their differences, these theoretical positions all recognize that labor-market segmentation builds on those differences based on objective social and cultural attributes: race, gender, ethnicity, class, legal status. These theoretical positions can be criticized on at least two related grounds, however. First, they put the intentions and behaviors of the firm at the heart of the construction and transformation of labor markets, paying scant attention to the resistance of workers who are victimized by these processes or the influences of cultural backgrounds on the way the industry goes about its business in rural America. Second, they have not successfully merged labor-market dynamics with the growth of transnational households, networks, and communities or the corresponding cycles of injury and therapy that result in the multiple survival strategies developing in what June Nash (1994:9) calls "the nexus between subsistence economies and market production." As companies further manipulate labor and embark on more comprehensive labor-control strategies, workers grow less likely to consider their occupations or even their union membership as a central part of their identity. Allegiance, loyalty, and affiliation run in other directions, toward the "imagined communities" of ethnicities and diasporas (Anderson 1983; Chavez 1994). If companies do little to show loyalty to or establish roots in communities, surely their workers cannot be expected to show loyalty or put down roots in the company. In a most contradictory manner, these forces bring labor and management together in ways that encourage them to pull apart.

Back in "The Jungle"

The chapters in this volume begin with insights from segmented labor-market theory while striving to carry these insights further, beyond the confines of the labor process. They constitute studies of communities within communities: of the constructed communities of food-processing plant workers, managers, and their families within the larger communities with names like Garden City, Lexington, Storm Lake, Gainesville, and Oriental. As community studies of sorts, they cannot confine themselves to mere tests of segmented labor-market theory. Instead, they address the more diffuse, comprehensive transformations taking place as food-processing plants relocate in new rural areas or initiate demographic and cultural changes in communities they have inhabited for decades.

This manner of exposition—community-within-community studies—derives from the professional orientation, common among anthropologists, to consider local and apparently small-scale processes in relation to national and international developments. We understand that community processes reflect, yet deviate from, changes taking place throughout the nation. Particularly alarming has been the expansion of food oligopolies into supplying agricultural producers with feeds, chemicals, and other inputs necessary to raise cattle, poultry, hogs, and aquacultured fish. This has consolidated contract production (subcontracting) in the poultry industry and encouraged the growth of contract production of hogs and cattle as well. By standardizing the production of birds and meats, these companies have created products recognized by most consumers, including intermediate consumers such as grocers and restaurant owners, thus setting industry standards and forcing other producers to conform to the large processors' practices. These practices include how firms interact with labor and with the communities that host the plants.

The following two chapters set the stage for the community studies: Michael Broadway's overview of structural and locational changes in food processing and Steve Bjerklie's assessment of major problems facing the meat and poultry industries. Broadway explores how major technological innovations within the meat-, poultry-, and fish-processing industries have altered the relationship between capital and labor and given companies greater geographic mobility in selecting sites for their facilities. As firms become more vertically integrated and capital more concentrated, productivity gains have compromised worker safety. Broadway provides a national perspective on shifting plant locations within each of the industries and the role of local factors in industry decisions. Within beefpacking, for example, a plentiful water supply is essential for a modern plant with a large slaughter capacity. But many communities, while possessing the necessary physical attributes to attract a plant, frequently lack access to a sufficient supply of labor for industries with high turnover. To resolve this problem, workers are recruited from outside the region, often from refugee and immigrant populations.

Bjerklie describes the tendency of the meat and poultry industries to withdraw into themselves, adopting defensive positions toward government inspectors, critics, and those who know little about the industry from the point of view of the head office. Again and again he raises the industry's vulnerability to commodity economics and profit margins of 1 to 2 percent, presenting these against a background of the difficulties of marketing, international competition, and product safety. Backed against a wall of governmental regulation and negative public image, the meat and poultry industry, Bjerklie argues, has become entrenched in rural secrecy and adopted a hard line against any public scrutiny.

Between Bjerklie's defense of the industry and the community studies, Stull and Broadway focus more narrowly on the occupational illness and injury that plague meatpacking, arriving at solutions based on expansions and revisions of current attempts to improve worker safety. Among the industry methods of dealing with worker safety are strategies designed to keep the reporting of injuries (and insurance premiums) low, encouraging workers to avoid filing workers' compensation claims. Stull and Broadway note that the drive for higher productivity and continued high rates of worker turnover undermine any earnest attempts to reduce occupational hazards. With this focus, they raise the issue of how worker safety becomes enmeshed in other concerns and dependent on state and local custom and law. This theme is retrieved in each of the community studies that follow.

Gouveia and Stull document the varied forces that gave rise to beef processing on the High Plains, and then turn to the problems surrounding the construction of new IBP plants in Lexington, Nebraska, and Garden City, Kansas. Both cities have experienced rapid multicultural growth accompanied by stresses on housing stocks, school systems, and volunteer agencies that serve those who, injured in the plants, find themselves unemployed. The consequent paradox of increased employment combined with increased poverty and occupational injury is, according to Gouveia and Stull, indicative of the growing "post-Fordist" model of development.

Primary among social and cultural stages on which this paradox is performed daily are the networks that form among meat, poultry, and seafood workers. Most food-processing plants rely heavily on network recruiting, which effectively "subcontracts" to workers a portion of the time and effort it takes to locate, relocate, train, and supervise new employees. When network recruiting occurs among new immigrants and refugees, cultural translation may become a central component of the labor process. Grey documents this process in Storm Lake, Iowa, with the emergence of a Tai Dam personnel manager as an intermediary between plant management and recent Lao refugees. The personnel manager, communicating management's positions to labor and labor's positions to management, possesses the capability to represent or misrepresent one to the other based on personal needs. More significantly, this creates a context for cultural brokerage services to extend well beyond the physical and temporal boundaries of the plant. In fact, this Lao personnel manager has taken on a variety of brokerage services for the refugees, using each of the services to his own advantage. Further, when such services become important in the homes of workers as well as in the plant, they begin to assume paternalistic dimensions and draw upon authority based on age and gender in the household (cf. Ong 1987; Griffith 1987, 1993).

The use of labor intermediaries and labor subcontracting has been well documented in labor markets where workers and managers come from different social, cultural, and linguistic backgrounds. U.S. agriculture, which has drawn heavily on immigrant workers on and off since the nineteenth century, is a prime example (Griffith and Kissam 1994). In farm labor, contracting has become so institutionalized that several pieces of legislation have been enacted to regulate contractors. More subtle but equally pervasive labor contracting practices follow immigrants and refugees into food-processing industries, some drawn directly from agriculture. Griffith's chapter on poultry processing in northwestern Georgia and North Carolina notes that poultry plants often draw heavily on workers legalized under the immigration reforms of 1986 and 1990. At least for a time, these workers continue to move between agriculture and food processing.

Similarly, Griffith's chapter on seafood processing examines the use of a little-known "H-2" visa classification to bring in workers from Mexico for seasonal crab picking in Pamlico County, North Carolina. In both the seafood and poultry cases, the use of workers from Mexico and Central America has Latinized workforces, resulting in distinctly new cultural developments in plants and neighborhoods and in increased cyclical migration between sending and receiving regions.

Following the community studies are two chapters that consider public policy in light of the hazardous nature of food processing and other problems associated with the industry. The first, by Robert Hackenberg and Gary Kukulka, address the inherent difficulties of providing adequate primary health care to workers who not only routinely suffer from occupational injuries but also move from place to place in a new kind of transhumance they call "industrial nomadism." They view injury, unemployment, therapy, and reemployment as a cyclical process that facilitates the continued transience of this population, arguing that health problems stem from a severe lack of preventive intervention and routine primary health care. The second in this pair of chapters is by Bob Hall, who, like Steve Bjerklie, comes from a background in journalism. His work constitutes an alternate voice within the more measured, academic texts of the other sections. Hall's article is a condemnation of company practices, followed by recommendations for change. As such, it offers a contrast to the earlier chapter by Bjerklie, which defends many industry practices.

Finally, Robert Hackenberg concludes the volume by comparing and contrasting points raised in the previous chapters. He does this by placing the findings of the community studies squarely within debates over free trade, political economic theory, and the past demise and future promise of labor organizing in the face of increasing international labor migration.

Conclusion

Several themes emerge again and again throughout this volume, all in some way related to our collective attempt to address the central paradox of rural community development based on the routine victimization of workers and communities. High injury rates in food-processing industries inevitably beg questions about the strategies managers and workers adopt to deal with injury. The public subsidies extended to food-processing firms in the form of tax incentives and holidays, job training, and commodity programs call attention to the conflicting roles that state and local governments play in the process of luring hazardous and polluting industries into their midsts. The growing importance of immigrants in these processes ties our discussions into immigration policy, trade negotiations, and economic restructuring.

In most of the chapters, we address these issues as they affect local settings in Kansas, Iowa, Nebraska, Georgia, and North Carolina. But as the chapters by Broadway and Hackenberg demonstrate, the problems confronted by workers and local communities are attributable to powerful macro-level forces, which, nevertheless, can be tempered by creative local responses. Over 15 years ago, in a review of the anthropology of industrial work, Burawoy (1979:233) noted: "In striving for ahistorical generalizations appropriate to all organizations, the concrete world was left behind and industrial anthropology disappeared in a welter of abstract categories." In this volume we hope to reintroduce concrete materials into the work on industrial capitalism without becoming too enmeshed in the detail of the local.

Note

1. The agencies designated by these acronyms are the Occupational Safety and Health Administration; the Immigration and Naturalization Service; the Department of Labor; the U.S. Department of Agriculture; the Food and Drug Administration; Health and Human Services; and the Health Care Finance Act.

References

Anderson, B. 1983. *Imagined Communities.* London: Verso.

Bonacich, E. 1972. A Theory of Ethnic Antagonism: The Split-Labor Market. *American Sociological Review* 37:547–49.

Broadway, M. J., and D. D. Stull. 1991. Rural Industrialization: The Example of Garden City, Kansas. *Kansas Business Review* 14(4):1–9.

Brown, D., M. Petrulis, and A. Majchrowicz 1991. Outlook Dim for Food-Related Job Growth. *Agricultural Outlook* 173:28–30.

Burawoy, M. 1979. The Anthropology of Industrial Work. *Annual Reviews of Anthropology* 8:231–66.

Chavez, L. 1994. The Power of the Imagined Community: The Settlement of Undocumented Mexicans and Central Americans in the United States. *American Anthropologist* 96:52–73.

Daniel, P. 1972. *The Shadow of Slavery.* Urbana: University of Illinois Press.

Edwards, R. 1973. The Labor Process. In *Labor Market Segmentation,* edited by R. Edwards, M. Reich, and D. Gordon. Lexington, Mass.: D. C. Heath.

Gordon, D., R. Edwards, and M. Reich. 1982. *Segmented Work, Divided Workers: The Historical Transformation of Labor in the United States.* New York: Cambridge University Press.

Griffith, D. 1985. Women, Remittances, and Reproduction. *American Ethnologist* 12:676–90.

———. 1987. Nonmarket Labor Processes in an Advanced Capitalist Economy. *American Anthropologist* 89:838–52.

———. 1989. *The Impact of the Immigration Reform and Control Act's Employer Sanctions on the U.S. Meat and Poultry Processing Industries, Final Report.* Binghamton, N.Y.: Institute for Multiculturalism and International Labor, State University of New York.

———. 1993. *Jones's Minimal: Low-Wage Labor in the United States.* Albany: State University of New York Press.

Griffith, D., and E. Kissam. 1994. *Working Poor: Farmworkers in the United States.* Philadelphia: Temple University Press.

Hage, D., and P. Klauda. 1988. *No Retreat, No Surrender: Labor's War on Hormel.* New York: William Morrow and Co.

Kwik, P. 1991. Poultry Workers Trapped in a Modern Jungle. *Labor Notes* 146:1, 14–15.

Massey, D., R. Alarcon, J. Durand, and H. Gonzalez. 1987. *Return to Aztlan: The Social Process of International Migration from Western Mexico*. Berkeley: University of California Press.

Nash, J. 1994. Global Integration and Subsistence Insecurity. *American Anthropologist* 96:7–30.

Ong, A. 1987. *Spirits of Resistance and Capitalist Discipline: Factory Women in Malaysia*. Albany: State University of New York Press.

Reichert, J. 1981. The Migrant Syndrome: Seasonal U.S. Wage Labor and Rural Development in Central Mexico. *Human Organization* 40:56–66.

Rhodes, R. 1978. Intra-European Return Migration and Rural Development: Lessons from the Spanish Case. *Human Organization* 37:95–106.

U.S. Bureau of the Census. 1993. *Census and You*. March. Washington, D.C.: U.S. Government Printing Office.

U.S. Department of Labor, Bureau of Labor Statistics. 1992. *Occupational Injuries and Illnesses in the United States by Industry*. Washington, D.C.: U.S. Government Printing Office.

2 | From City to Countryside

Recent Changes in the Structure and Location of the Meat- and Fish-Processing Industries

Michael J. Broadway

SINCE 1945 AMERICAN INDUSTRY has undergone a number of structural changes. Employment in agriculture and manufacturing has shifted to services, due to the substitution of machinery for labor. Production within individual sectors of the economy is increasingly characterized by oligopoly as a result of mergers and acquisitions. Capital has been redeployed at national and regional levels by corporations as part of a continual search for cheaper production locations (Knox and Agnew 1989). While these structural changes were occurring, the U.S. economy experienced a prolonged crisis. The period from 1972 to 1982 saw high inflation, increased energy costs, international competition, and slow economic growth. In dealing with this crisis, new relationships between capital and labor emerged, with capital recapturing the initiative over wages and regulations (Castells 1988). These changes are exemplified by the U.S. meat- and fish-processing industries. During the 1970s and 1980s, when oligopolies were emerging in the processing of beef, pork, chicken, and among some types of fish, workers' wages declined, while productivity and work-related injuries increased. This chapter examines the geographic consequences of this new relationship between capital and labor in meat and fish processing. Prior to analyzing the geographic dimensions of this restructuring process, some of the technological innovations and corporate strategies that altered the relationship between capital and labor in these industries will be briefly examined.

Technological Innovations

In beefpacking, the innovations associated with the founding of Iowa Beef Packers (now renamed IBP) and its subsequent cost-cutting strat-

Kansas City Stockyards, 1986. The stockyards closed in 1991. (Photograph by Michael J. Broadway)

egies are major factors behind the industry's restructuring. The company was initially financed by a $300,000 grant from the U.S. Small Business Administration in 1960. Twenty years later, IBP had become the largest producer of fresh beef products in the United States (Skaggs 1986). IBP's first plant in Denison, Iowa, revolutionized the industry. Previously, cattle had been shipped by rail from producing areas to terminal locations like Chicago, Kansas City, and St. Paul, where they were then sold and slaughtered in multistoried packinghouses. The Denison plant, by contrast, was located in the center of a large cattle-producing area. This enabled the company to purchase cattle directly from the farmer, eliminating the need for middlemen, and reducing transportation costs and the shrinkage and bruising associated with transporting animals long distances. The plant itself was a one-story structure, which allowed greater automation and the development of a disassembly line, whereby individual workers would be responsible for one task in the preparation of the carcass. This innovation reduced the need for highly skilled (and paid) butchers. Indeed, IBP's founder, A. D. Anderson, admitted, "We've tried to take the skill out of every step" of butchering (*Newsweek* 1985).

In 1967 IBP opened a plant in Dakota City, Nebraska, to produce a new product—boxed beef. Boxed beef increased the company's market share and lowered its transportation costs. Instead of shipping carcasses to its customers, IBP removed fat and bone at the plant, thereby retaining valuable waste materials, such as entrails for pet food, and shipped vacuum-packaged portions according to retail specifications. Vacuum packaging appealed to customers, since it reduces shrinkage, which is caused by exposure to air, and adds to the product's shelf life. The innovation also allowed meat wholesalers and supermarkets to lower their labor costs by eliminating most of their skilled butchers and contributed to an increasing demand for the product. IBP responded by constructing additional large slaughter–capacity plants close to feedlots in the High Plains during the 1970s and 1980s (Broadway and Ward 1990). This type of plant is more economical to operate than smaller packinghouses (Miller 1986).

IBP entered pork processing in 1982 and began applying the same cost-cutting strategies it had pioneered in the beef industry. IBP either constructed large-capacity plants or acquired previously owned plants close to principal hog-producing areas. Worker productivity rose with increased chain speed. The Oscar Mayer plant in Perry, Iowa, slaughtered approximately 750 hogs an hour in the early 1980s; when IBP operated this plant in 1990, the equivalent figure was 900 hogs an hour (Broadway 1992a). The company also replicated its success in boxed beef by producing vacuum-packed pork products.

Innovations in chicken processing followed vertical integration (Heffernan 1984). Poultry firms like Tyson, ConAgra, and Perdue oversee each stage of operation from the hatchery through slaughter to shipping their product to grocery stores. Innovations in genetics and poultry management techniques have halved the time required to raise broilers from 14 weeks in 1940 to 7 weeks or less (Bishop and Christensen 1989). The typical poultry producer contracts out the job of raising the birds to individuals. The firm provides the chicks and feed to the grower and then processes the fully grown bird in its own facilities. Poultry-processing plants share many similarities with beef- and pork-packing facilities: plants with large slaughtering capacities are more economical than smaller ones; the disassembly line is automated; workers are required to make a single defined movement, such as a cut with a knife or scissors; lines are fast—they can run up to 5,400 birds an hour.

Technical innovation has been slower to come to fish processing; it is difficult to produce a standardized product, and harvests vary seasonally and yearly. Companies have found it uneconomical to invest in large-capacity processing plants and not have them operate year-round. Fish processing is also characterized by a wide array of qualitatively and quantitatively distinct entities, from small scallop-shucking houses to tuna canneries and the freezing and breading facilities for producing packaged fish products (Griffith 1993 and this volume). Despite these and other differences between meat and fish processing, the two industries share an obvious similarity—the kill floor. Workers in both industries are required to make split-second cuts along a rapidly moving disassembly line. The result is often personal injury.

Aquaculture is among the most significant innovations in recent years in the fishing industry. In aquaculture, fish are raised in an artificial environment. Catfish, trout, and baitfish are the three leading U.S. aquaculture products by value; catfish is the most important (Dicks and Harvey 1989). Despite rapid growth during the 1980s, the industry still accounted for only 7 percent of all fishery products consumed in the United States by the end of the decade (Wineholt 1990). The industry is vertically integrated, with companies controlling the cost of feed and owning processing plants. These plants are organized like meat-processing facilities with a high-speed disassembly line. Workers are expected to gut 2,000 fish an hour (Bates 1991).

The preceding technical innovations have all helped to increase productivity (Ahmed and Sieling 1987), yet processing workers in all four industries are subject to some of the most unsafe conditions in the American workplace. Injury and illness rates for meatpacking (beef and pork) workers have increased since the 1970s, and meatpacking proved to be the most hazardous industry in America throughout the 1980s. Its incidence rate for injuries and illnesses was triple that for manufacturing as a whole (Personick and Taylor-Shirley 1989). The most common injury among line workers is carpal tunnel syndrome, a disorder that occurs when too much pressure is put on the median nerve that passes through the wrist to the hand. The rapid, repetitive nature of work on the disassembly line is generally credited with the syndrome's high incidence in this industry (see Stull and Broadway, this volume).

TABLE 2.1. Occupational Injury and Illness Rates for Meat- and Fish-Processing Workers, 1975–90 (per 100 full-time workers)

| | INDUSTRY | | | |
	Meatpacking	Poultry Processing	Fish Processing	Manufacturing
1990	42.4	26.9	22.5	13.2
1989	35.1	22.8	24.3	13.1
1988	39.2	19.4	19.7	13.1
1987	38.4	19.0	18.8	11.9
1986	33.4	18.5	18.2	10.6
1985	30.4	18.3	19.2	10.4
1984	33.4	18.8	17.3	10.6
1983	31.4	18.7	17.9	10.0
1982	30.7	17.9	17.1	10.2
1981	32.8	19.3	18.6	11.5
1980	33.5	22.1	19.4	12.2
1979	36.9	23.9	22.0	13.3
1978	32.8	23.6	20.4	13.2
1977	33.6	23.6	20.7	13.1
1976	34.7	23.1	17.7	13.2
1975	31.2	22.8	18.9	13.0

Source: U.S. Department of Labor, Bureau of Labor Statistics, *Occupational Injuries and Illnesses in the United States by Industry* (various years). Washington, D.C.: U.S. Government Printing Office.

Injury and illness rates for poultry- and fish-processing workers in 1990 were only slightly above the levels of the mid-1970s (Table 2.1).[1] Nevertheless, working conditions similar to those in meatpacking prevail in fish- and poultry-processing plants. According to an internal memo at a Perdue poultry-processing plant in North Carolina, it is normal procedure for about 60 percent of the workforce to visit the company nurse each morning to get painkillers and have their hands wrapped (Goldoftas 1989). In Hamlet, North Carolina, in September 1991, 25 workers were killed and 56 injured as a fire swept through the Imperial Food Products chicken-processing plant—many of the workers died at locked exit doors. The plant had not been inspected by the state occupational safety office during its 11 years of operation (Kilbourn 1991). In 1990, Delta Pride was cited by the Occupational Safety and Health Administration (OSHA) for exposing employees to dangerous working conditions and fined $12,000 for failing to report injuries. Despite such fines, the nature of work in processing plants remains largely unchanged.

Worker productivity remains the key to profits—and survival—in a fiercely competitive business. Worker productivity is a function of line speed; speed it up, and productivity increases. Such increases have contributed to the success of companies like IBP and ConAgra and the emergence of oligopolies within individual segments of the meat- and fish-processing industries.

Corporate Reorganization

IBP's cost-cutting innovations in the beef and pork sectors forced the old urban-based packers to try to cut their costs. Wilson Foods, one of the "Big Four" meatpacking companies in the first half of the century, negotiated a 44-month wage freeze with the United Food and Commercial Workers (UFCW) in December 1981. Eighteen months later, Wilson filed for bankruptcy, repudiated its union contract, and cut wages by 40 percent (*Business Week* 1983). In 1982, Rodeo Meats, a subsidiary of John Morrell & Company, closed a plant in Arkansas City, Kansas. Nine months later, this plant reopened as Ark City Packing Company, offering wages at $5 an hour instead of the previous union wage of $11 an hour (Skaggs 1986). Greyhound Corporation used a similar strategy when it closed its Armour packing subsidiary in 1984 and paid severance to its union workforce. It then sold Armour to ConAgra, which reopened the 17 plants and hired a nonunion workforce. The same year, Hormel cut its wages by 23 percent (Houston 1985). Despite such cost cutting, many packers were handicapped by older and inefficient plants and were forced to either close down or sell out to the new packers. By the late 1980s, IBP, ConAgra, and Excel (a subsidiary of Cargill, Inc.) controlled over 70 percent of the beef slaughtered in the United States.

ConAgra and Excel, in contrast to IBP, attained their dominance through acquisitions. ConAgra, for example, purchased Monfort of Colorado, Inc., and E. J. Miller in the late 1980s, while Cargill purchased Missouri Beef Packers Excel Corporation (MBPXL) in 1978 and renamed the company Excel in 1982.

Pork is following the beef industry's example. The "Big Three" in beef are also the "Big Three" in pork, although they account for only 34 percent of all hog slaughterings (*Journal of Commerce* 1990). Much of ConAgra's and IBP's expansion has been accomplished by purchasing old unionized facilities and reopening them at lower wage levels. IBP bought an old Oscar Mayer plant in Perry, Iowa, in 1989: when the company reopened the plant, the starting wage of $5.80 an hour was nearly $4.00 *less* than Mayer's starting wage. The company first used this strategy in 1982 when it purchased an idle facility in Storm Lake, Iowa (see Grey, this volume).

The cost-cutting innovations associated with a vertically integrated poultry industry have favored well-financed companies and enabled them to purchase existing companies, build new large-capacity processing plants, and contract with more farmers to grow chickens faster and cheaper. This process has reduced the number of firms selling fryers to retailers from 286 in 1960 to 48 in 1989 (Hall 1989). Tyson Foods, Inc., has been one of the principal beneficiaries of restructuring; between 1963 and 1991, it acquired 17 other companies to become the nation's largest chicken-processing company (Forrest 1991). ConAgra's status as the second-largest chicken-processing company has been accomplished in the last 10 years. In 1982 ConAgra launched its own poultry company, Country Poultry, Inc. Two years later, it purchased Country Pride, which specialized in value-added chicken products, like marinated breasts (Ivey 1987). The result of these and other acquisitions is that the eight largest poultry companies have increased their share of broiler sales from 18 percent in 1960 to 55 percent by 1990 (Hall 1989; Barkema, Drabenstott, and Welch 1991).

Mergers and acquisitions in fish processing led to the emergence of oligarchies among certain segments of the industry. ConAgra, for example, became the largest U.S. shrimp processor when it purchased Singleton Seafood and Sea Alaska Products in 1982. It is also a major competitor with General Mills and Campbell Soups in the frozen seafood market (Mirabile 1991). Three companies—Delta Pride, ConAgra, and Hormel—account for 85 percent of the catfish sold in the United States. This oligarchic structure comes from efforts to control costs. The biggest cost for catfish farmers, once the ponds are constructed, is feed. Recognition of this fact led some producers to establish their own cooperative feed mill. Three companies now produce over 90 percent of the catfish feed in the United States. Producers' desire to set prices for their products also resulted in the establishment of a cooperative processing company, Delta Pride. Since its founding in 1981, this company has grown through acquisitions to account for 40 percent of catfish sales (Wineholt 1990).

TABLE 2.2. Meatpacking and Poultry-Processing
Production Workers, 1960–90

Year	Meatpacking	Poultry Processing
1990	117,000	180,000
1980	131,300	102,500
1970	143,700	83,500*
1960	164,800	—

* The Bureau of Labor Statistics did not begin compiling
poultry-processing employment data until 1972.
Source: U.S. Department of Labor, Bureau of Labor
Statistics, *Employment Hours and Earnings, United States,
1909–84,* and *Supplement to Employment and Earnings,*
Washington, D.C.: U.S. Government Printing Office.

In conjunction with the growth of these oligarchies, workers' relative wages have either remained below national averages or deteriorated. This is most evident in meatpacking, which lost 46,000 production workers between 1960 and 1990 (Table 2.2). In 1960 the
average hourly wage of meatpacking production employees was 15
percent higher than the overall average for manufacturing; by 1990 it
was 20 percent less. In absolute terms, meatpacking hourly wages
peaked in 1983 at $8.83; seven years later they remain below this
figure (Table 2.3).

Wages have always been much lower in poultry processing because
many of the plants are nonunionized and located in the rural South, a
low-wage region. Although poultry-processing employment has increased (Table 2.2), wages have remained far below the national average for manufacturing employees. In 1972 poultry production-workers'
hourly wages were 62 percent of the overall average for manufacturing
employees. Eighteen years later, the equivalent figure was 63 percent.

In fish processing there is a wide disparity in income levels between
regions, reflecting levels of unionization and the scale and type of production. Wages are generally much higher in the North than in the
South. In 1990, in Massachusetts, the average annual income of fish-
processing workers was over $28,000; the corresponding figure for
North Carolina was $8,600 (Table 2.4). In Mississippi, when 1,000 Delta
Pride workers went on strike in 1990 to protest a 6.5-cents-an-hour wage
increase and poor working conditions, most were earning $8,100 a year
(Bates 1991).

TABLE 2.3. Meatpacking and Poultry-Processing Hourly Wage Levels, 1960–90

Year	Meatpacking	Poultry Processing	Manufacturing Production Workers
1990	8.74	6.84	10.83
1980	8.49	4.47	7.27
1970	3.98	2.39*	3.35
1960	2.60	—	2.26

* The Bureau of Labor Statistics did not begin compiling poultry-processing wage levels until 1972.
Source: U.S. Department of Labor, Bureau of Labor Statistics, *Employment, Hours and Earnings, United States, 1909–84,* and *Supplement to Employment and Earnings,* Washington, D.C.: U.S. Government Printing Office.

In all four industries the relationship between capital and labor has undergone dramatic transformation in the past 20 years. The establishment of low-cost competitors like IBP has led to a massive restructuring of beef and pork processing. Wages have been slashed, working conditions have deteriorated, and injury rates have increased, while at the same time production has become concentrated among a few companies. In poultry and aquaculture, attempts at cost containment have resulted in a few vertically integrated companies' controlling each step of the production process. For workers, this has meant low wages, hazardous working conditions, and high injury rates. The next section will examine the geographic consequences of these structural changes for each industry.

Beefpackers' Rural Industrialization Strategy

In beefpacking, IBP's decision to locate its first plant close to cattle supplies dramatically altered the location of future packinghouses. Prior to the construction of IBP's Denison plant, most packinghouses were located near railroad terminals in urban areas. The savings associated with IBP's rural industrialization strategy resulted in the closure of older urban plants and the construction of new plants close to where cattle are fattened. During the 1970s and 1980s, cattle feeding shifted westward from the Corn Belt to the High Plains (Table 2.5). This is attributable to the availability of large quantities of water from the Ogal-

TABLE 2.4. 1990 Average Wages of Fish-Processing
Workers by State (in dollars)

Region/State	Weekly	Annual
New England		
Maine	266	13,807
Massachusetts	544	28,294
Rhode Island	418	21,759
Mid-Atlantic		
New York	228	11,830
New Jersey	424	22,068
Pennsylvania	405	21,083
South Atlantic		
Florida	277	14,442
Maryland	276	14,332
North Carolina	166	8,630
South Carolina	229	11,893
Virginia	169	8,777
Gulf Coast		
Alabama	197	10,236
Louisiana	176	9,143
Mississippi	197	10,242
Texas	222	11,553
Pacific		
Alaska	401	20,581
California	265	13,787
Oregon	252	13,111
Washington	535	27,794

Source: U.S. Department of Labor, Bureau of Labor
Statistics, *Employment and Wages, Annual Averages, 1990,*
Washington, D.C.: U.S. Government Printing Office,
1991.

lala Aquifer and the subsequent adoption of center-pivot irrigation
technology. Widespread cultivation of feed grains followed. The availability of feed and water attracted feedlots and packinghouses. The result is that meatpacking employment has declined throughout most of
the United States, with the exception of Kansas, Texas, and Virginia
(Broadway and Ward 1990; Virginia's growth is from the expansion of
hog processing in the southeastern portion of the state [Reier 1988],
and as this text goes to press North Carolina is becoming a major producer of pork products). The largest employment declines have oc-

TABLE 2.5. Cattle on Feed by Region, 1960, 1990

	1960		1990	
Region	Number	Share of U.S.	Number	Share of U.S.
Northern Plains North Dakota, South Dakota, Nebraska, Kansas	1,330,000	18.4%	3,955,000	34.0%
Southern Plains Oklahoma, Texas	308,000	4.3	2,425,000	20.9
Eastern Corn Belt Wisconsin, Illinois, Michigan, Indiana, Ohio	1,357,000	18.8	1,095,000	9.4
Western Corn Belt Minnesota, Iowa, Missouri	2,224,000	30.1	1,370,000	11.8
Other Remainder of U.S.	1,987,000	28.4	2,741,000	23.5
Total	7,206,000	100.0	11,626,000	100.0

Source: U.S. Department of Agriculture, *Agricultural Statistics.* Washington, D.C.: U.S. Government Printing Office, 1960, 1990.

curred in the traditional midwestern meatpacking states of Iowa, Illinois, Minnesota, Ohio, and Wisconsin.

The effects of the beefpackers' rural industrialization strategy are evident in Kansas and Nebraska. Since the late 1950s, Kansas has witnessed packinghouse closures in Kansas City and Wichita, while new plants opened in the southwestern portion of the state in Finney, Ford, and Seward Counties. In Nebraska, plants closed in Omaha and Lincoln, while new ones have opened in rural communities like Norfolk and Lexington. These small communities have attracted the packers by their close proximity to feedlots and their plentiful water, since a plant utilizes between 400 and 650 gallons per head of cattle slaughtered and processed.

Local officials have welcomed the packers by providing them with a variety of tax breaks. In the case of IBP's Finney County plant, county commissioners provided $3.5 million in property tax relief for 10 years and helped finance plant construction with $100 million in industrial revenue bonds. In Lexington, Nebraska, the site of IBP's newest beefpacking plant, the company used the provisions of the state's 1987 Employment and Investment Growth Act to reduce its county property tax

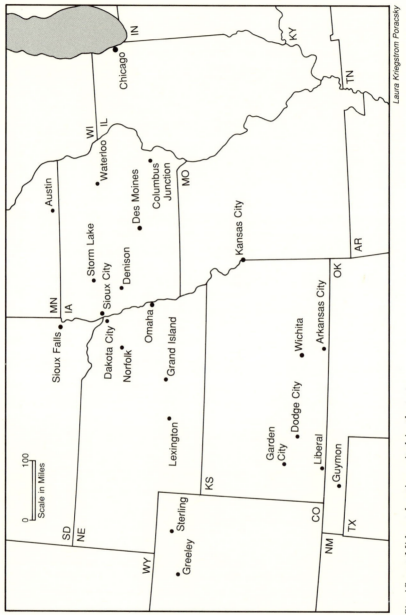

Significant Midwest locations cited in the text.

Laura Kriegstrom Poracsky

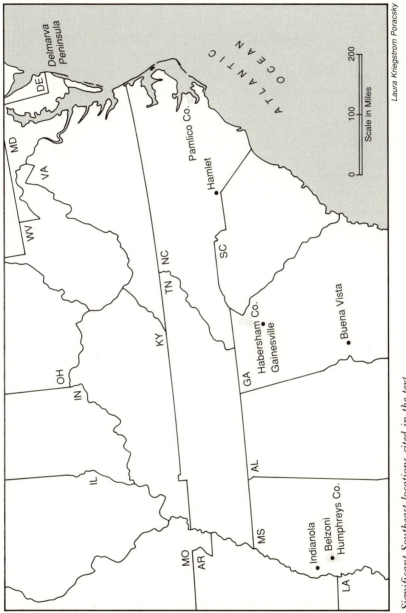

Significant Southeast locations cited in the text.

Laura Kriegstrom Poracsky

bill. The city of Lexington removed the plant from its tax rolls, while local taxpayers helped pay for infrastructure improvements associated with the plant's operation, such as the widening of a highway (Broadway 1992b).

The physical and financial attractions for the packers in these and other rural communities are readily apparent. Because of their size, however, these towns do not offer a traditional attraction for a manufacturer—surplus labor. In 1979, when IBP announced it would build its Finney County plant, unemployment in the county was 3.3 percent, or 432 persons. This small pool of surplus labor could not supply a plant that would eventually employ over 2,700 workers. A similar situation was evident in the late 1980s in Lexington. Unemployment in surrounding Dawson County averaged 4.0 percent, or 366 persons, in 1989; this, too, would be inadequate to meet the labor needs for a plant employing over 2,000 workers.

IBP has a publicly stated policy of recruiting workers from surrounding areas. Yet packinghouse work is physically demanding, dangerous, and low-paying, which contributes to high employee turnover. At IBP's Finney County plant, turnover among line workers averaged between 6 and 8 percent a month 10 years after the plant opened (Stull and Broadway 1990). This means that over 5,000 workers come and go each year, forcing the company to recruit from beyond the surrounding region. In the case of the Finney County plant, recruiters traveled to Texas, Alabama, and New Mexico in search of employees. The company also attracted Southeast Asians from Wichita, which in the early 1980s had Kansas's largest refugee population. The 1981–82 recession saw layoffs in the aircraft industry, the principal employer in Wichita, and plant closures in meatpacking. These factors combined to "push" migrants out of Wichita, while the opening of the Finney County plant "pulled" them to the area (Broadway 1987). A similar recruitment strategy is evident at IBP's Dakota City plant, where signs are in English, Spanish, and Vietnamese. As a result of this recruitment strategy, small rural towns with packing plants in the Great Plains have been transformed by this wave of "new immigrants." In Finney County, for example, the minority population increased from 16 percent to 31 percent between 1980 and 1990; the corresponding figures for Seward County, home of National Beef, were 15 and 28.5 percent, respectively. The social and economic changes associated with the

Sign at Dakota City beef plant. (Photograph by Michael J. Broadway)

plants and the influx of new immigrants will be discussed in the following chapters.

Hog Processing and Rural Areas

Hog processing has not experienced the same regional shift in plant locations as beefpacking, in part because hog farming remains concentrated in the western Corn Belt (Table 2.6). Within Iowa, packing plants have closed in Des Moines, Waterloo, and Sioux City, while they opened in rural communities like Storm Lake (1990 pop. 8,769) and Columbus Junction (1990 pop. 1,616). In 1990, IBP countered this pattern when it opened the world's largest hog-processing plant in Waterloo (1990 pop. 66,467).

The packers have generally been welcomed in rural Iowa. They provide a payroll at a time when farm income is declining and farmers are declaring bankruptcy. In Columbus Junction, the president of a local bank actively recruited IBP to take over the old Rath plant, because, in

TABLE 2.6. Hogs and Pigs: Number on Farms by Region, 1960, 1990

Region	1960		1990	
	Number	Share of U.S.	Number	Share of U.S.
Northern Plains				
North Dakota, South Dakota, Nebraska, Kansas	5,139,000	8.8%	7,835,000	14.3%
Eastern Corn Belt				
Wisconsin, Illinois, Michigan, Indiana, Ohio	16,924,000	28.9	14,450,000	26.5
Western Corn Belt				
Minnesota, Iowa, Missouri	20,869,000	35.7	21,300,000	39.0
Southeast				
Kentucky, Virginia, Tennessee, North Carolina, South Carolina, Georgia, Alabama, Mississippi	9,464,000	16.2	6,829,000	12.5
Other				
Remainder of U.S.	6,068,000	10.4	4,148,000	7.7
Total	58,464,000	100.0	54,562,000	100.0

Source: U.S. Department of Agriculture, *Agricultural Statistics*. Washington, D.C.: U.S. Government Printing Office, 1960, 1991.

the words of his son, "When Rath closed the plant down, this town was going to die and for those of us with roots in the community we couldn't allow that to happen. We have lived here all our lives, and we want our children to have some opportunities so they don't have to move away" (Broadway fieldnotes, July 12, 1991).

In Perry, a town of 7,000 situated 38 miles northwest of Des Moines, the local chamber of commerce helped recruit IBP to take over its vacant Oscar Mayer plant in the late 1980s. The town had lost nearly 1,000 jobs during the previous decade, with layoffs on the railroad and in meatpacking and a depressed farm economy. Although IBP's starting wage of $5.70 an hour was nearly $4.00 less than the Oscar Mayer starting wage, local business and community leaders generally welcomed the plant's reopening. Indeed, they note as evidence of the town's improving economic conditions the construction of a new McDonald's restaurant and a Super 8 motel (Broadway fieldnotes, July 11, 1991).

Like beefpacking, work in a pork plant is physically demanding, dangerous, and relatively low-paying. Turnover is high, and packers soon exhaust local labor supplies, forcing them to recruit from beyond the region. This labor shortage is exacerbated by the reluctance of former union employees to work for companies like IBP. At the Oscar Mayer plant in Perry, over half the former employees opted for some form of retraining rather than take a pay cut and work for IBP (Iowa Department of Labor 1991). During the summer of 1991, IBP actively recruited for its Madison, Nebraska, and Perry plants from southern California and Louisiana. Workers at its Columbus Junction plant have been recruited from the Rio Grande valley in Texas, Michigan, and inner-city Chicago (Farney 1990). Most of the workers recruited from these areas are Hispanics and African Americans.

The effect of these recruiting practices upon the ethnic makeup of individual communities appears to be a function of the town's situation, housing availability, and the length of time the plant has operated. In the Columbus Junction school district, which serves a large portion of Louisa County, the percentage of minority students increased from 7 percent in the year before the plant opened to 18 percent five years later. By contrast, the year before IBP opened its Perry plant, minority enrollment in the local school district was approximately 2 percent; two years later, the corresponding figure was 4 percent. This small increase is attributable to a shortage of rental housing and the fact that IBP runs a daily bus service for many of its Hispanic workers from Des Moines (Broadway 1992a).

The influx of newcomers is only one of many social and economic changes that rural packing towns experienced during the 1980s. They also experienced increased demands for health care, housing, second-hand clothing, food-pantry items, bilingual education, and ESL instruction (Broadway and Stull 1991; Broadway 1992a).

Poultry Processing and the Rural South

Employment in poultry processing, unlike meatpacking, has increased over the past 20 years (Table 2.2), reflecting changes in the American diet. In 1970, per capita consumption of chicken amounted to 28 pounds a year; by 1989 it had increased to 47 pounds. By contrast, equivalent figures for beef declined from 80 to 65 pounds (U.S. Bureau of the Census 1991). Poultry processing is concentrated in Arkansas,

North Carolina, Georgia, and Alabama. At the time of the last census of manufacturing in 1987, these four states accounted for 44 percent of poultry-processing employment. These same states accounted for 54 percent of the broilers produced in the United States in 1990 (U.S. Department of Agriculture 1991).

Poultry's rise to prominence in the South stems from several factors. The region's mild climate provides year-round growing conditions and low energy costs for heating and cooling the houses where broilers are raised. Most of the nation's small farmers are also found in the South. Seventy percent of the farms in Alabama, Arkansas, Georgia, and North Carolina are less than 179 acres in size, compared with 59 percent of all American farms. The presence of so many marginal farms is considered a key factor in the success of the poultry industry (Shand 1983). Many of these farmers use family labor to raise chickens under contract to the large processing firms like Tyson and ConAgra. Processors provide farmers with baby chicks, feed, and medication. Growers are judged on how much feed is used to grow each bird. The objective is to grow big birds with as little feed as possible. If the processing company finds the farmer's work unsatisfactory, it is unlikely to provide additional flocks, leaving the farmer with a $90,000 investment for a chicken house (Yeoman 1989).

Processing plants are located in rural areas close to where chickens are raised. In Georgia the leading producer is Habersham County, in the northeastern corner of the state, with nearly 44 million chickens sold in 1987. The county is also the site for a poultry-processing plant employing over a thousand workers. As Georgia's population has increased and urban areas have encroached upon traditional poultry-raising areas northeast of Atlanta, plants and poultry raising are shifting to more rural areas. During the 1980s, Hall, Forsyth, and Cherokee Counties all experienced declines in the numbers of broilers sold, while the more rural counties of Habersham, Madison, and Gilmer saw substantial increases (U.S. Bureau of the Census 1987a). Large-capacity plants have also been built outside the traditional broiler belt, northeast of Atlanta. These new plants have been constructed in diverse areas (Table 2.7). Some have been built in counties that have experienced minimal population growth (Marion, Evans); others have been constructed in more urban counties with large African-American populations (Bibb, Clarke); still others in rural counties with few African Americans (Habersham, Jackson).

TABLE 2.7. Characteristics of Counties in Georgia with Newly Constructed
Poultry Processing Plants

County	NUMBER OF PLANTS		POPULATION		PERCENT BLACK	
	1960	1990	1960	1990	1960	1990
Bibb	0	1	141,249	149,967	33.4	41.6
Clarke	0	2	45,363	87,594	25.4	26.2
Coffee	0	2	21,953	29,592	27.2	25.3
Evans	0	1	6,952	8,724	37.2	34.0
Forsyth	0	1	12,170	44,083	0.0	0.0
Habersham	0	1	18,116	27,621	5.0	5.6
Hall	1	2	49,739	95,248	10.8	8.6
Jackson	0	1	18,499	30,005	12.8	9.7
Marion	0	1	5,477	5,590	60.1	41.2
Walton	1	0	20,481	38,586	29.9	18.4
Georgia	2	12	—	—	28.5	27.0

Note: Only plants employing more than 500 workers are included.

Sources: Bureau of the Census, *Georgia County Business Patterns 1960, 1990.*
Washington, D.C.: U.S. Government Printing Office. Bureau of the Census, *Census of
Population, Georgia 1960, 1990.* Washington, D.C.: U.S. Government Printing Office.

Rural locations, beside providing access to where the birds are
raised, also give processors access to cheap labor. In Buena Vista, Georgia (1990 pop. 1,472), hourly wages at a chicken plant averaged between $5.10 and $5.60 in 1989—the highest in the surrounding region
(Goldoftas 1989). The positive economic benefits of processing plants
in providing a payroll and supporting local farmers are often grounds
for lax enforcement of environmental regulations. Fieldale Farms, a
poultry processor in northeastern Georgia, dumps waste from its plants
directly into creeks that flow into Lake Lanier, a popular swimming resort and major source of drinking water. The State of Georgia has cited
the company for violating water-quality standards but has allowed the
plants to continue operating because if the plants were closed "the
community would lose jobs" (Giardina and Bates 1991).

Aquaculture and Fish-Processing Employment

Employment changes in fish processing are related primarily to availability of raw materials. From 1977 to 1987 the amount of fish and shell-

TABLE 2.8. Amount of Fish and Shellfish Caught
by Region, 1977, 1987 (in millions of lbs.)

Region	1977	1987
New England	581	545
Middle Atlantic	213	163
Chesapeake Bay	668	791
South Atlantic	345	235
Gulf States	1,476	2,501
Pacific Coast	1,777	2,493

Source: U.S. Bureau of the Census. *Statistical Abstract of
the United States 1982, 1990.* Washington, D.C.: U.S.
Government Printing Office.

fish landed in New England and the Middle and South Atlantic regions
declined along with employment (Table 2.8). Employment increased in
areas where the catch increased, such as Washington. In Maryland, employment in fish-processing plants declined by over 1,000 jobs during
the same period (U.S. Bureau of the Census 1977, 1987b). These job
losses have been attributed to a reduction in the oyster catch and the
fact that some of the region's fish and shellfish are shipped to North
Carolina for processing (Griffith 1993). Average wages in North Carolina's processing plants are the lowest in the nation, which may serve to
attract firms. In 1988, firms in Maryland, North Carolina, and Virginia
began importing workers from Mexico to work in crab-picking plants
(see Griffith, this volume).

In Mississippi, increases in fish-processing employment are related
to expansion of catfish farming in the state's Delta region. Traditionally,
Delta farmers have depended upon cotton, but in the late 1970s declining cotton prices forced them to diversify or face bankruptcy. The poor
drainage and clay soils in the eastern portion of the Delta are ideal for
fishponds. Humphreys County, 60 miles northwest of Jackson, the state
capital, is the center of Mississippi's catfish farming industry; more catfish are raised in this county than anywhere else in the world.

Start-up costs for a catfish farm are high. A State of Mississippi document in 1988 estimated that it would cost a farmer $400,000 to dig eight
ponds, each covering 15 acres, fill them with water, stock them, and
feed the fish for a year until harvest. The yearly return on this investment, assuming the fish survived, would be about $120,000 (Schweid
1991).

The industry is vertically integrated; farmers own feed mills and a processing company. Delta Pride, ConAgra, and Hormel also control feed supplies and processing plants. The processing plants are close to where fish are processed, in towns like Belzoni (1990 pop. 2536), Sunflower (1990 pop. 729), and Indianola (1990 pop. 11,809). Local communities have welcomed the plants. Sunflower's $6 million facility was constructed with the assistance of a $1.6 million Urban Development Action Grant from the federal government. In 1989 the Farmers Home Administration approved a loan guarantee of $2 million to help finance a processing plant outside of Belzoni, home of the World Catfish Festival (Schweid 1991).

Unlike meatpackers, catfish processors have not had to recruit from outside the region. Almost all workers in processing plants are African-American women, and many are single mothers. Plant owners and catfish farmers are predominantly white. Low wages and dangerous conditions have led workers in several plants to unionize. Indeed, the largest strike by African Americans in Mississippi occurred among Delta Pride workers in 1990 (Bates 1991).

Conclusion

Restructuring in meat, poultry, and fish processing has followed a similar pattern. Worker productivity has been augmented by developing a disassembly line and increasing line speeds. A by-product of these innovations has been an increase in injury rates. Production costs in beef and pork processing have been lowered by shifting plant operations from urban to rural areas to be closer to raw materials. Rural communities have provided packers with tax reductions and other financial inducements. Local businesspeople welcome the packers since their payrolls provide an additional demand for goods and services. Many small midwestern towns with new packing plants have experienced an influx of newcomers due to labor shortages and high employee turnover associated with meatpacking. In recruiting workers, packers have focused on minorities in areas of high unemployment, such as the Rio Grande valley and inner cities.

Controlling costs in chicken and catfish processing has led to vertical integration, with producers controlling each step of production. Unlike the beef and pork industries, there has been little geographic mobility in the location of plants. Processing plants for both industries have remained close to their supply of raw materials in low-wage regions of the rural South. Despite low wages and hazardous working conditions in both industries, there is little indirect evidence, in the form of census data, that either industry has been confronted with labor shortages or has had to recruit workers from outside the region.

Rural industrialization is common to all four processing industries. Indeed, many policymakers regard the creation of these value-added manufacturing jobs as a panacea for rural America's endemic problems of poverty and underemployment. The community studies that follow consider the validity of this viewpoint by examining the social and economic consequences for workers and rural communities as a result of the opening of a meat- or fish-processing plant.

Notes

The author is grateful to Don Stull for his assistance and guidance in preparing this chapter. Any mistakes or omissions are, of course, the author's sole responsibility.

1. The year 1990 was selected as the cutoff point for the various tables and figures that follow. However, it was not possible to provide data for 1990 in all instances, since some census material is not collected on an annual basis.

References

Ahmed, Z. Z., and M. Sieling. 1987. Two Decades of Productivity Growth in Poultry Dressing and Processing. *Monthly Labor Review* 110(4):34–39.

Barkema, A., M. Drabenstott, and K. Welch. 1991. The Quiet Revolution in the U.S. Food Market. *Federal Reserve Bank of Kansas City Economic Review,* May–June:25–41.

Bates, E. 1991. The Kill Line. *Southern Exposure* 19(3):22–29.

Bishop, R. V., and L. A. Christensen. 1989. America's Poultry Industry. *National Food Review* 12:9–12.

Broadway, M. J. 1987. The Origins and Determinants of Indochinese Secondary Immigration to S.W. Kansas. *Heritage of the Great Plains* 20(2):17–29.

———. 1992a. Hog Wild: Community Change in Three Midwestern Meatpacking Towns. Paper presented at the annual meeting of the Association of American Geographers, San Diego, April 18–21.

———. 1992b. Economic Development Programs in the Great Plains: The Example of Nebraska. *Great Plains Research* 1:324–44.

Broadway, M. J., and D. D. Stull. 1991. Rural Industrialization: The Example of Garden City, Kansas. *Kansas Business Review* 14(4):1–9.

Broadway, M. J., and T. Ward. 1990. Recent Changes in the Structure and Location of the U.S. Meatpacking Industry. *Geography* 75:76–79.

Business Week. 1983. The Slaughter of Meatpacking Wages. June 27:70–71.

Castells, M. 1988. High Technology and Urban Dynamics in the U.S. In *The Metropolis Era.* Vol. 1, *A World of Giant Cities,* edited by M. Dogan and J. D. Kasarda. Newbury Park, Calif.: Sage, pp. 85–110.

Dicks, M., and D. Harvey. 1989. Catfish Leads the Way as Aquaculture Booms. *Farmline* 10(3):8–11.

Farney, D. 1990. Price of Progress. *Wall Street Journal,* April 3.

Forrest, S. A. 1991. Tyson Is Winging Its Way to the Top. *Business Week,* February 25:57–58.

Giardina, D., and E. Bates. 1991. Fowling the Nest. *Southern Exposure* 19(1):8–12.

Goldoftas, B. 1989. Inside the Slaughterhouse. *Southern Exposure* 17(2):25–29.

Griffith, D. 1993. *Jones's Minimal: Low Wage Labor in the U.S.* Albany: State University of New York Press.

Hall, B. 1989. Chicken Empires. *Southern Exposure* 17(2):12–17.

Heffernan, W. D. 1984. Constraints in the U.S. Poultry Industry. *Research in Rural Sociology and Development* 1:237–60.

Houston, P. 1985. The Pork Workers' Beef: Pay Cuts That Persist. *Business Week,* April 15:74–75.

Iowa Department of Labor. 1991. *Oscar Mayer Project.* Des Moines, Iowa: Dislocated Worker Center.

Ivey, M. 1987. How ConAgra Grew Big—And Now Beefy. *Business Week,* May 18:87–88.

Journal of Commerce. 1990. Meat Packing Industry Competition Probed. October 17:6A.

Kilbourn, P. T. 1991. In the Aftermath of Deadly Fire, a Poor Town Struggles Back. *New York Times,* November 25.

Knox, P., and J. Agnew. 1989. *The Geography of the World Economy.* London: Edward Arnold.

Miller, B. 1986. Why the Packer Crunch Will Continue. *Farm Journal Beef Extra,* June/July:19.

Mirabile, L. 1991. *International Directory of Company Histories.* Chicago: St. James Press.

Newsweek. 1965. Color It Green. March 8:76–77.

Personick, M. E., and K. Taylor-Shirley. 1989. Profiles in Safety and Health: Occupational Hazards of Meatpacking. *Monthly Labor Review,* 112(1):3–9.

Reier, S. 1988. High on the Hog. *Financial World,* June 28:26–31.

Schweid, R. 1991. Down on the Farm. *Southern Exposure* 19(2):14–21.

Shand, H. 1983. Billions of Chickens. *Southern Exposure* 11(6):76–82.

Skaggs, J. M. 1986. *Prime Cut: Livestock Raising and Meatpacking in the United States, 1607–1983*. College Station: Texas A&M University Press.

Stull, D. D., and M. J. Broadway. 1990. The Effects of Restructuring on Beef-packing in Kansas. *Kansas Business Review* 14(1):10–16.

U.S. Bureau of the Census. 1977. *Census of Manufacturers*. Washington, D.C.: U.S. Government Printing Office.

———. 1987a. *Census of Agriculture*. Washington, D.C.: U.S. Government Printing Office.

———. 1987b. *Census of Manufacturers*. Washington, D.C.: U.S. Government Printing Office.

———. 1991. *Statistical Abstract of the United States*. Washington, D.C.: U.S. Government Printing Office.

U.S. Department of Agriculture. 1991. *Agricultural Statistics*. Washington, D.C.: U.S. Government Printing Office.

Wineholt, D. 1990. Cooperation Builds Delta Catfish Industry, Brings Price Stability, Assured Market. *Farmer Cooperatives* 57(4):14–18.

Yeoman, B. 1989. Don't Count Your Chickens. *Southern Exposure* 17(2):21–24.

3 | On the Horns of a Dilemma

The U.S. Meat and Poultry Industry

Steve Bjerklie

THE MEAT AND POULTRY INDUSTRY spends a good deal of time talking about itself. Among the things industrymen like to say to each other are these: This is the second-most regulated industry in America (nuclear power is first); the public outside the industry cannot ever truly understand it; and it's a damn hard way to make a buck. In the hallways at industry meetings and conventions, the most common spoken mantra is "It's a tough business." There's a pause. "Maybe the toughest of all."

The high degree of regulation of the meat and poultry industry is inarguable. Its primary regulator is the Food Safety and Inspection Service (FSIS), an agency of the U.S. Department of Agriculture (USDA) that has been in existence in one form or another since 1906, when public clamor following publication of Upton Sinclair's book *The Jungle* caused Congress to establish, by means of the Federal Meat Inspection Act, a comprehensive regulatory program for the industry. Sinclair had intended his book to be an indictment of what he felt were the woeful working conditions under which much of blue-collar—especially immigrant blue-collar—America labored; he chose meatpacking plants in Chicago as the example to prove his hypothesis. But public response to the book focused not on Sinclair's social agenda but on his sometimes sensational descriptions of "routine" conditions in the packinghouses: frequent maimings of workers by dangerous equipment, saws, and knives; severed human body parts commingling with pieces of meat; and such inadequate refrigeration that many of the meat products shipped from the plants left them in a semirotten condition.

The basic tenet of the Federal Meat Inspection Act requires that every meat carcass and every processed meat product destined for interstate commerce be manufactured under the continuous, organoleptic inspection of a government-paid inspector (i.e., what can be seen, smelled, or otherwise detected through the five senses). This essential requirement of the act (which was paired with similar requirements in the Poultry Products Inspection Act in 1957; both were amended by the Wholesome Meat Act in 1967) has not been changed in nearly 90 years. Experiments with less-than-continuous inspection have been conducted in "good" meat plants over the past 20 years, and recent outbreaks of meat-caused bacterial contamination have brought the adequacy of organoleptic inspection into serious question, but no legislation altering the Federal Meat Inspection Act's continuous-inspection requirement has ever passed Congress. Thus, FSIS-inspected meat and poultry plants are the only food-manufacturing plants in the United States required by law to operate with a government inspector on the premises at all times; as a result the greater percentage, by far, of the industry's own discussion of its problems centers on inspection and regulatory matters, though greater problems and matters loom.[1]

The difficulty of making a profit in this industry is also hard to argue. The traditional rule of thumb used by industry executives and observers is that meatpacking (technically, the slaughter—or "harvest"—and disassembly of livestock) provides a margin of 1 percent; meat processing (the manufacture from raw meat of products such as sausage, ham, sandwich meats, snack foods, deli items, prepared foods such as microwaveable entrees, and myriad other products) yields 2 percent. Poultry companies, which usually slaughter and process at the same facility (as well as "further process" poultry meat into batter-and-breaded precooked products, analog products such as turkey ham and chicken-meat frankfurters, and many types of skinless-boneless cuts and portions), operate under somewhat different economics, but poultry processing, too, is not a high-margin business.

Several factors account for the narrow margins. Red-meat slaughtering, for instance, is a cash-intensive business dependent on livestock supply, which is vulnerable to volatile price swings. While accurate records are difficult to obtain, a general industry-used estimate is that 70 percent of all expenditures made by a packing company are for livestock procurement. Processors are in a similar situation, spending a like amount for raw materials to process into sausage and other items. Production labor accounts for 10 percent of the ledger-sheet expenditures of most meat companies. Livestock prices and, less directly, raw materials prices for processors are driven by herd size, demand, consumer confidence, the price of feed grains, weather, and exports and imports. All of these factors are beyond the control of any single meatpacker. In addition, the volume-and-commodity nature of meatpacking has encouraged concentration in beef, especially, of a few large packers, who hold among themselves more than 70 percent of the U.S. packinghouse capacity. According to 1993 figures compiled by *Cattle Buyers Weekly*, an industry newsletter, the top 20 beef packers have a total daily slaughter capacity of 120,175 head; of this, the top three packers—IBP, ConAgra's Red Meat Cos., and Cargill's Excel division—have a capacity of 83,750 head. No wonder they are called the "Big Three." In pork packing the top 20 firms have a combined daily capacity of 346,912 head, according to 1993 figures from Iowa State University; the four largest pork packers—IBP, ConAgra, John Morrell, and Excel—hold a 48 percent share of this total. Under these conditions, competition is fierce and margins slim.

The fact that processing companies tend to be longer-lived than packing firms is evidence that operating with even an average 2 percent return on sales allows better absorption of the vicissitudes of business and commerce. Several major meat processors, including Oscar Mayer and Hormel Foods, are more than 100 years old. By contrast, IBP, which is the largest fresh-meat packer in the world, was founded in 1960. Poultry-processing companies are also among the relative newcomers because the modernization of the poultry sector did not begin in earnest until the 1960s.

The impact of narrow margins on working conditions for hourly employees at meat and poultry plants is palpable. In a commodity business, the common wisdom calls for increasing productivity to eke out gains in margins. In the meat and poultry industry, the search for faster and better ways to slaughter and process meat and livestock is relentless, and has resulted in line (or "chain") speeds of unimaginable rapidity in packinghouses: more than 1,000 hogs per hour at the fastest pork-packing plants; 400 head per hour at the fastest beef plants; and literally thousands of broilers per hour at the poultry plants. Experiments with robotic equipment to speed the lines even further and reduce dependence on human labor in tedious and dangerous "kill floor" jobs have not proved commercially successful to date; the variability in the basic raw material is simply too great. Market-weight steers, for instance, can easily range over a 300-pound differential.

While the market forces and macroeconomics of agriculture may be too large for the meat and poultry industry to control or even influence, the same must be said for the industry's ability to control or influence its own public image. "The public doesn't understand us" is probably the greatest understatement commonly made in an industry prone to understatement. Part of the reason this is true is the industry's own insular and provincial nature; it seeks answers to its problems from itself. It tends to be distrustful of outside suggestions and advice. Recent media coverage, including a spate of negative television reports focusing on working conditions in packinghouses, provides evidence that those outside the industry who claim to know something about it are almost always critics and naysayers—a situation causing industry executives to murmur among themselves that no one truly understands what they do and what the industry as a whole does.

While the industry is insular and provincial, it is also an ugly example, to most Americans, of the industrial economy. Packinghouses, even under the best conditions, are not pretty; the meat industry is not a photo opportunity for the documentation of American enterprise and commerce. It is an industry based upon the killing, evisceration, and disassembly of animals—most of them large. The industry acknowledges the gruesomeness of its task with its own nomenclature: the area of a packinghouse where animals are killed and eviscerated is the "kill floor"; on the kill floor, workers "stick" carcasses to bleed them; eviscerators "drop bungs," "pull sweetbreads," and perform "head workups." Even the animals have been made, in this argot, to seem less individual and thus less alive. Most foremen and supervisors working on kill floors refer to a single steer or carcass as "a cattle." Moving animals through production is called "getting blood on the kill floor." Because steers, as well as hogs and lambs, are large warm-blooded creatures, red-meat kill floors tend to be hot and humid. Moisture rises from the hot, fat outside coverings of carcasses like vapor from a swamp. The brownish air in slaughterhouses stinks of opened bellies, half-digested cud, and manure.

Poultry plants, while cooler and fresher-smelling, nonetheless have an eerie quality all their own. Automated slaughter and evisceration equipment has been developed to a high degree; even in the largest and fastest poultry plants there is a startling lack of workers on the kill floor. Machines click, whir, clank, and hiss rhythmically and mysteriously.

For logical reasons, then, most American consumers choose not to be reminded of the "facts" of the meat and poultry industry, though these reasons are not necessarily in consumers' best interests. The removal over the course of the twentieth century of a large part of the population from rural to metropolitan and suburban settings has created a void in the knowledge of Americans of where food comes from and how it is prepared in a processing plant. When meat and poultry were slaughtered on farms, as was common until the middle years of this century, the "fact" of meat and how it got that way was obvious. Now meat slaughter and processing are performed, for the most part, in huge, faceless buildings beyond the edge of town. And most Americans know little of meat and poultry processing, or of the jobs of the workers in the plants.

The nature and condition of the meat and poultry industry have served, over time, to obscure its long and fascinating history, but that history is key to understanding the dilemmas that confront today's industry. Escaping commodity economics is, albeit arguably, the most important of these for the large packers, for producing and selling meat as a commodity both drives the packers to become ever larger and more efficient and yet holds margins to a minimum. The dilemma is clear. If packers try to add value to their products and thus improve margins, they risk a return by food retailers to doing their own processing, and possibly even consumer backlash against higher prices; if the packers likewise try to improve margins by building larger and more efficient plants, the huge production of these plants guarantees continuance of commodity pricing. In terms of the labor force, commodity economics holds down wage rates while increasing the pressure for greater production, thus forcing the industry to grow ever more dependent on cheap, and most often immigrant, labor.

The delicate balance between domestically produced meat and imported meat creates another dilemma (virtually no poultry is imported into the United States). Nearly all the meat imported into this country is considered inferior to U.S.-produced fed beef and pork, and thus is used for the production of fast-food hamburgers, sausage products, and other manufactured items.[2] But cheap imported meat holds down domestic prices; if domestic prices climb too high, buyers turn to the imports—even retail buyers. If high-quality meat is imported, it competes directly with U.S.-produced product. Further, some exporting nations subsidize their meat industries with government funds; the United States does not, but does subsidize portions of the feed-grain industry, and communities subsidize many plants with tax breaks.

Increasing demand at the consumer level is another dilemma with which the industry struggles. Experience proves that sale prices and discounting are the best ways to spark slack demand in the short term, but discounting erodes margins. The packers, one or two steps removed from consumers in the distribution of meat to the supermarket, have no brand-name presence and thus no consumer-visible marketing programs. To fill this void, generic beef and pork promotion campaigns (e.g., "Real Food for Real People," "Pork: The Other White Meat") have been developed, but these are funded by checkoff programs based on cents or dollars per head of livestock sold and thus are controlled by livestock producers, not the packers. Red-meat processors such as Oscar Mayer, Hillshire Farm, and Bar-S have high-visibility brand names, of course, but their marketing campaigns are devoted to increasing their own sales. The poultry companies somewhat solved the marketing problem in the early 1960s when Perdue and others sought to differentiate their poultry from store-packed product with brand names and at-the-plant packaging. Retail butchers at the time did not generally care to handle poultry (it was regarded as an inferior, second-grade protein), and so the centrally packaged and branded poultry was welcomed with relief. Soon, store-packed poultry disappeared altogether, replaced by branded products. This poultry was often slaughtered, eviscerated, processed, and packaged for retail at an individual plant.

Maintaining the safety of meat and poultry products creates a three-sided dilemma. On one side, commodity economics pressures the packing companies to produce greater amounts of meat more efficiently. But increased production increases the opportunity for bacterial contamination of meat and poultry products, since research has shown that most bacterial contamination is the result of spillage onto meat of eviscerated stomach contents, hide removal, and worker-to-meat-transferred bacteria. The faster the production, the greater the chance of contamination. However, the federal meat and poultry inspection program is based on organoleptic inspection, and bacteria, at least until they sufficiently contaminate meat or poultry to cause a telltale putrid smell, cannot be detected organoleptically. To date, no rapid method of bacteria detection for meat and poultry that can function at commercial volumes has been developed. Thus, the FSIS continues to inspect meat and poultry organoleptically, while commodity economics requires greater production in the face of increasing incidence of bacterial contamination. Failure is dangerous and costly: the outbreak of contamination of ground-meat patties caused by the O157:H7 strain of

Escherichia coli in the Pacific Northwest in January 1993 resulted in the deaths of four children and the hospitalization of several dozen others. Over the past two years, industry spokesmen have talked often of irradiation as a solution to the bacterial contamination problem, since the irradiation process in effect sterilizes products, but irradiation has not been approved by the federal government for use on beef, though it is approved for pork and poultry. Questions remain about the wisdom of sterilizing microbiologically vulnerable products such as meat and poultry; the opportunity for recontamination in the distribution pipeline might be great. Even if irradiation receives blanket approval for use on all flesh-protein products, consumer acceptance of irradiated food products in the United States is still an unknown factor.

According to USDA production statistics, the meat and poultry industry is the largest single segment of U.S. production agriculture as measured by gross receipts. [Total annual sales for the 100 largest meat and poultry companies in the United States, as published in the July 1993 issue of *Meat&Poultry*, are nearly $77 billion.] Yet the public posture of the industry is one with its head down to avoid attention and scrutiny. This creates difficulties in cultivating a good public image and has invited activists, from consumer organizations to animal rights groups, to set the public agenda. A long history of siege grips the industry into stasis; response to animal rights groups, for instance, has been largely sullen. Attacks made against the industry on moral grounds are somewhat indefensible; activists who believe it is morally wrong to kill an animal to provide human food can never accept the industry's position that its production of products from livestock is necessary and morally viable. Further, the meat and poultry industry, especially the red-meat segment, is an old industry, part of "smokestack America," without the glamour of modern industries such as computer manufacture or genetic engineering. Meat-plant scenes in the popular imagination comprise bellowing livestock, blood and juice-splattered workers, and noisy, clamorous plants. But creating an improved public image risks exposing the weaknesses, such as a high-volume orientation and dependence on unskilled (and sometimes undocumented) labor, that have given rise to the public perception of the industry.

Finally, the pressures of commodity economics, coupled with the unskilled labor needs of high-volume plants where a single worker performs a single function, create a situation where wages and skills must be kept to a minimum even as the need for safer food products and a better public image requires better, and more visibly improved, management of the workforce. Packers, devoting so much of their capital to livestock procurement, say they cannot devote more than 10 percent of their cost of production to labor. In addition, they say the cost of training skilled workers is too high, and in any case the high-volume "disassembly" plants are not designed for a skilled workforce. Plus, most hourly workers do not stay with one company for very long; turnover at some large plants has been documented at better than 100 percent per year. With economic pressure holding the 10-percent-of-cost in place, packers are reluctant to improve wages or change the jobs.

The dilemma of wages and skill in the meat and poultry industry is real and measurable. According to U.S. Department of Labor statistics published by the American Meat Institute (1993), in 1965 the average hourly wage of a packinghouse worker was $2.99, and that of a meat-processing plant worker was $2.78. In the same year, the average hourly wage of a worker in the broad food industry was $2.63, while that of a worker in American manufacturing was $2.61. Thus, an employee at either a meat packinghouse or meat-processing plant was among the best-paid hourly workers in all of American industry. Ten years later the ranking was identical: in 1975 the average hourly wage was $5.67 for a packinghouse worker and $5.36 for a processing-plant employee. Poultry-plant employees earned an average hourly wage of $3.03 (1965 statistics for the poultry industry are not available from the Labor Department). Employees at food plants in general averaged $4.61 an hour, and all manufacturing employees averaged $4.83. In 1992, however, the ranking was almost exactly reversed: the average hourly wage for all manufacturing employees was $11.45; for employees in food plants, $10.19; for meat-processing plant employees, $9.61; and for packinghouse workers, $9.13. Poultry-plant employees, who often work in plants located in southern right-to-work (and thus generally nonunion) states fared the worst in 1992 relative to these wages, with an average hourly wage of $7.26. At the same time, the rate of injuries and illnesses, as well as rates for lost workdays, has been steadily increasing from 1981 through the present, according to Labor Department statistics.

The issues and dilemmas facing the meat and poultry industry today can be summed up as follows: economic conditions pressuring production upward and margins downward; price volatility within a delicately balanced but still uncontrollable supply of domestically produced meat and poultry and imported product; uncontrollable demand; increasing product-safety concerns even as economics pressures production rates to increase; the need for a better public image though the industry isn't "pretty"; and falling hourly wage rates and skill levels relative to those for food-processing and manufacturing in general. In short, to escape these dilemmas the meat and poultry industry needs to clean up its economy, its image, its plants, and its working conditions.

To some degree the industry has always felt under siege. Publication of *The Jungle,* as mentioned earlier, caused the first great public outcry against conditions the industry assumed were "normal." The impact of that clamor reverberates still, and not simply in the strictures of the Federal Meat Inspection Act and the Poultry Products Inspection Act. Actually, there had been a formative government meat-inspection program as early as the 1890s, but the act passed in 1906 was the first in the U.S. food industry to firmly establish the continuous-inspection rule. (Only meat and poultry plants are inspected by an agency of the U.S. Department of Agriculture; all other food-processing plants, with the exception of seafood plants, are inspected on a random, noncontinuous basis by agents of the Food and Drug Administration. Seafood plants are presently inspected on a voluntary basis by inspectors from the U.S. Department of Commerce.)

Sinclair's book served to create in the popular imagination an image of the meat industry as an enterprise of exploitation, unsanitary conditions, low wages, and sometimes shocking incidents and product adulterations. While part of the reason Congress acted in response to the book was to restore confidence in the meat supply (another part of the reason was pure politics; 1906 was a congressional election year), Congress itself was disturbed by the allegations and descriptions it was hearing in committee and subcommittee testimony. Not only were meat-plant conditions apparently deplorable, but the operations of the companies themselves begged for investigation. By the mid-1920s, Congress, enforcing antitrust laws, passed the Packers and Stockyards Act. The act was the visible portion of an all-out government effort to break what investigators believed was a stranglehold by five meat companies on the nation's meat supply. The five companies—survivors into the latter part of the twentieth century included Swift, Wilson, Armour, and Cudahy (Armstrong was the fifth)—were effectively barred from controlling the means of distribution of their products (i.e., owning railroads), from controlling the means of sale of their products (owning grocery stores), and, by implication (though not by law), from controlling the production of livestock. The act established the Packers and Stockyards Administration at the Department of Agriculture; this agency's primary task is to protect the interests of livestock producers from packers.

Even at this early date, the industry had a high-volume orientation. The typical meat plant of the age was a gigantic brick structure located next to the stockyards. Animals—and most plants at the time slaughtered steers, hogs, veal calves, and lambs at the same facility—were mechanically conveyed to a top floor for killing and evisceration, the meat then working its way down through the floors for processing into various products, until arriving at the shipping bays on the street level. The labor needs of such plants were tremendous, but the influx of European immigrants into the United States in these years, and the post–World War I migration of African Americans northward out of the South, provided ready supplies of unskilled workers willing to submit to long days at low wages. In these years communication within the plants among workers and supervisors could be difficult: a sizable plant might include among its workforce native speakers of German, Polish, Gaelic, and Italian. Literacy was low.

These conditions proved ripe for union organizing. While the federal government investigated alleged front-office price-fixing and monopolies, union representatives sought to organize workers in the plants. The effort was effective and swift: by the time of the Great Depression, nearly all the workers in meat plants in Chicago and other big cities were members of unions, the most prominent of these being the Amalgamated Meat Cutters, forerunner of today's United Food and Commercial Workers.

Virtually every one of these situations—government investigation, questionable plant conditions, and labor organization—proved to be a harbinger for later issues and problems. Upton Sinclair's investigative journalism is the ancestor to the meat-industry reporting of Jonathan Kwitney of the *Wall Street Journal* and Jimmy Skaggs, who wrote a history of the industry entitled *Prime Cut* in 1986, and, less directly, to the criticism of the industry voiced by Jeremy Rifkin in *Beyond Beef* (1992). The trust-busting investigations of the federal government in the 1920s gave way to investigations of beef industry concentration in the 1970s and 1980s by Congressman Neal Smith from Iowa. To a lesser degree, the earlier investigations also heralded the efforts by cattlemen in the 1980s to investigate alleged beef price-fixing by large supermarket chains. Exposure of unsanitary and unwholesome manufacturing conditions created the opportunity for continued investigation into the safety and wholesomeness of meat and poultry products, leading to today's research into the causes and effects of *E. coli* and other contamination. Meat-plant working conditions, exposed at the turn of the century by workers and union organizers as well as by journalists, have been exposed again in recent years by the Occupational Safety and Health Administration. The activities in the early 1990s of animal rights activists are without precedent for the industry, but in this case precedent could have proved helpful: in the face of charges of a basic immorality, the industry has no historic moral position to take other than that meat and poultry have always been a part of the Western diet, and thus the industry has always had to exist.

[While *The Jungle* created an image of the industry in the mind of the public, the book at the same time created an image of the media in the mind of the industry. Suspicion and distrust have governed this relationship ever since.]In 1992, in the wake of yet another televised investigation of unsanitary conditions at a meat plant, an industry representative publicly accused the television reporters of using vanilla pudding to create the appearance of abscesses on beef carcasses.

In Chicago today the only remnant still standing of the city's meatpacking heritage is the ceremonial gate at the entrance to the old stockyards. In New York City the United Nations Building stands on the site of Manhattan's old "butchertown." In San Francisco the Giants major-league baseball team plays in Candlestick Park, less than a quarter mile away from where livestock were unloaded two generations ago from rail cars and ships for the city's nearby butchertown plants. In Fort Worth the stockyards have been transformed into an upscale district of boutiques, bars, and restaurants.

At one time in this century, virtually every major American metropolis had a butchertown community of meatpacking and meat-processing plants to fulfill the meat needs of the population. Except for still-thriving meat-purveying companies and plants, which service the hotel and restaurant trade, the butchertowns of yesteryear have completely disappeared. While a host of generic macroeconomic and social factors can be included among the reasons for these closures (departure to the suburbs of a large portion of big-city populations, increasing inner-city crime rates, rising land values that made the property meat companies

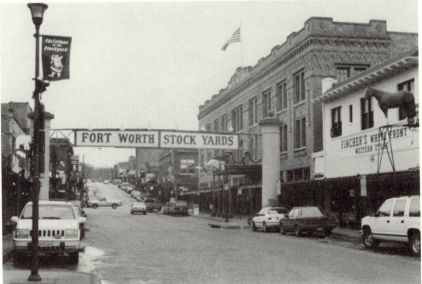

Fort Worth stockyard district, 1995. (Photographs by Laura Kriegstrom Poracsky)

sat on more valuable than the companies themselves), the demise of big-city butchertowns can largely be traced to a fateful meeting in the late 1950s of two men, Currier Holman and Andy Anderson. Both had backgrounds with Swift & Co., the meat-industry giant at the time, and both were frustrated by the inefficiencies of big-city multistory meat plants, of which Swift owned and operated several. Why, they asked themselves, should meat companies pay to have livestock shipped to the cities for processing? Why should meat companies still ship whole sides by inefficient railroads? Why should meat companies remain wage-locked in heavily unionized cities when unorganized workers could be hired at far lower wages out in the country?

In March of 1960 Holman and Anderson incorporated their ideas into a new company. They would slaughter and "fabricate" meat in the regions of the country where livestock was raised, saving transportation costs on the front end. "Fabrication" meant breaking down carcasses into "primals" and "subprimals," vacuum-packaging these, and shipping the pieces in boxes. Shipping would be by truck on the then-new interstate highway system. Out in the country they would take advantage of cheaper land to build their plants, which would be manned by country-raised workers used to low, country-style nonunion wages. They would not process meat into sausages and hams; they would specialize in slaughter and fabrication, gaining better margins through control of wages, access to livestock supply, and high-volume plants built on "economies of scale."

Holman and Anderson named their new venture Iowa Beef Packers, Inc. In March of 1961 they opened their first plant in Denison, Iowa.

Iowa Beef Packers—soon to be called Iowa Beef Processors, and today known simply as IBP—set into motion a series of changes transforming the meat industry from a city-based business of big, do-it-all plants operated by big, do-it-all companies into an industry of specialists scattered all over the nation. IBP challenged the assumptions governing the way the industry's big operators had conducted business for more than half of the twentieth century, and in so doing grew big itself. In addition to a working familiarity with the industry's traditional dilemmas and problems, Holman and Anderson anticipated a new dilemma for the big-city packers—how to fulfill an expanding market beyond the cities while still paying big-city wages and operating old, big-city plants—before anyone else did, and they profited mightily because of it. IBP's basic product, boxed beef, had so many advantages for the industry's supermarket-chain customers that even skeptical retail executives soon jumped on the bandwagon, though union labor behind the meat counters in the stores remained steadfastly opposed to boxed beef. The butchers saw boxed beef as a threat to their jobs, for much of the basic carcass-cutting work would be removed to the meat plant rather than be performed at the store. But boxed beef allowed the stores to order the kinds of meat they wanted when they wanted it, making specials and discounting much easier to manage. In the battle over boxed beef between in-store butchers and the big beef plants, the butchers lost, so that today boxed beef, as well as boxed pork, is the industry-standard basic product; Holman and Anderson's company transformed an entire industry.

IBP led the way, and others followed. The Missouri Beef Packing Company was established in the early 1960s; eventually it merged with another packer, Excel, to become MBPXL Corporation, and is now known again as simply Excel, owned by grain giant Cargill. A family of ranchers in Colorado named Monfort built a beef plant in the flat-pan landscape outside the town of Greeley, Colorado, and in the 1970s opened other operations, including a high-volume beef plant in Grand Island, Nebraska. After years of fierce, rancher-born independence, Monfort of Colorado Beef sold out in the late 1980s to agribusiness giant ConAgra, which was already beginning to collect meat companies such as Armour, E. A. Miller, and remnants of the old Swift & Co. In 1990, according to figures published by *Meat&Poultry*, ConAgra became the largest single meat processor in the world, and later added to its holdings meat concerns in Australia and other foreign nations. In addition to its substantial presence in beef packing, pork packing and processing, as well as poultry, ConAgra controls 75 percent of the United States' total lamb-slaughter capacity.

These new-era meat companies all own and operate plants in rural locations. Not one of them operates any facility more complex than a distribution center in any large American city. They also share the dimension of size. IBP, which is publicly held, reported gross sales of $11.1 billion for the fiscal year ended December 27, 1992, as reported in the July 1993 issue of *Meat&Poultry*. ConAgra, which lumps sales from its meatpacking division together with sales from its meat-processing and poultry-processing holdings, reported overall sales from its various animal-protein divisions of $16.2 billion for the fiscal year ended May 31, 1992, making it the largest combined packing and processing company in the world (IBP is the largest fresh-meat packer). Excel showed estimated sales of $8 billion for the year ended May 31, 1992, as reported in *Meat&Poultry*. Growth by these companies has been steep and steady: 10 years ago, IBP, even then the largest of the beef packers, reported sales of $5.0 billion, less than half its sales today, and Excel reported sales of $2.2 billion, barely more than a quarter of its present sales volume. Ten years ago, ConAgra wasn't even in the meat business.

At its 17 beef and pork plants IBP employs 27,500 workers, according to company-supplied figures. Excel employs 17,000 at 21 facilities, and ConAgra, company-wide for all divisions, employs 80,000.

The poultry industry has likewise experienced growth and concentration, though this was not precipitated by a wholesale move to the country, as happened in the beef and pork sectors; the poultry sector has always been rural-sited, with its home region being the South. The largest poultry-processing company today is Tyson Foods, reporting annual sales of $4.17 billion for the year ended September 29, 1992. Gold Kist and Perdue Farms both reported annual sales of $1.3 billion for fiscal 1992, and Seaboard Corporation, the fifth-largest poultry processor in 1993, reported sales of slightly more than $1 billion for the year. Ten years earlier, in 1983, the largest poultry company in the United States, ConAgra's Country Poultry, Inc., reported sales of $1 billion, as published by *Meat&Poultry*. Tyson Foods the same year reported sales of $559 million.

While the red-meat sector's story is one of exodus and rural rejuvenation, the poultry sector's story is one of taking advantage of rural opportunities. A largely segmented business until fairly recently, divided among poultry slaughterers, poultry processors, feed-grain mill operators, and independent poultry farmers, the poultry processors in the early 1960s began buying the feed-grain mills and contracting with the independent farmers, making them, in effect, contract workers for the company. Thus, the larger poultry companies emerging in the South became "vertically integrated": they controlled their product from fertilization of the eggs through hatching through "grow-out" to market weight and on through slaughter and processing. The cost advantages are obvious, and by the late 1970s the price differential between poultry and red meat began to be taken seriously by consumers. According to U.S. Department of Agriculture statistics, in 1975 U.S. per capita consumption of chicken stood at 26.4 pounds; beef was at 83.0 pounds, and pork at 38.7 pounds. By 1992 per capita beef consumption had dropped to 62.8 pounds, pork had climbed to 49.5 pounds, and chicken had risen dramatically to 45.9 pounds, a gain of more than 60 percent over 7 years (U.S. Bureau of the Census 1994:147).

Thus, over the course of approximately 35 years, dating back to 1960, both the red-meat and poultry sectors of the meat and poultry industry remade themselves, albeit in different fashions, and in so doing they left behind some old problems such as inefficient operations located in expensive neighborhoods. At the same time, the industry as a whole remains sensitive and vulnerable to long-standing issues and dilemmas, particularly with regard to commodity economics and production labor.

The siege mentality is a factor. Insular and parochial from what it regards as a long history of unjust attacks by government, unions, activists, and the media, the industry, despite the business success and growth it has enjoyed over the past three decades, is reluctant to search outside itself for answers to dilemmas, such as the squeeze produced by commodity economics, that are tightly woven into the very fabric of the industry's commerce. In the face of moral accusations regarding treatment of workers and care and handling of livestock, the industry is defensive and obstinate. And to a large degree, the industry's leadership is inbred and loyal only to the nearest enterprise at hand—the company.

The issues and dilemmas facing contemporary U.S. meat and poultry companies boil down to three critical subjects: economics, product safety, and labor management. It is clear from the history of the industry over the past 30 years that remolding and recreating its companies and way of doing business do not necessarily address or respond to these dilemmas. However, several factors suggest now that these dilemmas must be addressed soon or the industry risks suffering a forced downsizing.

One important factor is rapidly changing consumer demand. Reduced red-meat consumption in recent years is only one bit of evidence of a developing and changing consumer. Yet the industry, locked into high-volume production at huge plants, finds it difficult to manufacture the wide variety of new products consumers seem interested in. In addition, reduced fat consumption for the sake of healthier diets has caused turmoil within the pork and beef sectors, where fat is figured into the price of lean. These economics determine that heavier and fattier livestock benefit producers and packers, but retailers, sensitive to calls from consumers for leaner cuts, are encouraged to buy leaner beef and pork. (Poultry does not have this problem, since poultry meat does not contain fat to the degree of beef and pork. The fattiest part of a broiler is its skin, which is easily removed.) But because consumers ultimately hold the power in this equation, since they control demand, they will win the argument over pricing, and the industry will have to adjust accordingly.

The 1993 *E. coli* outbreak in the Pacific Northwest was only the first of several publicized incidents of bacterial contamination traced to beef and beef products. The primary focus for the past three years of the U.S. Department of Agriculture's FSIS has been improved product safety, since the Federal Meat Inspection Act and Poultry Products Inspection Act both give FSIS responsibility to "guarantee the wholesomeness, safety and proper labeling" of all meat and poultry products manufactured under federal inspection. Rapid line speeds in red-meat and poultry packinghouses will likely come under scrutiny as possible causes of unacceptable rates of bacterial contamination. Should this scrutiny result in data confirming the line-speed cause, the industry, from a regulatory standpoint as well as politically, will not be able to prevent legislative momentum to slow down chain speeds. And rapid chain speeds are only one factor in processing microbiologically cleaner and safer meat and poultry products. Labor management and equipment maintenance, as well as careful record keeping and attention to distribution, have all been shown to influence the microbiological profiles of the products.

Finally, the supply of cheap, unskilled labor, which the industry has taken for granted since the Chicago stockyards days, is drying up. Research has shown that the large packing companies have had to recruit far and wide to fill jobs at their labor-intensive plants. Much of this labor is immigrant and non-English-speaking, coming from Mexico, Central America, and Southeast Asia. Communication remains as difficult as it was when immigrants from Europe and the Middle East filled meat-plant jobs 80 years ago. Yet commodity economics drives the meat and poultry companies to build ever-larger plants. IBP's newest beef plant in Lexington, Nebraska, requires more than 2,000 hourly employees to operate at its full 250-head-an-hour capacity.

To respond productively to these issues, the meat and poultry industry must challenge itself to do the following:

Reduce dependence on commodity-priced volume. Despite the changes of the past 30 years—arguably, *because* of these changes—the meat and poultry industry remains price-driven. It has not been able to significantly improve margins, opting instead to earn profit by processing more tonnage at a smaller profit per pound than by adding value to a reduced volume. The result is a necessity for high-volume plants, which can be afforded by only the largest companies, thus concentrating the industry in the hands of a few players while at the same time increasing the need for unskilled labor and increasing dependence on a volatile livestock supply. Commodity economics create a pincer squeeze on meat companies. Since they are vulnerable to livestock prices, the companies cannot easily pass on price increases to supermarket meat buyers who have been trained to accept a low-bid formula and may be locked into discounting in any case. Poultry companies have moved away from commodity economics by vertically integrating, but in the battle for more per capita consumption the poultry sector has deliberately held down retail prices to attract price-sensitive consumers. Thus, the poultry companies escaped one kind of commodity economics while making another.

Improve the safety of products. The legal responsibility for safe and wholesome products resides with the FSIS, but at the same time it is the industry that suffers image problems, in part, from food safety issues. It makes sense, therefore, for the industry and the FSIS to work together to improve the safety of meat and poultry products. Consumers have come to believe that pure food products are a right, not a privilege. The inspection acts support this conclusion. But consumers' allegiances are fragile, their tastes fickle. Safer meat and poultry products can keep both for the industry. One approach: slow down production and retrain unskilled one-task workers as skilled food technologists.

Improve labor management. Begin by paying more—reduced dependence on commodity economics will open up the 10 percent slice of business cost that packers and processors say they can afford to devote to labor. Further, reduced volume will decrease dependence on repetitive and dangerous high-volume jobs for hourly workers. Research by the Department of Labor shows that most complaints from plant employees stem from perceived physical hardships on the job. Improve the jobs and the complaints will diminish. Follow up with more training. Workers in meat and poultry plants, who work with one of the most microbiologically volatile, and thus microbiologically dangerous, raw materials in all of nature must be considered technologists of a sort, not "disassembly grunts." Better pay and better training will bring more worker allegiance and employment longevity, thus reducing the need for continuous remedial training. And an operation peopled with "technologists" rather than mere "workers" will exhibit a better attitude and loyalty to the industry.

In 1990 Robert Peterson, chairman of IBP, made this prediction for the future of his company: "We'll be bigger. We'll be smarter. Nobody should feel sorry for us. We have to do what we have to do. If we don't do it, somebody else will" (Bjerklie 1990).

Whether Peterson knows it or not, the "it" he mentions in his last sentence must refer to the challenge of solving the issues and dilemmas of the meat and poultry industry. He is in one of the best positions to effect the changes required, but if he doesn't do "it," then "somebody else will." For if the issues and dilemmas continue to go unmet and unchallenged, the "somebody else" will not be a member of the meat and poultry industry, but in all likelihood will be part of some other food-manufacturing enterprise—or the government.

Notes

1. In addition to the FSIS, portions of the industry's commerce and management fall under the regulatory umbrellas of the USDA's Animal and Plant Health Inspection Service, the Agricultural Marketing Service, the Labor Department's Occupational Safety and Health Administration and Immigration and Naturalization Service, the Environmental Protection Agency, and numerous state and local agencies.

2. Major suppliers of beef are Canada, Australia, and New Zealand; Canada supplies pork and hogs.

References

American Meat Institute. 1993. *Meat and Poultry Facts*. Washington, D.C.: American Meat Institute.

Bjerklie, S. 1990. Straight Talk from Bob Peterson, Part 2. *Meat&Poultry* 36(8):33–34.

Rifkin, J. 1992. *Beyond Beef: The Rise and Fall of the Cattle Culture.* New York: Dutton.

Skaggs, J. M. 1986. *Prime Cut: Livestock Raising and Meatpacking in the United States, 1607–1983.* College Station: Texas A&M University Press.

U.S. Bureau of the Census. 1994. *Statistical Abstract of the United States: 1994.* Washington, D.C.: U.S. Government Printing Office.

4 | Killing Them Softly

Work in Meatpacking Plants and What It Does to Workers

Donald D. Stull
Michael J. Broadway

In the beginning he had been fresh and strong . . . but now he was second-hand, so to speak, and they did not want him. He was a damaged article, to put it exactly. And yet it was in their service that he had been damaged! They had got the best out of him, there was the truth—they had worn him out, with their speeding up and their damned carelessness, and now they had thrown him away! . . . The packers had gotten the best of them all. . . . Some had been frankly told that they were too old, that a spryer man was needed; others had given occasion, by some act of carelessness or incompetence; with most, however, the occasion had been the same as with Jurgis. They had been overworked and underfed so long, and finally some disease laid them on their backs; or they had cut themselves, and had blood-poisoning, or met with some other accident. When a man came back after that he would get his place back only by the courtesy of the boss. The only exception to this was when the accident was one for which the firm was liable; in that case they would send a slippery lawyer to see him, first to get him to sign away his claims, but if he was too smart for that, to promise him that he would always be provided with work. The promise they would keep strictly and to the letter—for two years. Two years was the "statute of limitations" and after that a man could not sue.

—Upton Sinclair, 1906

WHEN UPTON SINCLAIR wrote this passage in 1905, work in a meatpacking plant was difficult, dangerous, debilitating. It still is:

The case was that of a black man in his mid-30s, who now shines shoes in a carwash in Amarillo. At the time he was injured at Swift, on April 18, 1988, he was making $252 a week. He was stabbed in his forearm, but soon went back to work on light duty. But the injury was to his "hook hand" and it kept swelling. He was then assigned to splitting forequarters but he couldn't perform the job satisfactorily and was terminated. The scar is an impediment to getting a good-paying job. Employers see it and shy away from hiring him. (Stull fieldnotes, 1989 [workers' compensation hearings, Garden City, Kansas])

Reading and rereading *The Jungle* over the last six years, while studying beefpacking and beefpacking workers, we have been struck with how little has really changed. "Knockers" still start the killing, but now they use a "stun gun" instead of a sledgehammer. "Splitters" are still the most expert and highly paid workers on the "kill floor," deftly splitting carcasses with Jarvis Buster V band saws on moving platforms, where once they used massive cleavers. "Boners" and "trimmers" still turn cattle into meat with razor-sharp knives.

Beefpacking plants are massive factories, employing hundreds or even thousands of workers on "disassembly" lines, killing, bleeding, skinning, gutting, cutting, trimming, shrink-wrapping, and boxing hundreds of cattle an hour, 16 hours a day, 6 days a week. Beefpacking has always been labor-intensive, and, despite impressive technological advances, including computerization, laser technology, and robotics—the knife, the meat hook, and the steel remain the basic tools of the industry.

Immigrants continue to fill its ranks. No longer the Lithuanians, Bohemians, Poles, and Slovaks of Sinclair's day, today's packinghouses are crowded with Mexican migrants, with refugees from Laos and Vietnam, Guatemala and Nicaragua, with blacks, whites, and Latinos from America's farms and cities. And the respectable citizens of packinghouse towns still look askance at these workers in their midst, even as they fret about plant closings.

But the nine decades since the publication of *The Jungle* have also brought change. Modern plants slaughter only cattle or hogs, not both. Cattle are no longer shipped in by rail to stockyards and slaughterhouses in Chicago, Kansas City, and Omaha—and are no longer shipped out by rail as hanging beef to be broken down by butchers in shops and groceries. The packinghouses have moved to rural areas on the High Plains adjacent to centers of cattle feeding, where feedyards fatten cattle. Finished animals are transported from feedyards to slaughter over shorter distances—four hours or so at most in lightweight cattle trailers. Each day as many as 100 semis pull into the larger plants to unload cattle, which are then transformed into boxed, shrink-wrapped beef, that leaves the plant in refrigerated trailers for major markets hundreds of miles away (Broadway and Ward 1990).

Inside the plant, meat moves along "chains" or down conveyors,

Fabrication floor of a modern beef plant. (Courtesy of Meat&Poultry*)*

where once men moved rapidly from carcass to carcass. Workers now wear color-coded hard hats to mark their job status, and they are bedecked like gladiators in safety equipment costing hundreds of dollars to reduce the ever-present risk of injury.

Changes are also evident among the workers. Women now wield hooks and knives alongside men, skinning and trimming in Slaughter, boning and trimming in Fabrication. In 1992, the workforce at IBP's Finney County plant was 26 percent female, up from 20 percent in 1984 (Stull 1994). At its new beef plant in Lexington, Nebraska, which opened in November 1990, IBP has tried to attract female employees by providing the first on-site day care in the industry. One-quarter of the new hires in its initial 21 months were women (Gouveia and Stull, this volume).

One aspect of meatpacking that stubbornly remains is danger on the line. Meatpacking had the highest injury and illness rate of any industry in America during the 1980s—well ahead of poultry processing and more than three times greater than the overall manufacturing average (Broadway, this volume). The most significant illnesses are those associated with repeated motion and, in particular, carpal tunnel syndrome—"a condition in which the nerve passing through the wrist to the hand is pinched and compressed because of fast repeated forceful motions" (Personick and Taylor-Shirley 1989:5). It "can frequently lead to severe nerve damage, and the crippling of the hand or wrist, making it impossible for workers to grip or pick up everyday objects" (Brooks 1988:13). The incidence of repeated trauma disorder among meatpacking workers increased by nearly 300 percent between 1979 and 1986. By 1986 the rate of repeated trauma disorder for meatpacking workers was 479/10,000 full-time workers, while the comparable rate for manufacturing workers was just 22/10,000 (Personick and Taylor-Shirley 1989). Osborn (1992) reports an astounding rate of repeated trauma disorders for meatpacking and poultry-processing workers: 1,336/10,000 and 696/10,000, respectively—far ahead of any other industries. (For a summary of recent information on the causes and incidence of cumulative trauma disorder, as well as the controversy surrounding this occupational hazard, see Eicher 1994.)

In this chapter we examine some of the reasons behind meatpacking's high injury and illness rate and consider institutional responses to worker safety. We conclude with some recommendations for improving the industry's record.

Legal Controls and Worker Safety

Until the mid–twentieth century the principal compensatory mechanism for a worker injured on the job through employer negligence was tort law—a civil action for injury caused by wrongful conduct. Under tort law, a large proportion of any award to an injured employee goes to the lawyer who brought the action. This factor, combined with employers' mounting costs of defending civil suits, made workers' compensation an attractive alternative for settling disputes between employers and employees. By 1949 every state had instituted a workers' compensation system. Under workers' compensation, employers are required to carry insurance so that, in the event of work-related injury, the employee is entitled to compensation. This system is supposed to encourage the reduction of injuries, since insurers have an incentive to contain costs by implementing safety programs. Critics of workers' compensation argue that benefit levels are usually low and workers are required to forfeit their opportunity to utilize the tort system to gain a potentially higher award. Moreover, employers sometimes dispute applications for compensation on the basis that the injury was not work-related or that it is not covered by the compensation law. Such disputes have been especially common among cases involving occupational diseases (Frank 1993:110–12).

In response to increasing public concern about occupational hazards, Congress first enacted legislation to deal with mine safety in 1969; a year later a wide range of workplaces were included under the Occupational Safety Health Act of 1970. This act established the Occupational Safety and Health Administration (OSHA) and gave it certain rule-making and enforcement responsibilities, such as establishing standards for handling hazardous chemicals. Under the act, enforcement responsibilities are shared with states. OSHA has the authority to approve state enforcement plans, so long as they are considered as effective as federal enforcement. Currently, 23 states have federally approved state enforcement plans (Frank 1993:113). Some experts consider these plans far less effective than the federal system (Garland 1991). A 1992 OSHA review of state enforcement plans found deficiencies in workplace safety and health regulations in a number of states (Karr 1992). The problems associated with state enforcement were dramatized when 25 workers died in a fire at the Imperial Food Products poultry-processing plant in Hamlet, North Carolina, in 1991. Many of those who perished were prevented from escaping by locked doors. North Carolina has its own safety standards and enforcement program that require employers to keep exit doors clear, but the plant had never been inspected. Indeed, the state legislature cut the safety budget by 40 percent during the previous decade, leaving just 27 inspectors and trainees to monitor 180,000 employers (Garland 1991).

At the federal level, critics of OSHA argue that it has relied too heavily upon industry's voluntary compliance and has not been sufficiently vigorous in enforcing standards. During the early years of the Reagan administration, for example, the number of OSHA enforcement personnel decreased, along with the number of workplace inspections, violations, and imposed penalties (Claybrook 1984). When two workers died at National Beef's plant in Liberal, Kansas, in 1983, overcome by toxic fumes while trying to clean a blood-collection tank, OSHA fined the company $960 and asked that the cleaning routine be made safer. OSHA followed up with one routine safety visit. Eight years later, three workers died while trying to clean the very same tank. This time OSHA fined the company $1.5 million, but that doesn't mean the company will end up paying that amount, since OSHA has a long history of reducing its fines (Painter 1991; Freedman 1992).

OSHA and the Packers

Through 1987, OSHA focused primarily upon the underreporting of work-related injuries in packinghouses. Since 1988 the agency has shown a much greater concern with injuries caused by repetitive motion. Tom Lantos, house chairman of the Employment and Housing Subcommittee of Government Operations, drew attention to both issues when he held hearings in 1987 on alleged record-keeping violations and assertions of unsafe working conditions in the meatpacking industry, particularly IBP's Dakota City, Nebraska, plant (*New York Times* 1987; Brooks 1988). The first packing company to be cited for alleged record-keeping violations was John Morrell. OSHA proposed a fine of $690,000 for 69 violations at the company's Sioux Falls, South Dakota, plant (*Wall Street Journal* 1987). Three months later, OSHA proposed a $2.6 million fine against IBP for deliberately concealing worker injury and illnesses at its Dakota City plant. IBP was charged with "willfully failing to record 1,038 job-related injuries and illnesses in 1985 and 1986." Going unreported were knife wounds, concussions, burns, hernias, fractures, and carpal tunnel syndrome (Shabecoff 1987).

In 1988 OSHA proposed a $3.1 million fine against IBP for requiring employees to do repetitive motions that endanger their health. The fine was based upon the results of an ergonomics study of the Dakota City plant. According to the study, 620 workers at 45 workstations were at "grave risk" of developing repetitive motion illnesses. The $3.1 million fine represented a $5,000 fine for each of the 620 workers (Associated Press 1988). This fine and one of $2.6 million from the previous year were subsequently lowered to $975,000, when IBP agreed to redesign its disassembly line and other production areas to reduce job injuries. The agreement required IBP to establish a three-year education program for its managers and workers on the causes and prevention of carpal tunnel syndrome at all its meatpacking plants (Noble 1988). A similar arrangement was reached between OSHA and John Morrell in

1990, when the agency agreed to lower an earlier $4.3 million fine for violations at the firm's Sioux Falls plant to $990,000. In return, Morrell agreed to hire a neurologist from Johns Hopkins Medical School to oversee medical operations at the plant; conduct an ergonomics study of the plant; and allow injured workers to seek treatment from their own physicians, instead of company doctors (Swoboda 1990).

Other packers have also been fined by OSHA. In March 1991, Monfort was fined $1.1 million for "egregious violations of safety laws" at its Grand Island, Nebraska, beef plant (Swoboda 1991). A year later, Monfort's parent company, ConAgra, Inc., the nation's largest meat and poultry firm, agreed to pay $425,000 for violating record-keeping and other safety regulations at its turkey-processing unit (*Wall Street Journal* 1992). This litany of violations, fines, and subsequent "agreements" attests to the dangerous nature of meat-processing work and calls into question the packers' commitment to safety.

Fines and associated adverse publicity have forced the industry to address some of the issues surrounding worker safety. According to J. Patrick Boyle (1992), president and CEO of the American Meat Institute: "In recent years, the meat industry has reemphasized its long-standing commitment to preventing workplace accidents. . . . As a result, the meat industry has made substantial progress in reducing accidents." Citing the Bureau of Labor Statistics, he asserts that accidents dropped 14 percent and combined injuries and illnesses declined 10 percent from 1988 to 1989. He attributes this dip to greater cooperation with OSHA and the United Food and Commercial Workers (UFCW) in information and training programs. Our own examination finds that the occupational injury and illness rate for meatpacking did indeed fall between 1988 and 1989, but only by 4.1 percent. In 1990, however, it climbed to 42.4 per 100 full-time workers, 7.1 percent above the 1989 figure and 8.9 percent higher than it had been a decade earlier (see Table 2.1 in Broadway, this volume). If the meat industry is in fact more aware of and concerned with worker safety, why have occupational injuries and illnesses continued to climb steadily?

Getting It Out the Door

As injuries and illnesses rose throughout the 1980s, so too did packer productivity: by 21 percent between 1980 and 1986 (Austin 1988c). For management, productivity means "getting it out the door." Production quotas, tied to supply of fat cattle and demand for boxed beef, both of which fluctuate seasonally, even daily, apparently take precedence over safety and perhaps even product quality and purity.

Productivity is measured by "chain speed"—the number of carcasses processed in an hour. Chain (or line) speed is regulated by management. Debbie Berkowitz, the UFCW's health and safety director, maintains that speeds have increased by 50 to 80 percent in the past decade (Osborn 1992).

When the chains run too fast, line workers sacrifice safety and quality to keep up. But keep up they must.

> The fact is that they don't take time enough to explain something to you so that you can do a good job for them, you know. They're always in such a hurry 'cause the line runs so fast. . . . The production, when I left was 352 head an hour. Now they've upped it to over 400 an hour. (Stull interviews with former IBP slaughter worker, August 16 and September 16, 1988)

The packers get more out of each worker, in part through technological innovations that allow machines to do more of the work. But, more importantly, when the packers "speed up the chain," workers must produce more just to keep up—and to keep their jobs. Some quit; others are let go; many are injured.

> [The floor is a dangerous place to work] because of, one, the fast paced orientation of it. You know, trying to shove that meat through there as fast as they can. That sounds kind of bad to say, but basically that's what it's all about. . . . There is so much equipment involved and it's all enclosed in such a small area. I mean, it's a big plant, but on the other hand, compared to what's there, it's a small area, and you're confining people in those areas, plus you have people that are working with sharp instruments. I mean, you know, you have people that are standing shoulder to shoulder working with knives and things of that nature, so naturally they're going to be prone to something happening, especially with guys not paying attention to what he's doing or got something else on his mind, you know, the usual things. The push of "we've got to get the product out the end of the door" can at times be trouble because you're putting everybody on that edge of they got to get it done. And you have to have that to a certain degree and then again, you can go beyond that into where it becomes so much of an ideal thing to simply shove that stuff out the door that they start forgetting safety, they

start forgetting, and you start cutting shortcuts to what you're supposed to do as a rigid routine. And that can hurt you pretty bad. You're working around very dangerous equipment, equipment that can maim or kill you, you know, in a matter of a split second. (Stull, interview with IBP maintenance worker, May 9, 1989)

Turnover

The Current Population Survey for January 1991 found meat-products industries to have the lowest median employer and occupational tenure of all occupations surveyed (Maguire 1993:33). This should come as no surprise to anyone familiar with meatpacking. The five beef plants in southwest Kansas report average *monthly* turnover of between 6 and 8 percent (Wood 1988:76). Such turnover, 72 to 96 percent annually, is considered acceptable, even low, by industry standards; the National Institute for Occupational Safety and Health reported rates between 200 and 400 percent at the John Morrell plant in Sioux Falls, South Dakota, for the year ending April 30, 1988 (NIOSH 1989).

Turnover in meatpacking, as in any industry, includes workers who do not make probation, those who are fired, and those who quit. Managers and workers agree that the line is unpleasant and distasteful. Most of all it is hard—not everyone can "pull count."

> Our jobs kind of center on the ability to utilize their various instruments, cutting instruments basically, either saws or knives, and to be able to keep pace. . . . The work is physical in nature and it's very tough work as compared to some other industries. (Director of personnel at a Kansas beef plant interviewed by L. Boitano, KANZ Radio, June 12, 1989)

> The skinning line is the hardest part to work in the whole killfloor because of the hide. The hide is the hardest part, the toughest thing to cut. Those knives have to be pretty sharp in order to do a good job, and then to be tired. So if you're working with the butt knife, man, your hands swell, get blisters and everything. And finally they have to either move out or they have to tell the foreman they want to move out, [they want] some other job that you don't need to use a knife. It's up to them. A lot of people quit. (Stull interview with slaughter worker, June 19, 1989)

To keep their jobs, workers must "hang with it." It is a tough business, and little sympathy is given to those who cannot "pull their count." Management, from line supervisors to plant managers, wants efficient and compliant employees, workers who will do as they are told: "They can fire anybody. That's no problem for them. They tell you, if you can't do it, I'll get somebody else that can. . . . They can write you up for anything . . . three times and you are gone" (Stull interview with slaughter worker, June 4, 1989:37).

Industry critics and many workers say that high turnover benefits the packers, and they encourage it. Arden Walker, former head of labor relations for IBP, had this to say in a 1984 National Labor Relations board proceeding (Brooks 1988:11):

> COUNSEL: With regard to turnover, since you are obviously experiencing it, does that bother you?
>
> MR. WALKER: Not really.
>
> COUNSEL: Why not?
>
> MR. WALKER: We found very little correlation between turnover and profitability. An employee leaves for whatever reason. Generally, we're able to have a replacement employee, and I might add that the way fringe benefits have been negotiated or installed, they favor long-term employees. For instance, insurance, as you know, is very costly. Insurance is not available to new employees until they've worked there for a period of a year or, in some cases, six months. Vacations don't accrue until the second year. There are some economies, frankly, that result from hiring new employees.

Walker's testimony is borne out in figures on worker longevity. Only 48 hourly production workers, out of more than 15,000 IBP employees, received retirement benefits between 1974 and 1986 (Brooks 1988:11).

But even among those who believe the packers encourage turnover, there is disagreement over who they target.

> Q: I've heard it said that they try to get rid of people before the six months, when they become eligible for health insurance.
>
> A: I would say that it's backwards. They try to get rid of people that has been long enough there, because the longer they are there, they have to be paying two weeks vacation . . . in three years. And insurance and everything, stuff like that, and I think that the company more feels that it's like way extra weight to carry when a person has been there longer. So I would tend to think, and I have seen it, they get on some people's cases more often that has been there the longest. . . . So what they do is . . . the longer a person stays there, he gets closer to being watched, like for unsafe acts, absenteeism, if they need one time to crawl on your ass. (Stull interviews with slaughter worker, June 4, 1989:47; July 16, 1989:11)

Working on the trim line. Note how worker is stretching and off balance. (Courtesy of Meat&Poultry)

Other industry executives refute such assertions. Testifying under threat of subpoena before the Lantos subcommittee, IBP chairman Robert Peterson contradicted his former head of labor relations by maintaining that high turnover is not in his company's financial interest (Brooks 1988:11). Regardless of whether packers encourage turnover or not, high turnover means that plants have many inexperienced workers, and an inexperienced workforce is at greater risk for elevated rates of work-related injury and illness.

Safety

Meatpacking has always been dangerous. Despite the hard hats, goggles, earplugs, stainless steel mesh gloves, plastic forearm guards, chain mail aprons and chaps, leather weight-lifting belts—even baseball catcher's shin guards and hockey masks—meatpacking remains America's most hazardous industry. It is also the most dangerous industry in

Kansas, the national leader in beefpacking. From 1980 to 1988, 17,000 Kansas meatpacking workers were injured on the job, more than one-third lost work time, and 8 died. One-third of these injuries involved cuts and punctures; almost one-quarter were due to carpal tunnel syndrome or cumulative trauma disorder (Austin 1988b). In the past five years, six more workers have died.

Record OSHA fines for underreporting injuries and unsafe practices, coupled with declines in their labor pool, have forced packers to pay more attention to safety. Ergonomists try to improve equipment and tool design, new workers receive training and conditioning to protect them from injury, supervisors are held accountable for accidents on their crews, and incentives are offered for reducing accidents.

But "getting it out the door" is still the order of the day. Packers readily admit that injuries cost them money—but the cost is a minor, and an acceptable, one. Industry-wide, payment for workers' compensation benefits, insurance, and hospitalization averaged $1.47 per $100.00 of sales in 1986 (Austin 1988c). As meatpacking's injury and illness rates have continued to rise through the 1980s and 1990s, so too have packers' concerns with the costs of workers' compensation. For some plants these expenditures now exceed 5 percent of total costs (Stull fieldnotes, March 23, 1994).

Workers' Compensation

a calculated trade-off b/w injury safety related costs & productivity gains

Injury and illness rates in the meat industry are shocking. The packers are on the defensive: demand for red meat is down among health-conscious consumers, and competition between firms—and meats—is fierce; recent fines for unsafe practices, underreporting, and negligence are unprecedented. Spokesmen defend their companies and their industry with arguments that they have "an extraordinary incentive to reduce costly accidents and illnesses in the workplace" and that they are spending "tens of millions of dollars . . . to improve worker safety"—a significant investment, they say, in an industry with an avowed profit margin of under 1 percent (Boyle 1992). But one must wonder as turnover and injury climb ever higher.

While statistics may surprise, even alarm, us, they cannot convey the pain and suffering of injured workers who often must live with their debilities long after the doctors and the lawyers have done with them. For such knowledge we turn to workers' compensation hearings, to see for ourselves the hurt visited on so many, and the working conditions that spawn it.

The following vignettes are taken from workers' compensation hearings Stull attended in Garden City, Kansas, in August 1988 and January–July 1989. To protect individual identities, names and occasional details have been changed.

The hearings began at 9:00 A.M. They are held the third Tuesday of the month in the city council chambers. The judge, the court reporter, and most of the lawyers came from out of town. All were Anglos; all but one were male. The judge wore a sport coat and tie; most of the attorneys wore dark suits and red ties, though one or two wore slacks and sport shirts, in deference to the August heat. Not counting the lawyers, there were about 10 people in the audience when the hearings began—most were claimants and their relatives. No one appeared to take notice of the anthropologist, sitting in the last row, taking notes.

The hearings were informal, and it was clear the attorneys knew each other very well. They called one another by first names; they smoked, they joked, they talked about their golf games and their cases as if the claimants were not there. While the hearings went on up front, in the back of the room and out in the hall waiting attorneys talked among themselves or to their clients.

The second case of the morning was a preliminary hearing for Hector Gomez, an IBP worker in his late twenties with a sixth-grade Mexican education who speaks no English. He was accompanied by a translator; his Anglo wife and baby were in the audience. He suffers from back problems, possibly a herniated disk, and had been to seven or eight doctors. They kept referring him back and forth and could not agree on what, if anything, was wrong, or what should be done about his condition. After hearing the recommendations of his most recent physician, the judge remarked, "My experience with Dr. Adams is that: one, he does not release people quickly; and, two, he likes to do surgery." The judge decided to send him back to Dr. X for more tests.

Hector's second hearing was not held until five months later. The company's attorney, Mr. Kimble, began by challenging the interpreter: "Are you related to the claimant? Are you a member of a union? [The interpreter, a Mexican American in his seventies, wore a postal-worker's union jacket—his son's.] How much are you paid?" Such challenges are standard, and the packinghouse lawyers are assertive and hostile toward claimants as a matter of course.

Hector testified he was not told what to do when he went to work at IBP; they just put him on the job. Meat came at him on a hook and he had to take it off and push it toward a saw. It came too fast, and as a result he hurt his back on October 8, 1987, or 11 months before his initial hearing. He was treated and released by several area physicians but still could not work because his back and legs hurt. Since his injury he had tried to do house and yard work, and a year after his injury he helped his landlord build a fence, but he could not sustain such activity for very long.

Before he took the job in which he was injured, Hector had cut meat at IBP, but he maintained he could no longer do that either because he couldn't stand for long. Before IBP he did cement work, lifted paper, planted grass. He didn't think he could return to any of his former jobs.

The judge ordered temporary total (TT) disability of $256 per week and vocational rehabilitation. The IBP lawyer wanted to send Hector back to his original job cutting meat, and the judge directed the attorney to refer him to a supervisor within 10 days to evaluate his ability to do such a job.

Two months later, Hector made his final appearance. His Anglo wife interpreted, though his attorney spoke Spanish and helped with a few words. He still could not work, and although he said he would try to find work, he thought he needed more treatment. The orthopedic surgeon to whom he was referred at his initial hearing, some eight months earlier, concluded he has 10 percent impairment and recommended that when he lifts he do so by bending his knees. Hector Gomez received a settlement for $7,500 and a "buena suerte" from the judge.

John Savage was 32 years old, an Anglo from the next county to the north, with long hair and tattoos on his forearms. He graduated from high school in 1974 and received an associate of arts degree in auto mechanics in 1986. Before he began working for IBP in September 1987 he was a manual laborer. He started as a knocker on B-shift. His first injury came in January 1988; at the time he was averaging $292.42 a week.

> JOHN: I was knocking—killing—cows. They run cattle through like a revolving chute, a restrainer, and the animals weren't being cleaned and the [stun] gun kept misfiring, so it bounced off most of the time. Instead of

knocking them once, you had to knock them two or three times. It kicked my right arm back into the cow's head.

ATTORNEY: As that occurred, did you have physical problems?

JOHN: My back hurt real bad, on my shoulder blade, the top part of my back.

ATTORNEY: Did you report that to anyone?

JOHN: Yes, the foreman and then the nurse.

ATTORNEY: As a result of notifying the foreman and the nurse was your job changed in any way?

JOHN: Yes, ma'am. I went home the night my back was hurting and I saw the nurse, and then I came [in the next night] and then I had to cut ears and tails.

ATTORNEY: What happened on January 12, 1988?

JOHN: The trolley that lowered the cows, that the cows were hanging from, came loose at the back. It's like a roller, it's got a hook in it. The hook goes through the cow's leg. It weighs about 5 or 6 pounds, and it came down and hit me in the shoulder blades.

ATTORNEY: Did you report the incident to anyone?

JOHN: There was a foreman standing right beside me when it happened.

ATTORNEY: Did you receive medical treatment as a result of that injury?

JOHN: No.

ATTORNEY: Did you request medical treatment?

JOHN: No.

ATTORNEY: Why didn't you request treatment?

JOHN: I was scared.

ATTORNEY: What do you mean, you were scared?

JOHN: When I went in the first time, and they sent me into the nurse, they just kept telling me that if I couldn't tell them what it was that happened to hurt my back I couldn't see the doctor. And I kept saying, "The guns aren't going off right." And they said that I had to be more specific, and I didn't know how to be more specific.

On February 2 John slipped and fell in a pool of frozen blood, landing on his buttocks and then his back. The next day he couldn't get out of bed. IBP did not at first provide medical treatment, so John went on his own. His doctor prescribed painkillers and nothing more. IBP subsequently sent him to the company doctor. He referred him to another physician for examination, who diagnosed a soft-tissue problem and told John to go back to work. John did not feel able to go back to work; when he asked to see another doctor he was terminated on February 15.

ATTORNEY: Currently do you feel capable of employment?

JOHN: No.

ATTORNEY: Why not?

JOHN: I can't do anything. My back hurts, right above the belt line. I have to change positions, lay down for a while, sit for a while. Sitting, laying, I change positions about 20 to 30 times per night, walking. I don't pick up anything, and just sometimes, heck, one time that I wanted to get up and I just, everything didn't work, and I just fell flat on my face.

The final hearing in John's case took place the following March as his pregnant wife sat in the back row. The doctors had concluded that his lower back injury resulted in a 10 percent impairment. He was not working, but said he planned to go back to school to become an RN. The company offered to settle for $4,500 plus medical costs. His attorney opposed the settlement, but the baby was due in July and they needed the money. They planned to move to Texas after getting the settlement. The judge also tried to talk him out of it, but Mr. Savage replied, "I feel I'm entitled to more but I don't think I'll get any more." "All right then," the judge said. "Good luck to you. I came close to not approving this."

During the break that followed, the judge commented that he would have been more forceful in trying to convince Savage not to settle, but the firm representing him had argued hard against a settlement. IBP's attorney then said that "he got about what he deserved. We had an ace up our sleeve on that one."

Susan Ramirez is Hispanic and in her early thirties. She started at IBP on November 16, 1987; on March 22, 1989, she fell at work. She claimed several people were walking with her when it happened. At the time of the injury she was pulling flat meat on the straight line, and before the injury she had problems with her hand cramping up.

Her job involved trimming fat with a knife off a piece of flat meat approximately 18 to 24 inches by 12 inches. She reached out with either her hand or a hook, depending on how close the piece was to where she stood; trimmed the meat; then threw the fat down a hole and put the meat back on the line.

She testified that because of the fall her spine was stiff from the back of her head to her leg. She went to Dr. Anh the next day; one week later she went to Dr. Bernofsky; several weeks later she saw Dr. Smith. Bernofsky gave her pills to help her sleep, but she couldn't take them at work because they would make her drowsy. She went to Smith three or four weeks later; he also gave her pills, but they did not help. Before she went to Bernofsky she went to a chiropractor, who gave her ultrasonic sound and traction, which improved her ability to walk and helped her feel less stiff.

This week she was returned to regular duty from light duty, and her back hurts once again. She claims that Bernofsky returned her to regular duty too early.

Mr. Roper, IBP's attorney in this case, asked if she could identify the witnesses to her fall—she couldn't. She only knew them by first name and face, which is fairly common. He said she worked at her regular job for one week after the fall. He also stated that company policy prohibits going to unauthorized physicians for work-related injuries. In fact, he said she got written up for going to Dr. Anh, whereupon she demanded to go to an authorized MD, who was Bernofsky.

IBP then called a witness, Karla, an Anglo woman in her late twenties, who is the assistant employment manager—she interviews and hires new employees—a job she has held for four to five months. She was Susan's superintendent at the time of the injury (which would make it impossible for her to have had her present job for four to five months, but that's what she said). She testified that Susan told her she fell and would be late on the line. After she got there she worked fine; when Karla asked her several times if she was all right, Susan said yes. Karla read from a statement that she had been asked to prepare on the incident a week or so later.

After Susan was written up for failure to report the trip to Dr. Anh, she stayed late to help Karla clean up (a voluntary duty). She told Karla she was upset that she had been written up and said that "IBP will pay" for the write-up.

Karla testified that company policy requires the company nurse to determine if a worker can go to an MD for a work-related injury.

Susan denied saying that IBP would pay for the write-up; Roper then produced a written statement by a fellow worker stating that he overheard her make such a statement to Karla. Roper interpreted her statement to mean that she would get on light duty and run up lots of medical expenses.

The judge denied further treatment by the chiropractor and authorized continued treatment by Bernofsky.

The Vietnamese man suffered a back injury while working at IBP. He was very wan, walked with a cane, and claimed he had been unable to make any of the several treating physicians understand him. Through his interpreter, he asked permission to have one of the two Vietnamese physicians in the region diagnose him. The company doctors–both Anglo men—say he either is suffering from psychosomatic conditions or is malingering.

IBP's attorney strongly opposed the request, asking why he should be sent to either of the Vietnamese general practitioners, when three orthopedic surgeons had found him to be malingering. "We've already spent $4,454.24, and they want us to spend still more because there is allegedly a communication problem." There was no doubt that IBP did not like the local Vietnamese doctor; it felt he always sided with the worker. The claimant's attorney contended that there was not only a language barrier but a cross-cultural barrier that needed to be broached.

The judge wanted to know if the local Vietnamese doctor's English could be understood and if indeed he spoke adequate English. None of the attorneys seemed to know. He ordered 15 weeks of TT at $224.25 per week and an examination and evaluation only (no more tests) by the Vietnamese physician.

Ms. Rivera was Hispanic, obese, and in her late twenties. The claimant received an average weekly wage of $271.87 at the time of her injury; she had been paid TT at a rate of $181.26. Monfort sent her to Drs. Cortez, Jenkins, and Bernofsky. At the time of the hearing, the company claimed she quit and was not disabled. She said she had been returned to light duty but was terminated because she couldn't keep up. To no one in particular before the hearings began, Ms. Rivera said, "There ain't no light duty out there."

Her injury, repetitive trauma or carpal tunnel syndrome, was dated from November 1988. She worked in the trim department, putting lids on boxes, then putting them on pallets; she also trimmed meat, sometimes with a Whizard knife (an electric-powered hand knife with a rotating cutting blade), sometimes with a regular knife. In October 1988 she began getting cramps in her hands and she couldn't lift anything. She told the nurse about her problem, and the nurse told her to put a "jelly" like Ben-Gay on her wrists and wrap her hands—it didn't help; her hands still were swollen. She was then sent to Bernofsky, who put her on light duty, but at work she was told to go right back to weighing and lifting boxes (in the 60- to 70-pound range).

When a box fell because of her swollen hands and lack of grip, Ms. Rivera's supervisor told her to pick up the meat and wash it. Once again she told the nurse about her problem and was again sent to Bernofsky, who then sent her to Cortez, who took her off work and did surgery on her right hand (she told him she didn't want surgery on both hands at the same time because she wouldn't be able to care for herself). Nevertheless, the hand remained swollen. She returned to work on April 28. She was told to wrap her wrist, and she did so. After work she unwrapped it and found a lump under the wrapping. She was told to soak her wrist over the weekend and return to work. She did so.

The next week she was working on the line pulling fat, bones, and meat from the trim line; the meat line became stuck, and she waved at the supervisor to indicate the problem because he couldn't hear her. He paid no attention, so she figured he didn't care, and she left the line. She was called in to the office and told she was being suspended for failure to do her job. She refused to sign the write-up slip, told them she couldn't do her job because of pain, and left to see the doctor. She went to the doctor because of the pain in her hands; from there she called her supervisor to tell him she couldn't work. He told her to get down there or else she would lose her job. She did not go back in.

She said she was still on pain pills and did not feel capable of going back to work in a packinghouse.

During cross-examination she said she started on the line weighing and putting 60- to 70-pound boxes on a pallet. She claimed to experience pain from both hands extending up her shoulders to her neck. However, the Monfort attorney said that none of the doctors' reports mentioned neck or shoulder injuries.

She said she was first suspended because swollen hands prevented her from working. Her supervisor then told her when she called in from the MD's office that if she didn't show up right then she didn't have a job. The attorney said that at the time she was suspended she had been put on indefinite suspension because of excessive absenteeism— four write-ups in the previous year (four written warnings in one year is cause for termination).

The fabrication superintendent was called to the stand. He testified Ms. Rivera had been given three write-ups for "no call–no shows." She had been put on light duty, upgrading trim—separating fat from the 50–50 line to the 80–20 line. He refuted Ms. Rivera's testimony. When she had called from the doctor's office, he said he told her to come in and see the personnel director: "We don't fire people over the phone; they have to have a 'fair treatment hearing.' "

The judge gave her TT from June 2 at $181.26 per week until Cortez released her.

Conclusion

> I aimed at the public's heart and by accident I hit it in the stomach. (Sinclair 1962)

The price of the packers' hunger for ever greater productivity is evident in the industry's high injury and illness rate, and graphically detailed in the workers' compensation cases presented here. Federal and state governments, which are responsible for administering worker safety laws, are often reluctant to do so for political and economic reasons. In Kansas, for example, the packing industry has brought over 8,000 jobs to the southwest portion of the state and a payroll of over $118 million a year. The packers have invested over $1 billion in buildings and equipment, and purchase millions of dollars of cattle and local services every year. To accommodate the packers, the 1988 state legislature chose not to tax industrial cleaning businesses to satisfy packers trying to hold down costs. It also revised the workers' compensation law to reduce payments for carpal tunnel syndrome and other industrial injuries (Austin 1988a). The Kansas Supreme Court struck down this provision in 1992, ruling that it discriminated against workers suffering from the condition (Associated Press 1992). In response to pressure from employers to reduce the costs of workers' compensation, the state enacted a new law in 1993, which includes new limitations on carpal tunnel syndrome claims and settlements (Associated Press 1993).

Wages paid to packinghouse workers remain low, offering minimal security or hope for advancement. And jobs are still dangerous, leaving all too many injured or disabled. After fining John Morrell & Co. for safety violations at its Sioux Falls, South Dakota, plant, OSHA asked the National Institute for Occupational Safety and Health (NIOSH) to evaluate cumulative trauma disorders (CTDs) at the plant. NIOSH investigators examined OSHA logs over the course of a year (May 1, 1987 through April 30, 1988) and independently examined selected employees and jobs for health risk. Using OSHA logs, they calculated an upper-extremity CTD incidence rate of 41.7/100; this compares to the overall industry rate of 6.7, and 0.1 reported for all U.S. industries in 1987. Half of the 200 workers they selected for questioning and examination suffered from upper-extremity CTDs. Of the 185 jobs videotaped for ergonomic analysis, the investigators found 62 percent to be at intermediate risk and 31 percent at high risk for producing upper-extremity CTDs. Workers who used vibrating tools, such as Whizard knives and saws, were at greatest risk of developing hand-wrist CTDs. The investigators concluded that not only did most jobs put workers at risk for developing CTD, but John Morrell failed to allow injured workers sufficient recovery time (NIOSH 1989).

Solutions to many of the problems that plague the meatpacking industry are no mystery. And while turnover and health and safety risks that existed at John Morrell's Sioux Falls plant in 1988 were excessive, they are nevertheless representative of the industry. The industry is becoming more attentive to its problems and its image, forced by government fines and mandates, lawsuits brought by workers, and a changing labor force.

[margin note: unionization not mentioned among the solutions]

The industry has taken seriously the concerns of consumers, concerned with their health and safety. And it is beginning to respond to issues raised by environmentalists and those concerned with more humane treatment of livestock. Why, then, despite government fines and the new ergonomic awareness, do occupational injuries and illnesses continue to rise? Why does employee turnover that approaches, and often exceeds, 100 percent a year remain the industry standard? Do the packers really want to reduce turnover and injury, or are these empty platitudes?

The solutions are simple and well known. Provide better and longer periods of training. Adequately staff work crews. Vary job tasks to relieve muscle strain. Provide longer recovery periods for injured workers. But, most of all, slow down the chain. The packers defend their inaction with cries of "slim profit margins" and "fierce competition between firms." And there is much truth in their excuses. But if the public outcry was loud enough, if the pressure was strong enough, they would hear, and they would respond. What is our excuse? Will we never hear the beating of our hearts over the growl of our stomachs?

Note

The field research that forms the basis for this chapter was funded primarily by a grant from the Ford Foundation's Changing Relations Project.

References

Associated Press. 1988. U.S. Fines Meatpacker $3.1 Million over Injuries. *New York Times,* May 12.

_____. 1992. Court Strikes Carpal Tunnel Provision. *Garden City Telegram,* April 13.

_____. 1993. Workers' Comp Bill: Key Provisions. *Kansas City Star,* May 12.

Austin, L. 1988a. Rich Potential for Kansas Carries Risk. *Wichita Eagle-Beacon,* September 11.

_____. 1988b. Riskiest Job in Kansas Escapes Close Scrutiny. *Wichita Eagle-Beacon,* December 4.

_____. 1988c. Fines Push Packers to Forefront of Worker Safety. *Wichita Eagle-Beacon,* December 11.

Boyle, J. P. 1992. Worker Safety Still One of Top Meat Industry Goals. *Wichita Eagle,* January 9.

Broadway, M. J., and T. Ward. 1990. Recent Changes in the Structure and Location of the U.S. Meatpacking Industry. *Geography* 75:76–79.

Brooks, J. 1988. *Here's the Beef: Underreporting of Injuries, OSHA's Policy of Exempting Companies from Programmed Inspections Based on Injury Records, and Unsafe Conditions in the Meatpacking Industry.* Forty-second report by the Committee on Government Operations together with additional views. Washington, D.C.: U.S. Government Printing Office.

Claybrook, J. 1984. *Retreat from Safety: Reagan's Attack on America's Health.* New York: Pantheon.

Eicher, D. 1994. The Risk of Repetition. Part 1 and 2. *Denver Post,* August 22, 23.

Frank, N. 1993. Maiming and Killing: Occupational Health Crimes. *Annals of the American Academy of Political and Social Science* 525:107–18.

Freedman, A. 1992. Workers Stiffed. *Washington Monthly* 24(11):25–27.

Garland, S. B. 1991. What a Way to Watch Out for Workers. *Business Week,* September 23: 42.

Karr, A. R. 1992. Review by OSHA Finds Deficiencies in States' Regulation of the Workplace. *Wall Street Journal,* February 3.

Macguire, S. R. 1993. Worker Tenure in 1991. *Occupational Outlook Quarterly,* Spring:25–37.

National Institute for Occupational Safety and Health. 1989. *Health Hazard*

Evaluation Report: John Morrell & Co., Sioux Falls, South Dakota. HETA 88-180-1958. Washington, D.C.: U.S. Government Printing Office.

New York Times. 1987. Safety Panel Widens Inquiry at Largest U.S. Meatpacker. June 13.

Noble, K. B. 1988. Accord Is Seen Reducing Injury in Meatpacking. *New York Times,* November 23.

Osborn, M. 1992. Repetitive Stress Injuries Up During Downturn. *USA Today,* January 20.

Painter, S. 1991. OSHA Fines National Beef $1.5 Million. *Wichita Eagle,* December 6.

Personick, M. E., and K. Taylor-Shirley. 1989. Profiles in Safety and Health: Occupational Hazards of Meatpacking. *Monthly Labor Review* 112(1):3–9.

Shabecoff, P. 1987. OSHA Seeks $2.59 Million Fine for Meatpackers' Injury Reports. *New York Times,* July 22.

Sinclair, U. 1962. *The Autobiography of Upton Sinclair.* New York: Harcourt, Brace & World.

———. 1988. *The Jungle.* The Lost First Edition, edited by G. DeGruson. Memphis: St. Luke's Press.

Stull, D. D. 1994. Of Meat and (Wo)Men: Meatpacking's Consequences for Communities. *Kansas Journal of Law and Public Policy* 3(3):112–18.

Swoboda, F. 1990. Meatpacker to Expand Treatment of On-Job Injuries. *Washington Post,* March 21.

———. 1991. Meatpacker Fined $1 Million by OSHA for Safety Violations. *Washington Post,* March 28.

Wall Street Journal. 1987. United Brands Unit Faces $690,000 Fine for OSHA Citations. April 28.

———. 1992. ConAgra Inc.: OSHA's Charges on Safety Settled by $425,000 Penalty. January 30.

Wood, A. 1988. *The Beef Packing Industry: A Study of Three Communities in Southwestern Kansas.* Final report to the Department of Migrant Education. Flagstaff, Ariz.: Wood and Wood Associates.

5 | Dances with Cows

Beefpacking's Impact on Garden City, Kansas, and Lexington, Nebraska

Lourdes Gouveia
Donald D. Stull

[handwritten: Garden City IBP plant: 12/80]

The High Plains—Where Cattle Is Still King

If you want to start a fight just about anywhere from Amarillo, Texas, to Aberdeen, South Dakota, from the Sandhills of Nebraska to the Flint Hills of Kansas, just mention those crazy folks from New Jersey and their silly notion of a buffalo commons.[1] This is cattle country. Now more than ever. In 1989 four Plains states—Nebraska, Texas, Kansas, and Colorado—marketed over 70 percent of the 23 million fat cattle in the 13 cattle-feeding states (Krause 1991:iii). And Kansas, Nebraska, and Texas rank first, second, and third in beef slaughter as well.

In Nebraska, beef production and processing represent more than 22 percent of the gross state product, and beefpacking accounts for one-half of the state's manufacturing jobs (Ackerman 1991a). Since 1985 Kansas has been first in beef slaughter. Its six major beef plants *[handwritten margin: Kansas]* have a combined daily slaughter capacity of 24,100 head—almost one-fifth of the national output. Five of these six plants are located in three communities in southwest Kansas—beefpacking's "Golden Triangle." They have a combined daily slaughter capacity of 20,300 head, or 84 percent of the state's output (Dhuyvetter and Laudert 1991:8).

Over the past two decades, beefpacking has increasingly concentrated in the central High Plains, in a belt from the Texas Panhandle to northeastern Nebraska. The reasons are simple—plenty of fat cattle, water, and cheap feed grain; good weather for raising cattle; and no labor unions to speak of (Webb 1986). Cattle no longer come to the slaughterhouses of Chicago and Kansas City; the packers have moved to the cattle—largely to minimize transportation costs and damage.

In December 1980, IBP, Inc. (formerly Iowa Beef Processors, Inc.) opened the world's largest beefpacking plant 10 miles west of Garden

City, Kansas, in rural Finney County. In 1983 another plant, now owned by Monfort (a subsidiary of ConAgra Red Meats), opened on the town's eastern edge. Today these facilities combine to employ approximately 4,200 workers who slaughter and process up to 8,400 head of cattle per day, six days a week.

On November 8, 1990, IBP began slaughtering cattle in Lexington, Nebraska, in the first new beef plant to be built in the United States since the Finney County, Kansas, facility. IBP currently employs about 2,100 workers to slaughter and process up to 4,000 head of cattle a day.

Garden City emerged from the 1980s as the "trophy buckle on the beef belt." Lexington is looking to outshine it in the 1990s. They offer a "natural experiment"—a chance for comparison of two packing-house towns at very different phases of rural industrialization—Garden City a decade after industry expansion and Lexington during plant construction and start-up.

Methodology

From the summer of 1987 until February 1990, Stull directed five anthropologists and a geographer in an investigation of relations between Anglos, Hispanics, and Southeast Asians in Garden City as part of the Ford Foundation's Changing Relations Project. The team produced a community study, focusing on work (especially meatpacking), schools, neighborhoods, and community structure. Although emphasizing participant observation, the researchers conducted 260 formal interviews with a wide range of Garden Citians and collected an array of documents and numerical data (see Benson 1994; Broadway 1990, 1994; Broadway and Stull 1991; Stull et al. 1990; Stull 1990; Stull and Broadway 1990; Stull, Broadway, and Erickson 1992; and Stull 1994).

Late in 1988, IBP announced it would open a beef plant in Lexington, Nebraska. Lexington established a Community Impact Study Team (CIST), which visited packing towns and sponsored public forums. A CIST representative visited Garden City in January 1989. Researchers and community members from Garden City visited Lexington the following April to report on changes Lexington might expect. In the summer of 1990 the authors, along with Michael Broadway, began collecting baseline socioeconomic and demographic data in Lexington and conducting interviews. Since then we have monitored developments in the community and conducted intermittent fieldwork. From July through December 1992, Stan Moore, a Spanish-speaking doctoral student in anthropology at the University of Kansas, carried out fieldwork in Lexington, engaging in participant observation, interviewing workers, and gathering social and demographic data.

The Lexington team has cultivated contacts with and purposely sampled a cross section of established Lexingtonians for ongoing conversations and interviews: cattle feeders; packing-plant managers, professionals, and line workers; employers; social service providers; professionals; educators; and "everyday citizens." Of special interest to Gouveia are the experiences of new-immigrant Latinos and Latinas. She, along with Moore and their local interviewers, has completed 50 structured interviews with Latino/a heads of household and informally interviewed another 100 Latino newcomers (most employed at IBP).

Garden City and Lexington

Lexington is 220 miles west of Omaha and 320 miles east of Denver. Originally a stop on the Oregon Trail, today it straddles another major east-west transportation artery—Interstate 80. Garden City is on the old Santa Fe Trail, 215 miles west of Wichita and 309 southeast of Denver. Located some 85 miles south of Interstate 70, Garden City is much more isolated than Lexington.

Both communities lay in the valleys of two of the Plains' major rivers—the Arkansas and the Platte—and both are bordered by sand hills. Across the usually dry bed of the "Ark" to the south of Garden City, the desolate sandsage prairie is now checkered with 132-acre circles of alfalfa and corn, made lush throughout the growing season by huge irrigation booms. Lexington, by contrast, nestles in the verdant valley of the Platte, Nebraska's shallow, meandering Nile. Fifty miles or so north of town, the Sandhills begin, long a bastion of cattle ranching.

Beginning in the mid-1960s, center-pivot irrigation enabled farmers in southwest Kansas to tap the vast underground reserves of the Ogallala Aquifer and cultivate a variety of feed grains. The widespread availability of both water and feed spawned commercial feedyards. In 1964 there were 197,000 cattle fattened on grain in nine counties in southwest Kansas; by 1987 the figure stood at 2.5 million. Finney County is the top cattle-feeding county in Kansas, and over 100 feedyards are lo-

Ingalls Feedyard, southwest Kansas. (Courtesy of Michael J. Broadway)

cated within a 50-mile radius of Garden City. Average capacity is 13,000 head, but some can hold 100,000 animals (Laudert n.d.).

Dawson County ranks first in Nebraska in both fat cattle and irrigated agriculture. It, too, sits atop the Ogallala—in some places only a few feet below the surface. But most irrigation comes from ditches, not circles. And even though about the same number of cattle are fattened in Dawson County as in Finney County—between 415,000 and 470,000 head a year—the pattern is one of small farmer-feeders, not gigantic commercial yards. In fact, the largest feeding operations in Dawson County would be among the smallest in Finney County.

Nebraska's more restrictive anticorporate farming law certainly accounts for some of the differences (*Dawson County Herald* 1991). Since IBP announced it would open a beef plant in Lexington, however, the number of cattle on feed has steadily climbed, local feedlots have expanded, and new commercial ones are opening. Still, the biggest operations have one-time capacities of 30,000 head or less (Ackerman 1991a). Despite these surface differences, it is no wonder that both Garden City and Lexington have emerged as natural centers of beef-packing.

Garden City combines low-wage mfg growth + regional service + trade center.

With an official population of 24,097 in 1990, Garden City is the largest community in western Kansas. It holds three-fourths of the county's population (33,070), and no town of any size is closer than 24 miles. A decade of rapid growth has made it the primary trade and service center for the surrounding region, eclipsing its chief rivals— Dodge City and Liberal—for the capital of beefpacking's Golden Triangle.

Lexington, on the other hand, is but one in a string of small to mid-size settlements along the Platte River. At 6,601, its official 1990 population was about twice as big as Dawson County's two other primary communities, Cozad (pop. 3,823) and Gothenburg (pop. 3,232), but it holds only one-third of the county's population. Unlike Finney County, Dawson County was hit hard by the farm crisis of the 1980s—its population fell some 11 percent during the preceding decade, due largely to the closing of Lexington's Sperry–New Holland combine plant in 1986.

Not only do they differ significantly in size and settlement patterns, but Garden City and Lexington have very different demographic profiles. Nine months before IBP opened its Finney County plant, the 1980 Census enumerated 18,256 people in Garden City—82 percent were white. The largest minority was Hispanic (16 percent), who first came in the early 1900s to work in the sugar beet fields and on the railroad (Oppenheimer 1985). One percent was African American, and 0.5 percent each was Asian and American Indian.

Two beef plants and a decade later, Garden City had been transformed into a multicultural community, with the addition of Mexican and Central American migrants, Vietnamese and Lao refugees. Not only was Garden City the state's fastest-growing community in the 1980s, increasing by 33 percent, but it has become among its most ethnically diverse: 31 percent minority—25 percent Hispanic—according to the 1990 Census. School records reveal a higher and probably more accurate percentage of minorities—37 percent at the close of the 1990–91 school year (Broadway and Stull 1991:6).

In Lexington the 1990 Census, taken eight months before IBP opened on the site of the old Sperry–New Holland plant, counted 6,601 people, making it one-third the size of Garden City at the same point in its development as a packinghouse community (Loughry 1991a). Like Garden City, Mexicans settled in the Platte River valley in the 1920s, finding work harvesting sugar beets and potatoes and on the Union Pacific Railroad. But unlike Garden City, they were few and remained largely "invisible" to Anglos. The 1990 Census reported 4.9 percent of Lexington's population as Hispanic; 7.3 percent were classified as minority.

Social and Economic Changes in Garden City, 1980–90

Building on new jobs in beefpacking, Garden City and Finney County have sustained a prolonged period of apparent economic growth. Employment rose by 55 percent (4,200 jobs) from 1980 to 1988, and the gain in local payroll has received credit for much of the growth in the service and retail trades. Thirty-nine new retail stores opened, many in a new shopping center anchored by J. C. Penney and Wal-Mart; 17 new eating and drinking establishments opened; and four new motels opened (Broadway and Stull 1991).

But most of the new jobs pay low wages. The starting hourly wage for production workers at IBP is now $6.60, at Monfort $6.25. Gross annual income for IBP line workers ranges from about $15,500 to $22,000, depending on job grade and length of employment. Hours worked—and income—vary seasonally and even weekly depending on price and supply of fat cattle, consumer demand, and profit margins. Monfort closed its plants in Garden City and Dumas, Texas, for a week in mid-February 1992 and cut back hours at its other plants; IBP ran on reduced hours much of the winter of 1992 (Painter 1992). It was much the same in 1993. But the winter of 1994 found the plants running strong because of a drop in the price of fat cattle.

Most new jobs outside packinghouses are in the service sector and characterized by even lower pay and part-time employment. Many holding such jobs must rely on social service agencies for supplemental food, medical care, and other basic needs. The cumulative effect of this boom in low-wage jobs shows in per capita income: in 1980 Finney County's was 94 percent of the state average; by 1988 it had dropped to 91.5 percent, more than $1,300 below the state average and $2,111 below the national average (Broadway and Stull 1991:4).

Garden City's rapid growth created immediate demand for housing. While new construction has helped, most line workers live, at least initially, in mobile home parks on the outskirts of town. One-tenth of Garden City's population reside in one trailer park alone, built specifically—and reluctantly—to house IBP's expanding workforce.

Not surprisingly, school enrollment soared. From 1980 to 1990, it jumped from 4,535 to 6,600, an increase of 45 percent! Garden City voters responded by approving bond issues to build three new elementary schools and expand existing facilities. Minority enrollments roughly doubled, while bilingual and ESL programs greatly expanded. Recruitment of minority and bilingual teachers remains a serious problem, however.

In 1990, Garden City's school district had the highest dropout rate in Kansas, student turnover of almost one-third each year, and chronic absenteeism. Of ninth graders in 1986, 36 percent dropped out by the time their class graduated four years later. Underlying causes are complex, but poverty is clearly a factor—36 percent of the district's students qualify for the federal lunch program. It is not surprising, then, that many students must work: two-thirds of those in high school do—one-third for more than 35 hours a week. Officially none of the packers hire anyone under 18, but underage workers have been reported, and for a time Monfort even advertised for workers in the high school newspaper. Of course, many students are over 18, and some work the B-shift, going from school to the plant floor and arriving home after midnight (Broadway and Stull 1991:6).

Various social disorders rose dramatically in the 1980s. Both violent and property crime climbed throughout the decade in Finney County, while falling in the state. The incidence of child abuse more than tripled to exceed the state average by 50 percent (Broadway and Stull 1991:7).

Increased demands on service providers offer another, and more telling, barometer of the declining fortunes of newcomers and old-timers alike. Emmaus House opened in Garden City in 1979 amid a wave of newcomers drawn by the construction of IBP and a new power plant. Started by church volunteers, the house provides temporary shelter and hot meals for indigent transients and newcomers seeking work, and food boxes and commodities for the community's poor. In 1988 it sheltered 625 people, served a total of 69,000 meals, and gave out 3,614 holiday food boxes—a level of service two-and-a-half times greater than six years earlier (Broadway and Stull 1991:8).

The costs of a decade of economic expansion are also paid in declining levels of worker health and a growing crisis in access to health care. Meatpacking is America's most dangerous industry, as recent tragedies and record OSHA fines have reminded us. More than 4 out of every 10 meat-processing workers suffer injury each year (see Stull and Broadway, this volume). Attention focuses on injuries and unsafe practices on the floor; we don't hear much about packers' health insurance policies, however. If they can afford the premiums, and many cannot, coverage is minimal. It does not even begin for line workers at IBP's Finney County plant for six months. Even then, the individual deductible is $300, and a second family member must incur an additional $300 in covered expenses before the family deductible is satisfied; preexisting conditions, including pregnancy, are not covered; and if the carrier is not notified of pregnancy six months prior to the due date, benefits are reduced by $500 (IBP 1991).

IBP: health insurance plan

Line workers face occupational hazards and, along with their families, limited access to care. They are not alone. In Finney County the ratio of physicians to population has fallen sharply. In 1988 there was one physician for every 858 persons in Finney County; five years later, in 1993, there was only one physician for every 1,897 persons. Health care is even more remote for the poor: of Garden City's 15.8 full-time equivalent (FTE) primary-care physicians, only one's practice is devoted exclusively to the medically indigent, and only 2.96 FTE is available for persons at or below 200 percent of the poverty level (Kansas Department of Health and Environment 1993; United Methodist Mexican-American Ministries 1994). Thus, health care is increasingly remote for all Garden Citians, but especially for those with limited ability to pay.

Social and Economic Changes in Lexington, 1990–93

Unlike Garden City, Lexington knew what to expect and had time to prepare for IBP's coming. Financed in part by IBP, members of Lexington's Community Impact Study Team (CIST) traveled to Garden City, Dodge City, and Emporia, Kansas, and to Norfolk, Nebraska (at times flying in the company's plane), to see for themselves major packing plants and the towns that host them. In addition to the Garden City research team, they invited city and school officials from Garden City and Norfolk to speak in Lexington and provide reports on vital issues such as housing (Norfolk Area Chamber of Commerce 1989) and schools (Garden City School District 1989). Nevertheless, changes between 1988, when the new plant was announced, and 1993, three years after it opened, mirror those in Garden City.

The opening of IBP's plant in November 1990 fueled unprecedented growth, and the census data from the previous April were obsolete before they were released. Recognizing the inopportune and costly timing of the 1990 Census, county officials paid for a recount, conducted on February 24, 1993. This special census enumerated 8,544 persons in Lexington—an increase of 1,943, or 29 percent, in three short years. Hispanics, virtually all new immigrants, increased almost fivefold to 24 percent of the population (2,021 persons). Overall, Dawson County grew by 13 percent, making it and an adjoining county Nebraska's fastest-growing counties in 1990 and 1991 (Ackerman 1993a).

During IBP's start-up, unemployment in Dawson County fluctuated widely from month to month—from 2.3 percent in December 1990, for example, to 7.2 percent in May 1991. By 1993, however, average unemployment for the county had stabilized at around 3.3 percent (Nebraska Department of Labor 1990–93). Some businesses—banks, feedlots, food stores—have done well, and several have expanded. Storefronts downtown are all occupied, and new businesses have opened near the interstate.

industrial restructuring

But as in Garden City, most new businesses are in the service sector, where wages are low and employment generally part-time. Typical is Amigos, a franchise restaurant, that advertises pay "up to $5 per hour" plus benefits. The nature of the businesses that have recently opened in Lexington—fast-food franchises, liquor stores, a convenience store and service station, a pawn shop, a shoe-repair store, a warehouse discount store (Loughry 1992c)—suggest a working population earning wages considerably below those paid by Sperry–New Holland a decade earlier. As one prominent citizen put it, New Holland paid "higher wages than what normal people were making in this area at the time. . . . People went to stores and bought refrigerators and stoves and everything else on that credit . . . and [they thought] that money would always be there to pay off their debts" (Gouveia interview, May 7, 1991).

Lexington's annual net taxable sales have shown average increases slightly above those for the state as a whole, in contrast to decreases found in Dawson County's other communities. A 1993 survey conducted by Consumer Media Services for the local newspaper found that sales of televisions, stereos, washers and dryers, and automobiles rose by an average of 5.8 percent between 1990 and 1993. Furniture sales doubled during the same period. But much of the capital generated by new businesses, such as food franchises and large retail chains, leaves town. The same survey also found an increase in the number of people who go elsewhere to do their shopping: local retailers are often unable to match the prices and more convenient hours of discount malls in nearby larger communities. In contrast, the local Wal-Mart, located across the highway from IBP, and grocery stores have enjoyed significant increases in sales (*Clipper-Herald* 1993; Nebraska Department of Revenue 1993).

Wal-Mart + IBP [handwritten margin note]

According to the Nebraska Public Power District (1990), about 40 percent of Dawson County workers are employed in the retail and service sector; their average annual wages range from $5,000 to $15,000. Approximately 77 percent of the job openings in 1990 paid under $6.00 an hour. By 1992 these figures had changed very little: the average wage offered by employers listed with the Nebraska Job Service was $5.31 an hour. Forty-five percent of the openings in "high-growth occupations," such as clerical, sales, agriculture, and services, were part-time. Only processing (IBP) and construction posted high numbers of openings for full-time work (Nebraska Department of Labor 1992).

The impact of the "new packers" on their smaller, "old-line" competitors is well documented, and Lexington proved no exception. Cornland Beef Industries, a 30-year-old beef-slaughter facility that employed 180, closed in June 1991 (*Clipper-Herald* 1991; Ackerman 1991b). Even after extensive renovation in 1989, Cornland was unable to withstand upward pressures on wages and cattle prices accompanying IBP's move to Lexington. "IBP sure hasn't helped the situation with them coming in killing 4,000 a day. . . . I'd say the impact of IBP has been negative . . . they need so darn many cattle they go out and gather them and they set the price" (Gouveia interview with Cornland plant manager, May 9, 1991).

In spite of, or more likely because of, the relatively high starting wages at the Lexington plant ($7.15 to start and a $.40 raise after 30 days), many are ineligible for state aid but often cannot afford basic needs. As Amy Richardson, administrator of the Lexington office of the Nebraska Department of Social Services, remarked:

> We've gone from seeing people at poverty level as a result of joblessness to seeing more people who really are the working poor. These are people who are working and do not meet the poverty-level guidelines, but who are having a lot of difficulty making ends meet because of low wages or large families. (*Clipper-Herald* 1992a)

Preparing for the opening of Haven House, Lexington, Nebraska, June 1991.
(Photograph by Donald D. Stull)

By the end of 1990, when IBP opened, demand for social services was rising sharply. For Mid-Nebraska Community Services (MNCS), a state-sponsored agency, 1991 saw huge increases in demand for social services: referrals through its homeless program rose by 1,000 percent, and food pantry allocations were up 405 percent. Of the 27 counties MNCS serves, Dawson County had the highest increase—88 percent (*Clipper-Herald* 1992a). But in 1993 the number of families receiving allocations from the food pantry appeared to be leveling off, and a slight decline (2.3 percent) was recorded from the previous year. Nevertheless, demand remains high: 2.8 times greater than in 1989 (Dawson County Food Pantry 1989–93).

Haven House, founded in early 1991 to serve newcomers, provided 4,714 bed-nights and served 24,381 meals in its first year. Some 80 percent of guests were unaccompanied males (Haven House 1992). By 1993 the level of service had dropped off to 19,733 meals and 2,786 bed-nights (Haven House 1993). These declines in demand may reflect stabilization in Lexington's initial growth and stricter enforcement of Haven House's regulations on length of stay.

Crime has increased in Lexington: monthly police bookings jumped 63 percent between October 1988 and October 1991. Domestic violence and property crimes accounted for the largest increases (Loughry 1991c). Lexington's rising crime rate of 90.8 per 1,000 population was the highest in Nebraska in 1991, more than double the state average of 43.7 per 1,000 (Loughry 1992f). But in 1993 the overall crime rate fell 39 percent to 57.1 per 1,000 (*Clipper-Herald* 1994).[2] Nevertheless, traffic offenses and violent crimes continued to rise.

From 1989 to 1993, non-Hispanic whites accounted for most of the crime, but Hispanics are increasingly visible in crime statistics, especially traffic offenses. In 1989 Hispanics constituted 4.9 percent of Lexington's population and represented only 2.7 percent of the city's traffic offenses. By 1992, however, they accounted for 47.2 percent of such offenses, a rate almost double their proportion of the population (Lexington Police Department 1989–92).

The reasons behind this dramatic overrepresentation of Hispanics, most new immigrants, in traffic and other offenses are related to ignorance of local ordinances, lack of proper documents, and insufficient funds upon arrival to secure necessary insurance and driver's licenses. Recreational outlets are limited, especially for non–English speakers, and drinking at bars or private homes is a common source of entertainment. Excessive consumption of alcohol contributes to elevated rates of accidents, drunk-driving arrests, and domestic violence (Ackerman 1993b). Local law enforcement agencies, in cooperation with other groups, have produced a video in Spanish, which is designed to instruct new-immigrant Latinos in local ordinances and proper comportment. It remains to be seen whether it will have its intended effect.

School enrollments increased modestly at first, then accelerated to record levels. Enrollments in the Lexington schools rose from 1,670 in 1988 to 2,062 in September 1992, an increase of 23.5 percent (392 students). The first day of the 1993–94 school year saw 2,166 students enrolled in the Lexington schools, 5.9 percent above 1992 (Lexington Public Schools 1991–94).

Voters approved a bond issue in 1990 to renovate and expand two elementary schools, but overcrowding remains a problem: in the fall of 1991, elementary schools were at 88 percent capacity, the junior high at 98 percent, and the high school at 101 percent capacity (Loughry

1992b). Student turnover that same fall was 7.75 percent, but by the end of the school year it had climbed to 25 percent (Loughry 1992a, 1992e). New students made up 19 percent of total enrollment—they came from 20 states and five countries (Loughry 1992a)—and the new students are more ethnically diverse. Before IBP opened, minorities constituted 3.5 percent of the student body. By November 1991, IBP's first anniversary, minority enrollment had risen to 16 percent, and by September 1992 it stood at 23 percent (Loughry 1992d; Lexington Public Schools 1989–92).

Observers and many in the community agree that Lexington's transitional period could have been much worse; some even call it "smooth." Preparation is part of the answer, but so is the controlled flow of newcomers. Many were initially unable to settle in Lexington because of an acute housing shortage. In January 1990, citizens blocked the sale of city-owned land to a developer who planned to build a 40-unit apartment complex not far from the plant. By the summer of 1990, lack of housing forced IBP to buy a small motel to house construction workers. An 85-unit trailer court, built by out-of-town speculators who naively expected newcomers to move trailers into town, sat empty. An Arizona speculator teamed with a local farmer on a plan for a 240-unit "rental community" (rehabbed trailer park) in a bean field adjacent to the plant. Their request for rezoning included an impassioned warning by an IBP unit manager of "tent cities" if Lexington did not provide adequate housing. Like other plans for new housing, it did not materialize (*Dawson County Herald* 1990; Stull fieldnotes July 11, 1990).

In projecting housing demand, Lexington relied on a needs assessment conducted by an outside consulting firm. Based on figures provided by the company, the firm estimated IBP's workforce would be 1,400 and calculated that Lexington would need 334 new units by 1992. In a meeting with the housing consultants, local business and community representatives expressed their dissatisfaction with the housing shortage and related loss of revenues for the city. Some attributed this housing shortage to the fact that only those with limited purchasing power were moving to Lexington. As one prominent businessman put it:

> We need more housing for middle-income people, say in the $60- to $70-thousand dollar range. Maybe that's why [middle-income families] are not coming to town. When we first heard that IBP was coming, there was talk

about all the spinoffs that we were going to have. I really have not seen that except for fast-food restaurants. (Gouveia fieldnotes, July 1992)

Housing construction increased in 1991 and 1992, but it continued to lag behind demand. A housing study released in July 1993 concluded that Lexington was still experiencing a local housing "crisis" (Ackerman 1993c). An increased level of building activity is clearly evident in Lexington, however. Several new apartment complexes have been completed, some for low-income tenants, and the city has received grants for housing construction and renovation. The mobile home park is now full of rented units provided by a private contractor in cooperation with IBP, and other mobile home parks have expanded. The community has taken a prudent approach to new housing, emphasizing slow growth, rehab of existing rental units, and scattered-site development (Loughry 1991b). In 1992, IBP calculated that 1,600 of its 2,100 employees lived in Dawson County. As more housing becomes available, fewer workers will be forced to commute, and Lexington's growth will accelerate.

The Impact of Beefpacking on Workers: The New Faces of the Working Poor

IBP management has periodically given us summaries of the ethnicity, gender, and size of its workforce in Lexington. The company is not required to release details on its workforce, however, and it chooses not to do so (Tom Doering, Nebraska Department of Economic Development, personal communication). New employees fill out survey forms to determine employer tax credit (TJTC) eligibility.[3] IBP forwards these forms to the local office of Nebraska Job Services, which kindly made them available to us. Review of all applications from the plant's opening in November 1990 through July 1992 enabled us to measure hiring and turnover.

According to records provided by the local office of Nebraska Job Services, in its initial 21 months of operation, IBP-Lexington hired 5,004 workers. By February 1992 the plant's labor force leveled off at slightly over 2,000 workers (*Clipper-Herald* 1992b). With this figure as the denominator, we calculate that employee turnover during this period totaled 250 percent, or 12 percent per month. (This denominator

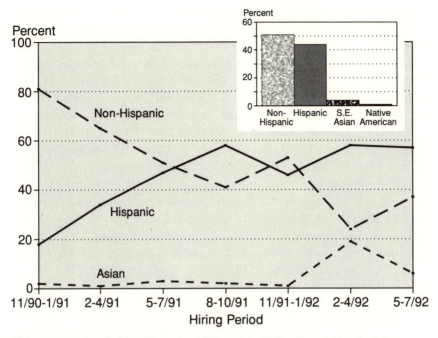

IBP new hires by ethnicity, November 1990 to July 1992. (From Nebraska Job Services, Dawson County, 1992.)

yields a conservative turnover rate, since it took some 16 months for the number of workers to reach this level.)

Using names to operationalize ethnicity, we found 51 percent of new employees were non-Hispanic (most are presumed to be Anglo, since few African Americans live in Lexington); 44 percent were Hispanic; 4 percent Southeast Asian; and less than 1 percent Native American.[4] But over time, a marked reversal in ethnic composition occurred: during start-up 81 percent of those hired were non-Hispanic; by the end of the study period that figure had fallen to 37 percent; conversely, the proportion of Hispanic new hires climbed steadily from 18 percent to 57 percent. Except for a sizeable influx in the winter of 1992, the number of Southeast Asians remained small.

The stereotypical meatpacking worker is a young, single male; however, packers admit targeting women in recruitment—they are seen as less mobile and more docile than their male counterparts. Company officials initially projected 60 percent of their processing workers (the majority of hourly employees) to be women, many single mothers. IBP also hoped that on-site day care—a first for the industry—might help lower turnover (Stull fieldnotes, June 28, 1990). But the day-care center has not been fully utilized, largely because workers cannot afford the fee IBP deducts from their wages (initially $9/day for the first child, $8 for the second; IBP now charges more). And IBP's workforce remains overwhelmingly male—76 percent over the study period. In fact, the proportion of women employees declined from 29 percent during the plant's initial three months to 20 percent at the end of the study period.

IBP takes a *Field of Dreams* approach to labor recruitment—"build it and they will come" (the company did, after all, start in Iowa). Company officials say they want to fill labor needs locally, but given plant size and the magnitude of turnover, everyone knows better. Word of mouth, enhanced by "bounties" offered to current employees for each new hire recruited, combine with advertisement in packing towns and pockets of high unemployment to bring in a steady flow of applicants. Recruiters take to the road as needed, and if labor supply is down they may offer to cover some initial expenses against wages. Many workers arrive in town broke, and even if they receive advances, the first few months are tough—both physically and financially. It appears that initial impoverishment is especially pronounced among Latinos, most of whom come originally from agricultural regions in Mexico, often moving from other jobs and locales in the United States. All workers interviewed cite either no work or poor wages and working conditions as reasons for picking up and moving to Lexington. Some have worked in other packing plants before.

In fact, interviews point to a circuit of Latino meatpacking workers, who regularly share information about wages and working conditions. For example, three Mexican IBP employees interviewed in the spring of 1991 said they left Monfort–Grand Island because workers with more seniority are given preferential treatment there. "They [Monfort] pay less, work you harder, and treat the newer worker with more disdain. . . . [The older workers] have their houses, their insurance, and the person that enters new is treated somewhat bad." At IBP "you can start working right away" (Gouveia fieldnotes, April 9, 1991).

But many of these same workers also tell of their frustration as they realize that wages and seasonally fluctuating work hours are insufficient to meet inflated housing, food, and medical costs typical of packing towns. The county assessor estimates that real estate prices have risen 20 to 30 percent since IBP came (Gouveia interview, March 20, 1992), forcing some to move into poorly insulated and run-down trailers, to share living quarters with many others, and to postpone sending for their families: "We pay too much here . . . and we don't even have beds to sleep on"; "I wouldn't bring my wife, they don't pay enough. . . . If I bring my wife, I can't live with a bunch of people" (Gouveia interview, April 9, 1991).

Men whose household members are able to work are more likely to bring their families with them and seem to be more optimistic about sticking it out for a year or two. But, as several women told us, Lexington offers fewer service-sector jobs in domestic work, motels, and laundry service than larger communities. Latino households in Lexington, as elsewhere, adopt survival strategies conditioned by documented status, access to child care, types of work available, and size. For example, young (often underage) male relatives come from other locales to help with additional paychecks when wives must stay home; young females or grandmothers take care of children when the wife can work outside the home. A single paycheck is insufficient for such families to survive. Native workers have access to alternative survival strategies, especially in small communities, including opportunities for alternative employment, access to well-established family and community support systems, and higher utilization rates of social services. Newcomers may not.

Uncertain legal status, low skill levels, and language barriers combine to force newcomer Latinos to accept employment often spurned by locals. Managers, workers, and service providers say that most documented Latino workers in Lexington are new immigrants legalized under the Immigration Reform and Control Act of 1986 (IRCA), primarily through its so-called agricultural amnesty provision. Others are undocumented or have false papers. Although far fewer, Salvadoreans and especially Guatemalans are increasingly noticeable; most of those we have interviewed are in the United States under temporary asylum programs.

By adding new and more complicated steps to the legalization process, and restricting access to cash assistance for five years, the IRCA inadvertently adds to the new immigrant's economic and social insecurity. Salvadorans and Guatemalans face even more uncertainty, as many risk deportation once their temporary permits expire. Most vulnerable of all are undocumented workers, who, because of IRCA's employers' sanctions, may be driven further underground and into even more dangerous and poorly paid jobs.

Conclusion

What can Garden City and Lexington tell us of the overall impact of beefpacking on the social and economic welfare of those who work in this industry and the communities that host its plants? Beefpacking creates jobs. Not just on plant floors, but in industries such as cattle feeding and trucking, and in the expansion of services that always come with population growth. Economic development is necessary if communities on the High Plains—or anywhere in America, for that matter—are to survive and prosper. We don't dispute that. But our research suggests that certain kinds of development—and certain industries—create not only new jobs but greater levels of poverty. They attract the working poor, increasingly immigrants, native minorities, and women, with jobs requiring no previous training. If that was all, then we might argue that we are witnessing nothing more than a redistribution of poverty from one locale to another. And we are. But today's beefpackers, even more than their predecessors, fail to offer most of their workers a viable way out of poverty.

Wages are said to be relatively high, but they soon peak and are not indexed to cost of living or seniority. Internal labor markets (like those the Mexican workers from Monfort complained about) are almost completely eroded, and worker turnover remains high. Lack of English skills effectively blocks many immigrant workers from supervisory jobs, for which Anglos and bilinguals are preferred. Beefpacking jobs are too dangerous and too harsh to offer a satisfactory alternative to those rural residents who adopted multiple-job occupational strategies following the farm crisis. The new packers' oligopoly reduces competition, which eventually deflates cattle prices without comparable price reductions for the consumer. Small feeders and packers disappear, and their workers join the ranks of the unemployed.

The packers' impact on workers and communities stems largely from high injury rates and turnover and their increasing tendency to replace even native minorities with new-immigrant workers. They provide a pronounced example of strategies of industrial restructuring that have been increasing since the 1970s.

"Fordism" has become a handy term for the economic model that dominated the U.S. economy between World War II and the early 1970s. It refers to the tight linkages between mass production and mass consumption as the engine of economic growth (Kenney et al. 1989). In today's "post-Fordist" era, mass production is no longer expected to be linked to mass consumption within the domestic sphere. Upward mobility and purchasing power of local workers and communities, states, and even whole nations are largely irrelevant when large corporations have the capacity to scout the globe for the most lucrative—if less massive—markets. And hiring vulnerable workers who are in no position to demand better wages has become an important part of restructuring in an era of heightened international competition. Employment of recent, often undocumented, immigrants is not unique to packers; one need only look to assembly and service-sector industries in the new "global cities," such as New York, Los Angeles, and Tokyo. Neither is heightened demand for economic concessions from financially strapped states and municipalities in the form of tax abatements, rezoning, and infrastructural development. But most research so far has concentrated on urban industrial settings and, more recently, on border areas. Researchers have focused on traditional manufacturing industries, such as automobile and electronic assembly. The study of food processing, especially meat, poultry, and fish processing, can expand our understanding of the consequences of new models of development. But, most importantly, it can direct our attention to largely neglected rural areas and the growing numbers and changing faces of the rural poor.

"You dance with the one that brung ya'." Garden City and Lexington are communities whose heavy dependence on the cattle industry is now being shaped to fit a new industrial world increasingly defined by the packers. They've been out on the dance floor with producers and feeders for a long time, but now the packers are calling the tune. The costs of this economic dance are becoming clearer in Garden City and Lexington—in overcrowding and increased turnover in the schools, greater demands on social service agencies, rising crime, and declining access to health care in the face of increased demands on already underserved care systems. It only remains for communities to determine how much they want to pay the piper. Workers, too, must pay to dance, but they have little to say about the price.

Notes

Lourdes Gouveia's research was supported by grants from the Ford Foundation/Aspen Institute and the University of Nebraska-Omaha. Donald Stull's research was supported by grants from the Ford Foundation's Changing Relations Project, the Ford Foundation/Aspen Institute, the General Research Fund of the University of Kansas, and a sabbatical leave from the University of Kansas. We gratefully acknowledge the assistance of a host of agencies and our many friends in Garden City, Kansas, and Lexington, Nebraska, who have given so freely of their time and knowledge. We are, however, solely responsible for the content of this paper.

1. Rutgers University professor of urban studies Frank Popper and his wife, Deborah, unleashed the fury of westerners when they published "The Great Plains: From Dust to Dust" in *Planning* (1987). In this widely circulated and much ballyhooed article, they argued that 150 Plains counties were in decline, by conventional measures of population and per capita income; another 40 were beyond redemption. The Poppers proposed the idea of a "buffalo commons" as a possible concomitant to what they saw as the natural—and inevitable—depopulation of certain portions of the Great Plains. Among the many volleys fired in answer to the Poppers' argument was that of the Center for the New West: *The Great Plains in Transition: Overview of Change in America's New Economy* (Shepard et al. 1992).

2. The 1991 and 1992 rates were inflated by the use of inaccurate 1990 Census figures as the denominator. The crime rates for 1993 use the larger, and more accurate, population figures from the recount of February 1993.

3. Targeted Jobs Tax Credit is a federal program that offers tax credits for employers who hire applicants from nine targeted categories, including persons receiving various types of social assistance, ex-offenders, and unemployed youth. Employers may qualify for tax credits of up to $2,400 per employee.

4. Hispanics in Lexington are overwhelmingly of Mexican origin, but Central Americans (primarily Guatemalans and a few Salvadoreans) are identifiable and growing. Vietnamese and Laotians predominate among Southeast Asians. "Anglo" refers to all non-Hispanic whites, and "non-Hispanic" is often a residual category (containing small numbers of African Americans and Native Americans). The problems associated with such groupings are well known. We also realize that surname is not a reliable indicator of ethnicity—false-

positives and false-negatives abound. Nevertheless, we believe the trends reflected in these data to be valid, and if systematic bias does occur, it is likely to be found in underreporting of minorities.

References

Ackerman, P. 1991a. Agriculture: Many Factors Contribute to Rebound. Special '91 Report. *Lexington Papers,* February 27.

_____. 1991b. 180 Lose Jobs as Cornland Permanently Closes in Lex. *North Platte* [NE] *Telegraph,* June 12.

_____. 1993a. 8,556! Preliminary Census Figures Show Lexington Grew by 1,955. *Clipper-Herald,* March 24.

_____. 1993b. County's DWI-Related Crash Rate 6th in State. *Clipper-Herald,* December 4.

_____. 1993c. Study Finds Local Housing "Crisis." *Clipper-Herald,* July 21.

Benson, J. E. 1994. The Effects of Packinghouse Work on Southeast Asian Refugee Families. In *Newcomers in the Workplace: New Immigrants and the Restructuring of the U.S. Economy,* edited by L. Lamphere, G. Grenier, and A. Stepick. Philadelphia: Temple University Press, pp. 99–126.

Broadway, M. J. 1990. Meatpacking and Its Social Consequences for Garden City, Kansas, in the 1980s. *Urban Anthropology* 19: 321–44.

_____. 1994. Beef Stew: Cattle, Immigrants, and Established Residents in a Kansas Beefpacking Town. In *Newcomers in the Workplace: New Immigrants and the Restructuring of the U.S. Economy,* edited by L. Lamphere, G. Grenier, and A. Stepick. Philadelphia: Temple University Press, pp. 25–43.

Broadway, M. J., and D. D. Stull. 1991. Rural Industrialization: The Example of Garden City, Kansas. *Kansas Business Review* 14(4):1–9.

Clipper-Herald [Lexington, NE]. 1991. '91 Marks Year of Progress, Growth. December 28.

_____. 1992a. What's Ahead in '92? Here's a Peek. January 1.

_____. 1992b. More than 2,000 People Now Working at IBP Plant. February 12.

_____. 1993. Lexington Net Taxable Sales Were Up 4.1 Percent in March. July 21.

_____. 1994. City's Crime Rate Drops 39 Percent. January 22.

Dawson County Food Pantry. 1989–93. Annual reports. Authors' files.

Dawson County Herald. 1990. Mobile Homes Called "Band-Aid." July 16.

_____. 1991. Initiative 300 Could Be Model for Other States. June 22.

Dhuyvetter, K. C., and S. B. Laudert. 1991. *Kansas Feedlot Industry: Facts and Figures.* Manhattan: Cooperative Extension Service, Kansas State University.

Garden City School District. 1989. Cattle Industry Impact on USD #457, Garden City, Kansas. Report to Lexington School District Representatives, Lexington, Nebraska. Typescript. Authors' files.

Haven House. 1992. 1991 Report. Typescript. Authors' files.

_____. 1993. Intake Data Summary. Authors' files.

IBP, Inc. 1991. Health Insurance Program for Hourly Production/ Maintenance of IBP, Inc., Finney County, Kansas. IBP Form no. 1359. October. Typescript. Authors' files.

Kansas Department of Health and Environment. 1993. *Primary Care County Analysis: Preliminary Report.* Topeka: Bureau of Local and Rural Health Systems, KDHE.

Kenney, M., L. M. Labao, J. Curry, and W. R. Goe. 1989. Midwestern Agriculture in U.S. Fordism: From the New Deal to Economic Restructuring. *Sociologia Ruralis* 29:131–48.

Krause, K. R. 1991. *Cattle Feeding, 1962–1989: Location and Feedlot Size.* Commodity Economics Division, Economic Research Service, USDA. Agricultural Economic Report no. 642. Washington, D.C.: U.S. Government Printing Office.

Laudert, S. B. n.d. Kansas Feedlot Industry: Facts and Figures. Manhattan: Kansas State University Extension. Typescript.

Lexington [NE] Police Department. 1989–92. Police and Communication Annual Summary. Authors' files.

Lexington [NE] Public Schools. 1989–94. Census Information System. Authors' files.

Loughry, M. 1991a. School Registrar Sold on Lexington, and Wants to Share That. Special '91 Report. *Lexington Newspapers,* February 27.

_____. 1991b. Podraza: An Exciting Time to Live in Lexington. Special '91 Report. *Lexington Newspapers,* February 27.

_____. 1991c. Crime Trend Leveling Off, Officials Say. *Lexington Clipper,* November 6.

_____. 1992a. Turnover Teaches Flexibility. *Clipper-Herald,* January 18.

_____. 1992b. Board Focusing on School Facility Priorities. *Clipper-Herald,* January 22.

_____. 1992c. City Can't Let Down Its Guard, Chamber Director Says. *Clipper-Herald,* January 22.

_____. 1992d. Schools Seeking "Partners" in Education. Special '92 Report. *Clipper-Herald,* February 26.

_____. 1992e. Lexington Enrollment Was 1910 on Last Day of the School Year. *Clipper-Herald,* May 30.

_____. 1992f. Crime Rate Troubles Officials. *Clipper-Herald,* July 22.

Nebraska Department of Labor. 1990. *Nebraska Survey of Average Hourly Wage Rates.* Lincoln: Administrative Services Division.

———. 1990–93. *Nebraska Monthly Report on Labor Force and Unemployment.* Lincoln: Administrative Services Division.

———. 1992. *1992 Nebraska Survey of Hourly Wage Rates.* Lincoln: Nebraska Department of Labor.

Nebraska Department of Revenue. 1993. *Comparison of Net Taxable Sales for Nebraska Counties and Selected Cities.* Lincoln: Nebraska Department of Revenue.

Nebraska Public Power District. 1990. *Industrial Facts.* Lexington, Neb.: Nebraska Public Power District.

Norfolk [Nebraska] Area Chamber of Commerce. 1989. Final Report of the Norfolk Housing Task Force. Typescript.

Oppenheimer, R. 1985. Acculturation or Assimilation: Mexican Immigrants in Kansas, 1900 to World War II. *Western Historical Quarterly* 16:429–48.

Painter, S. 1992. Packer Will Shut Down for a Week: Monfort Action to Idle 1,300. *Wichita Eagle,* February 6.

Popper, D. E., and F. J. Popper. 1987. The Great Plains: From Dust to Dust. *Planning* 53(12):12–18.

Shepard, J. C., C. B. Murphy, L. D. Higgs, and P. M. Burgess. 1992. *The Great Plains in Transition: Overview of Change in America's New Economy.* Denver, Colo.: Center for the New West.

Stull, D. D. 1994. Knock 'em Dead: Work on the Killfloor of a Modern Beef-packing Plant. In *Newcomers in the Workplace: New Immigrants and the Restructuring of the U.S. Economy,* edited by L. Lamphere, G. Grenier, and A. Stepick. Philadelphia: Temple University Press, pp. 44–77.

———, ed. 1990. When the Packers Came to Town: Changing Ethnic Relations in Garden City, Kansas. *Urban Anthropology* 19:303–427.

Stull, D. D., J. E. Benson, M. J. Broadway, A. L. Campa, K. C. Erickson, and M. A. Grey. 1990. *Changing Relations: Newcomers and Established Residents in Garden City, Kansas.* Report no. 172. Lawrence: Institute for Public Policy and Business Research, University of Kansas.

Stull, D. D., and M. J. Broadway. 1990. The Effects of Restructuring on Beef-packing in Kansas. *Kansas Business Review* 14(1):10–16.

Stull, D. D., M. J. Broadway, and K. C. Erickson. 1992. The Price of a Good Steak: Beef Packing and Its Consequences for Garden City, Kansas. In *Structuring Diversity: Ethnographic Perspectives on the New Immigration,* edited by L. Lamphere. Chicago: University of Chicago Press, pp. 35–64.

United Methodist Mexican-American Ministries. 1994. Application for Medically Underserved Population Designation. Authors' files.

Webb, T. 1986. No. 1 in Beef: Kansas Plants Lead Country in Production. *Wichita Eagle-Beacon,* January 25.

6 | Pork, Poultry, and Newcomers in Storm Lake, Iowa

Mark A. Grey

STORM LAKE is located in northwestern Iowa, approximately 70 miles northeast of Sioux City. With a thriving downtown, Iowa's fourth-largest natural lake, and streets lined with graceful old homes, it is a handsome, clean community that in many ways lives up to its designation as "the City Beautiful." The seat of Buena Vista County, Storm Lake is further enhanced by Buena Vista College, a small liberal arts college affiliated with the Presbyterian Church.

Belying this bucolic image is the world's second-largest pork-processing plant, only two blocks from the lake and eight blocks from downtown. The next block over is a turkey-processing plant. These food-processing factories dominate the east side of town, and many residents live within their shadows and smells.

With these plants, Storm Lake has become an important center for adding value to agricultural products. Although the lake provides opportunities for recreation and tourism, city officials have placed greater emphasis on developing agricultural resources.

Pork has been central to Storm Lake's economy for decades, and the community provides an opportunity to document recent changes in this processing sector. In 1981 the old-line Hygrade pork plant, with its stable, established-resident, unionized, and Anglo workforce, closed. The following year, IBP, Inc., purchased the facility and transformed it into a high-volume factory, dependent upon imported labor, in particular Lao refugees.

The turkey plant, owned by Bil-Mar Foods (a subsidiary of Sara Lee), also employs refugees as well as Latino immigrants. In fact, much of Bil-Mar's workforce is made up of former IBP employees who seek better working conditions.

Together IBP and Bil-Mar employ over 1,700 workers, of whom about 500 are immigrants and refugees. How these workers have affected this small, formerly homogeneous community is the subject of this chapter. Their impact on schools and health services is of specific concern, along with that on human services and law enforcement agencies. Community reactions to the influx of newcomers are also considered.

The Coming and Going of Hygrade

The Storm Lake economy relies heavily on meat and poultry processing—72 percent of its manufacturing jobs are in this industry, illustrating the community's overwhelming dependence on adding value to local agricultural products and its vulnerability to major economic shifts (Pilkington and Padavich 1989). The town's dependence on meat processing began in 1935, when Storm Lake Packing built the plant that later became Hygrade and IBP. Hygrade took over the facility in 1953. Throughout Hygrade's operations in Storm Lake, only one day was lost due to a labor strike, although the plant did shut down for nine months in 1975 because of inadequate hog supplies.

What happened to Hygrade was typical of the industry in the 1970s and 1980s. In May 1978 Hygrade announced the plant would close permanently if Local 191 of the United Food and Commercial Workers (UFCW) did not accept contract concessions. The workers refused, but the plant remained open. Hygrade demanded concessions again two years later. In response, Local 191 proposed elimination of incentive pay if Hygrade upgraded the plant and its sewage lagoon, a source of local complaint. The plant and local agreed on this compromise, but Hygrade's parent company, Hanson Industries, refused. In February 1981 Hanson gave the UFCW six months' notice of a planned shutdown of the Storm Lake facility. In August, as the shutdown approached, the company agreed to operate the plant for two more months and attempt to negotiate a new contract.

While Hygrade and the UFCW negotiated, community leaders made their own efforts to keep the facility running. The city offered concessions, including industrial revenue bonds to improve the plant's waste treatment system. In September the city council offered to pay—at an estimated cost of $1.4 million—the expense of upgrading the plant's sewage lagoons if it remained open (Osterberg and Sheehan 1982:11). A group of residents, "Concerned Citizens for Saving Hygrade," placed full-page ads in the local newspaper encouraging Hygrade and the union to resolve their differences. But their efforts were in vain. In October Hygrade demanded a $3.00 per hour pay cut *in all Hygrade plants* as a prerequisite for keeping the Storm Lake plant open. The UFCW refused, and Hygrade used the union's decision to justify closing the plant later that month (*Des Moines Register* 1981; Osterberg and Sheehan 1982).

Storm Lake had lost its largest industry, and with it some 500 relatively high-wage unionized jobs that formed the backbone of a stable local workforce. Fifty management jobs were also lost.

Several other meat plants also closed in Iowa during this time. In addition to Hygrade's Storm Lake facility, four large pork operations shut down between 1981 and 1982, and two other plants ceased hog-slaughter operations. About 3,300 jobs were eliminated. Another 1,500 other jobs were lost in cutbacks in other pork facilities. In all, 4,500 to 5,500 pork-packing jobs were lost between 1975 and 1982 (Lauria and Fisher 1983:41, 48). Job loss in Iowa's pork plants followed on the heels of similar developments in beef: between 1975 and 1979, eight plants shut down, with a net loss of some 2,450 jobs (Lauria and Fisher 1983:41). Old-line unionized plants were being replaced by a new breed of low-wage packers.

IBP in Storm Lake

IBP bought the Storm Lake facility in April 1982 for $2.5 million, a short six months after Hygrade closed its doors. This "modest" transaction "signaled the start of another revolution in the meatpacking industry" (Lippman 1982:1). IBP president Robert Peterson acknowledged that the purchase was "the first stage of a planned major expansion by Iowa Beef into the pork business" (quoted in Lippman 1982:1). In the decade following acquisition of the Storm Lake plant, IBP extended its pork operations to five more plants and became the world's largest producer of pork.

With the initial investment of $2.5 million and subsequent overhaul and expansion of the Hygrade plant, IBP has spent more than $30 million on the facility (Cullen 1992a). By 1989, hog slaughter and processing capacity rose to 13,400 head per day, or more than 3.35 million head per year (IBP 1990). The plant is now IBP's most profitable.

IBP is central to Storm Lake's economy. Since its opening in Sep-

IBP's Storm Lake plant. (Photograph by Mark Grey)

tember 1982, the plant has purchased 34 million hogs, 90 percent at farms or buying stations within 120 miles of the community. Local farmers can also sell hogs at the plant itself.

With more than 1,200 employees, IBP's payroll is $27.5 million per year. The size of the current workforce and payroll contrast with those of Hygrade, which employed 500 workers and had an annual payroll of $15 million.

Hygrade workers' average hourly wage was about $9.50, and production incentives as high as $200 a week were also available. Adding his hourly wage of $11.00 per hour and incentive pay, one former worker estimated his earnings during Hygrade's final year reached $45,000! The average employee earned about $30,000, however.

Today, IBP workers start at $6.50, up but 50 cents an hour from when the plant opened in 1982. The *highest* hourly wage available to line workers is $11.30. Although this wage is similar to rates paid to Hygrade workers, its net value is much less. First, turnover is now so great (about 10 percent monthly) that relatively few workers remain employed long enough to qualify for this wage. Second, new wages must be adjusted for inflation: average hourly wages for meatpackers in Iowa have fallen from $10.75 in 1980 to $5.65 in 1991. Finally, flexible productivity schedules that respond to market conditions (demand for boxed meat and the price of livestock) often mean employees work less than 40 hours per week.

Luring IBP: Costs to Storm Lake

While IBP is the backbone of Storm Lake's economy, its presence does not come without costs to the community. After Hygrade shut its doors in 1981, the city sought a replacement. IBP (then Iowa Beef Processors) expressed an interest, and negotiations began in December. City officials hoped to reduce local unemployment and increase economic activity, while maintaining the town's social character (Osterberg and Sheehan 1982:12–13).

To attract IBP, the city offered industrial revenue bonds, tax abatements, sewage changes, and favorable water rates. The first two concessions illustrate the lengths to which rural communities often go to attract big plants.

Storm Lake passed its tax-exempt status to IBP by issuing revenue bonds itself; in effect, a tax break granted by the U.S. Treasury was extended to the plant. IBP negotiated the ability to call upon $10 million of bonding, the maximum allowed by law (Osterberg and Sheehan 1982).

IBP took advantage of tax abatements to renovate the old Hygrade plant. Under Iowa's Urban Revitalization Act, Storm Lake was authorized to designate parts of the city as "revitalization" areas. Any improvements to real estate in these areas could be made eligible for tax exemptions. The Hygrade facility was chosen as one of these sites, and IBP could negotiate for reduced property tax rates. One estimate of the city's tax concession for a $3.9 million investment in the plant was $253,640 (Osterberg and Sheehan 1982). Substantially more has been invested in the plant, however, and lost revenues have increased proportionately. Altogether, over $30 million was invested in the plant, yet its taxable value in 1992 was only $9.7 million. In 1992, taxes paid to the county, city, and schools totaled $337,324 (*Storm Lake Times* 1992:4).

Despite these concessions, no formal study was undertaken to determine the costs and benefits of the plant to the community (Osterberg and Sheehan 1982). A local businessman, writing for the Storm Lake Industrial Commission, did issue a three-page report that focused primarily on tax consequences, but its assumptions were precarious. In general, projected tax benefits were overly optimistic: property tax abatements negotiated by IBP were not taken into account, and the report did not discount future benefits (Bauer 1982). "Rather than future tax benefits of around $1.9 million [as the report projected], Storm Lake will gain over the years 1983–1992 approximately only $750,000 from IBP's decision to locate in the community" (Osterberg and Sheehan 1982:30). This projection was high, but no one in 1982 could have anticipated that $30 million dollars would eventually be invested in the plant.

Residential property tax collection estimates were optimistic as well. IBP employees were projected to buy 388 homes valued at $50,000 between 1982 and 1992, adding $19,400,000 to local tax rolls and bringing in more than $2 million in taxes (Bauer 1982). These estimates assumed 1,000 new jobs, but IBP guaranteed only 350 production jobs when the plant first opened. A second shift was promised, but at an unspecified time.

The most spurious assumption, however, was that IBP workers could afford to buy $50,000 homes. With starting wages of $6.00 per hour, and 40-hour workweeks, an IBP employee would earn only $12,480, or $1,040 per month. Using a guideline stating that only 25 percent of gross monthly income should be committed to mortgage payments, only $260 would be available. Assuming 14 percent interest rates, the prevailing rate in the early 1980s, and a down payment of 25 percent, monthly payments on a $50,000 home would be $546, twice that available to a household dependent upon a single IBP employee. Even with 10 percent interest rates, an IBP employee could afford only a $30,000 house, assuming a down payment of $7,500 (Osterberg and Sheehan 1982:31–32). But given the company's high rate of turnover, most employees do not work for more than a year or two, much less the duration of a 30-year mortgage. With seasonal fluctuation in demand for meat, employees are not guaranteed a full 40-hour workweek throughout the entire year. And few, if any, meatpacking line workers have money for a down payment.

While the projected tax benefits to the community were based on questionable assumptions, the report did predict that many new jobs would be held by newcomers. Newcomers were expected to fill half the

400 jobs in 1983 and 600 of the 1,000 jobs to be created by 1992. These forecasts, like those on economic benefits, proved wrong on two counts: the number of jobs created at IBP exceeded predictions by 20 percent, and most of those who had worked at Hygrade did not go to work for IBP. Indeed, a significant proportion of IBP's workers today are new immigrants and refugees.

Diversified Labor at IBP and Bil-Mar Foods

While Iowa's population fell by 4.6 percent in the 1980s, Storm Lake lost only 0.5 percent (from 8,814 in 1980 to 8,769 in 1990). While the community's size did not really change during the 1980s, its composition did. The 1990 Census found that Asians (mostly Lao) made up 3.5 percent ($n = 304$) of the town's population, Hispanics, 1.1 percent, and African Americans, 0.4 percent. These figures are low, however. In April 1991, an Iowa Bureau of Refugee Services survey counted 504 Southeast Asians. More have arrived since then.

Other immigrant populations have grown as well. Some 70 Mennonites from Mexico and Texas live in the area; many were recruited by IBP to work at the Storm Lake plant. Latinos are also being drawn by the jobs at IBP and Bil-Mar, but accurate figures are not available.

Others have documented meatpackers' tendency to draw their labor from beyond their host communities (Stull et al. 1990; Broadway and Stull 1991), and Storm Lake is seemingly no different. According to the IBP personnel director, approximately one-third of IBP's workforce in 1992 consisted of immigrant minorities, many recruited from out of state.

Ethnic group	Employees (%)
Southeast Asian (Lao and Tai Dam)	300 (25.0)
Hispanic/Latino	80 (6.7)
Mexican Mennonites (German-speaking)	20 (1.7)
Anglo	800 (66.7)

Similarly, the personnel director at Bil-Mar Foods reports that 25 percent of Bil-Mar's workforce in 1992 were minorities.

Ethnic group	Employees (%)
Southeast Asian	50 (10.0)
Hispanic/Latino	75 (15.0)
Anglo	375 (75.0)

Unlike IBP, Bil-Mar does not actively recruit its workforce. Instead, it takes its workers from among the ranks of those who leave IBP. Starting wages are the same, but workers are attracted by better working conditions and benefits. For example, Bil-Mar provides a 40-hour workweek in five days, while IBP's workweek often includes Saturdays. Bil-Mar's hourly employees are eligible for medical and dental benefits after 90 days, instead of the six months mandated at IBP, and coverage is better in many respects. Of vital importance to worker health and longevity, the production line is halted at regular intervals for hand- and finger-stretching exercises. Given these conditions, Bil-Mar's annual turnover rate is only 25 percent, while IBP's turnover is about 120 percent.

Since Bil-Mar relies primarily on former IBP workers, it is IBP that is largely responsible for the influx of newcomers to Storm Lake. IBP's recruitment strategies vary with the ethnicity and location of potential workers. One IBP personnel director who deals with Southeast Asians said he has personally visited Tennessee and California to recruit Lao workers. In California he met with leaders of the Lao community. He confirmed that a mobile recruiting team has also been used to enlist Anglo workers from Missouri, Wisconsin, and Minnesota. This team, however, has traveled only on a seasonal basis as demand for workers dictates. Spanish-language television commercials are broadcast in Texas to attract Latino workers, and Spanish/German-speaking Mennonites have been directly recruited from their settlements in Mexico and Seminole, Texas (Grey fieldnotes, October 24, 1992).

Informal information networks account for much of the Lao migration to Storm Lake. Many have moved to Storm Lake in a process of secondary migration common among Southeast Asian refugees in the United States (Mortland and Ledgerwood 1987). A 1991 survey of Southeast Asians in Storm Lake by the Iowa Bureau of Refugee Services found that 47 of 149 households had arrived from 12 different states: Louisiana, Texas, California, Utah, Tennessee, Oklahoma, Idaho, Illinois, Minnesota, North Dakota, Ohio, and Missouri. Four families came from Washington, D.C. The remaining families were initially resettled in Storm Lake or other Iowa communities. Of the 149 families surveyed, 125 household heads were employed at IBP; 2 worked at Bil-Mar (Iowa Bureau of Refugee Services 1991).

Lao movement to Storm Lake is representative of strategies employed by refugees to confront the many challenges of life in a new country, particularly as their government benefits expire. Often persons with poor English-language skills cannot find employment. The availability of jobs requiring only minimal knowledge of English has led migrants to Storm Lake and other meatpacking communities in the Midwest and the Great Plains.

From the refugee's perspective, secondary migration is motivated not only by material needs but by cultural factors as well. These factors include kinship, patron-client relationships, and mobility as a historical and cultural condition (Mortland and Ledgerwood 1987). While kinship is necessary in understanding the flexible nature of familial patterns, the more important factor in Storm Lake seems to be the role of patron-client relations. Such relations are indicative of "nonmarket labor processes" (Griffith 1987) through which labor migration is often promoted.

To satisfy long-term material needs, most Lao in Storm Lake work at IBP. Sources for initial information about these jobs, however, and eventual adjustment to Storm Lake, often represent variations of patron-client relations. Contrary to predominant American expectations that emphasize *independence* for individuals and families, Southeast Asians seek greater *interdependence* among co-ethnics to access needed resources. "When a refugee is making the decision to secondarily migrate he is attempting to plug into one of these networks of interdependence, into a system that he recognizes and knows he can rely on" (Mortland and Ledgerwood 1987:313).

Personal contacts are essential for survival, and necessary information and assistance can often be obtained only through entering patron-client networks. For example, while information about work in Storm Lake has been transmitted by IBP itself—sometimes through contact with refugee "leaders" in other states—more often this information is spread through personal contact. These suppliers of job information gain the loyalty of new employees because of the latter's appreciation for help in finding a job, as well as for assistance in such essential matters as finding housing, obtaining driver's licenses, and enrolling children in school. A degree of trust must be developed as patrons convince clients to leave their homes and risk the move to Storm

Lake to find work at IBP. Once the move has been successfully accomplished, the patron's role is strengthened and his network of influence expanded.

IBP encourages this informal network through monetary awards to current employees who refer new workers. For every new hire who successfully completes the 90-day probationary period, the employee who recommends that person receives $150. Incentives for new workers to come to Storm Lake, such as $100 loans, are used as well.

IBP also encourages informal mechanisms of recruitment with its Southeast Asian personnel director: a Tai Dam man who has lived in Storm Lake since 1976, speaks English and Lao fluently, and has become an American citizen. He trains new employees and is instrumental in direct recruitment. IBP also encourages him to assist the Lao community and the Storm Lake health sector by providing translation (often in emergencies). This man is vital to the adjustment and maintenance of the Lao community: as long as the community has its essential needs met vis-à-vis the formal service sector and their employer with this IBP boss, he serves as their patron. Lao employees who do not speak English well—and few do—become his de facto clientele. Bilingual supervisors—like bilingual social workers—"may be in a position to actually decide who will receive services and who will not" (Mortland and Ledgerwood 1987:313). This bilingual personnel director is clearly in a position to decide who gets jobs.

Impact on Storm Lake Schools

The growth and changing nature of meatpacking labor has dramatically affected local school districts where new plants have been established (Broadway and Stull 1991; Grey 1990; Gouveia and Stull, this volume). In Storm Lake, enrollments have grown steadily from 1,462 in 1981 to 1,738 in 1991, a 19 percent increase. Despite this growth, the community has been reluctant to pass bond issues to build more schools and remodel old buildings. After three previous bond attempts had failed, the community approved funding for a new $5.5 million middle school in November 1991. School administrators warned that the space needs of other schools would be reviewed within a few years.

Many new students are limited English proficient (LEP). Immigrant and refugee students have been recorded since the 1970s with the

TABLE 6.1. Total LEP Student Enrollments:
1980–81 to 1992–93, Storm Lake Community
Schools

School Year	No. of LEP Students	Total Enrollment	Percent of Total
1980–81	21	1,395	1.5
1981–82	24	1,462	1.6
1982–83	28	1,500*	1.9
1983–84	28	1,424*	2.0
1984–85	No report	1,507*	—
1985–86	43	1,535*	2.8
1986–87	17	1,530*	1.1
1987–88	10	1,536*	0.7
1988–89	27	1,528	1.7
1989–90	88	1,558	5.7
1990–91	120	1,620	7.4
1991–92	211	1,730	12.2
1992–93	236	1,807	13.1

*Projected enrollments.

Source: Iowa State Department of Education, *Limited English Proficiency Student Count*, 1980–81 to 1992–93. Iowa State Department of Education, *Iowa Educational Directory*, 1980–81 to 1993–94.

settlement of Tai Dam refugees, but their numbers have risen dramatically since the 1987–88 school year (Table 6.1). This increase is due to an influx of Lao- and Spanish-speaking students (Table 6.2).

Increasing enrollments of LEP students have forced the school district to expand its ESL program. Two and one-half full-time instructors were hired, as well as seven paraprofessionals. During the 1992–93 school year, the district received $157,000 in federal funds to operate the ESL program. However, that funding will be cut by some $16,000 in 1993–94, and the school district has already warned that aides may be laid off as a result. Whether the school board will make up for this shortfall will provide some indication of the extent to which the community is willing to accommodate growth of an LEP population that shows no signs of slowing down.

Storm Lake schools have also experienced growth in the number of students who receive free or reduced-price lunches, an indicator that many new students are from low-income families. In 1983, 23 percent of

TABLE 6.2. Limited English Proficient Students, by Language

| Language | SCHOOL YEAR | | | | | | |
	86–87	87–88	88–89	89–90	90–91	91–92	92–93
Spanish	—	—	—	2	8	40	58
Percent	—	—	—	(0.1)	(0.5)	(2.3)	(3.2)
Lao	17	10	27	78	94	134	156
Percent	(1.1)	(0.7)	(1.7)	(5.0)	(5.8)	(7.8)	(8.7)

Source: Iowa State Department of Education, *Limited English Proficiency Student Count*, 1980–81 to 1992–93.

all students received free or reduced-price lunches. By October 1991 the percentage had grown to 30, nearly 6 percent above the state average.

Implications for Health Care

Among community services most affected by an influx of low-income workers is health care. Health services in Storm Lake/Buena Vista County have come under increasing stress as the number of immigrants and refugees and their unique health problems grow. Language and cultural barriers between established residents and newcomers limit the effectiveness of available programs.

Until recently, the proportion of the local hospital's care that went uncompensated remained at about 1 percent. In 1991, however, these costs rose to 13 percent of the budget, or about $1.2 million; 1992 saw a cash-flow deficit of some $122,000, and receipts ran some $300,000 behind those of 1991 (Cullen 1992b:1). This decline was publicly blamed on declining inpatient stays, but other factors—the low-income status of many newcomers, restrictions of IBP and Bil-Mar health insurance, and growing transiency in the community—also play a part.

Of the barriers to health care, language differences have proved particularly difficult for both the Buena Vista County Health Department and the hospital. These institutions need full-time translators to assist physicians, facilitate health education, undertake home visits, and encourage participation in available services. In the face of shrinking budgets, their boards have been reluctant to approve funding, and emergency translation is provided by the IBP Southeast Asian personnel director and on occasion by school district paraprofessionals.

The language barrier is often compounded by refugees themselves. One refugee leader noted that many Lao arrive with little or no understanding of community health services or how to access them. Provision of health care in their homeland relied more on interpersonal contact than on formal, bureaucratic organizations.

The county health department and hospital have noted other barriers. For example, they have difficulty putting their thumbs on the Lao "community." Without an identifiable population, it cannot be readily accessed for group preventive education. Group education would be preferable to and cheaper than home visits, but efforts to organize such meetings have proved difficult. Prenatal care among refugees has also been identified as essential. The hospital employs two maternal case managers who seek contacts with the Lao community, but their efforts have met with minimal success. A total of 310 babies were delivered at Buena Vista County Hospital in 1991, of which 22 were to Lao mothers. Only two of the Lao women received childbirth instruction and/or prenatal care, however. More nutritional and cancer-prevention education is desired, but language and cultural barriers hinder such efforts. In addition, many of the most recent wave of refugees are illiterate, negating use of health information written in Lao.

The county health department has identified what it considers to be the most pressing health issues in the Lao community (Grey fieldnotes, January 8, 1992):

1. Use of too much salt, promoting hypertension;
2. Many Lao believe they need less medication than Americans because of their smaller physical size;
3. Refugees occasionally do not use preventive or primary care, allowing treatable illnesses to develop into emergency cases in the hospital; and
4. Many Lao don't have a personal physician whom they see on a consistent basis.

Many of these concerns were echoed by the administrator of Buena Vista County Hospital. He also noted that Lao patients often have diseases unfamiliar to the hospital's physicians. One patient, for example, had three parasites never before seen in the community (Grey field-notes, January 8, 1992).

Health status is further affected by restrictions of IBP and Bil-Mar health insurance policies. These policies burden already low incomes by forcing workers to choose between receiving adequate care—and paying much of the expense themselves—or neglecting their conditions. IBP workers are not eligible for health insurance benefits during the first six months of employment. Bil-Mar employees become eligible after four weeks of perfect attendance and an additional 60 days on the job. During these waiting periods, workers are responsible for *all* medical expenses—unless injured on the job.

Once workers have secured health insurance from IBP, the $300 individual/$600 family deductible and coverage restrictions further contribute to debt incurred as a result of seeking medical treatment. The insurance plan covers 80 percent of most expenses incurred after the $300/$600 deductible has been satisfied. However, the uncovered 20 percent of catastrophic expenses—which the workers often cannot afford—will ultimately contribute to their debt as well (IBP 1992).

Bil-Mar's medical plan has deductibles of $200 per individual and $400 per family, after which 80 percent of doctor bills and other expenses are paid by the policy. Prescription plans are also available with which workers can purchase drugs for up to 90 days for $9.00. Although the company pays 80 percent of premiums, a family of four must pay weekly premiums of $14.13, or $734.76 per year. Despite better coverage than that offered by IBP, health care costs still bite heavily into a Bil-Mar worker's income.

Increasing debt burdens lead to inadequate and/or delayed treatment of conditions that are either uncovered or only partially covered by health insurance. Ailments are thus exacerbated, ultimately adding to the worker's debt. An example of this problem is provided by a Lao woman who gave birth in 1991. IBP gave her six weeks of unpaid maternity leave. Since she had been employed more than six months, her insurance covered the birth, which cost $1,400. Nevertheless, she was still responsible for 20 percent of this bill ($280) after the initial deductible of $300 was satisfied. Several other medical bills were also incurred *before* she was eligible for insurance coverage, including basic care for her two other children and her own prenatal doctor visits. During the seven months she had lived in Storm Lake, she estimated she paid $2,000 for medical bills!

This woman's experience illustrates the debt dilemma of workers with significant medical expenses. But even for those without major health concerns, IBP and Bil-Mar insurance assures that major proportions of their medical expenses will come out of already low incomes.

The recent release of figures for uncompensated-care expenses at the local hospital is a recognition of the added burden IBP's newcomer labor force places upon the community. Concern about this issue is growing; health administrators have recognized an influx of Latino workers whom they regard as more transient than refugees. Most Lao refugees remain in the community for years and are therefore available to pay their bills. Latino workers, on the other hand, are believed to stay for only a few weeks or months, not long enough to qualify for IBP health insurance that could pay the bulk of their care expenses. These expenses, whether incurred by refugee, Latino, or Anglo workers, are increasingly paid by the taxpayers of Buena Vista County.

Storm Lake's Changing Social Character

In their search for Hygrade's replacement, Storm Lakers could not foresee how deeply their community would be transformed by IBP. The community's initial experience with Southeast Asian refugees came when it was designated a "cluster community" for the settlement of Tai Dam refugees from the Laos-Vietnamese border. From 1975 to 1981, the Iowa Bureau of Refugee Services resettled 24 families, or 104 individuals, in Storm Lake. The majority of these families have since left the community.

Local churches sponsored refugees, who were assisted in finding housing and jobs. They were invited into the community just as the State of Iowa opened its arms to Tai Dam refugees not resettled in Europe. The community's goals for this small population were largely assimilationist as well as humanitarian. Perhaps most importantly for local residents, however, their presence did not disrupt the community.

The more recent—and much larger—influx of Lao refugees and other newcomers stands in sharp contrast. In addition to stress on schools and health services, other problems associated with a growing and increasingly transient population have developed. Crime has increased sharply. In the first nine months of 1992, for example, 124 burglaries were reported—four times the 1991 total. During the same period, prowler, assault, and disturbance reports all surpassed 1991 totals (Larson 1992). In one prominent case, four Lao men were arrested for possessing stolen property, transporting a semiautomatic pistol without a permit, and possessing an assault rifle.

The number of inmates in the Buena Vista County Jail has swelled. In 1992 the total number of inmates was 804, or 63 more than in 1991, and 211 more than in 1990. Substantial proportions of these inmates are minorities and newcomers. Of the 1992 inmates, 32 (4 percent) were Asian, 51 (6 percent) were African American, and 120 (15 percent) were Hispanic: 101 (13 percent) inmates were non–English speaking.

In response to rising crime, the city reestablished the Neighborhood Watch program that had failed several years previously, apparently because of lack of perceived need. In addition, the city council recommended hiring two new police officers, including a community services officer to work directly with minorities, educating them about the city's services and their responsibilities as citizens. The officer could also serve as a translator; however, he would not carry a gun or be a commissioned police officer.

Increased demands on schools, health services, and law enforcement have been compounded by a housing shortage and additional caseloads at human service agencies, which face new problems in a variety of languages. These emerging concerns prompted the organization of Lao language classes and the creation of a multilingual information display in the public library. The changes also led to the organization of the Buena Vista County Joint Task Force on Unmet Community Needs. Task force members included the school district superintendent, the police chief, clergy, the county attorney, social workers, school counselors, health administrators, and citizens. Noteworthy was the active membership of three IBP supervisors, including the plant manager, and the human resources manager of Bil-Mar Foods. Through a series of task force conferences, "town meetings," community surveys, and personal interviews, the task force identified a number of unmet community needs. These needs and recommendations to address them made up the group's final report, *Recommendations for Unmet Community Needs* (Blundall and Brown 1992).

Some of the task force's recommendations have already been implemented. For example, the police department has developed an informational pamphlet for newcomers that provides emergency phone numbers and information on municipal codes, and explains frequently violated laws. The pamphlet has been printed in English, Lao, and Spanish. Translation and printing were provided by IBP.

Regardless of how many of the task force's recommendations are accomplished, Storm Lake is a community whose identity is in the midst of a transformation. At the request of city leaders, the Iowa State University, University Extension undertook a mail survey of Storm Lake residents to determine their perceptions of community issues. In response to the survey's findings, one newspaper stated, "Two of America's most vexing problems—drug abuse and race relations—are coming home to roost, Storm Lakers believe." Indeed, one in five respondents felt that drug abuse was "severe," while one-third felt that alcohol abuse was severe. Forty-five percent of households with incomes less than $20,000 reported that drug problems were severe. In terms of "race relations," one-third of respondents felt that having a diverse population was a "disadvantage." Another third felt it made no difference. Forty-five percent felt Storm Lake could be doing more to promote equality, while 46 percent felt that Storm Lake did "better than most" (Ryan 1992).

While the community survey was distributed to a random sample of 440 households and enjoyed a 75 percent return rate, the instrument itself did not include a question about the respondent's race or ethnicity. There is no way of knowing how members of different populations perceived ethnic relations or other issues.

Conclusion

IBP is publicly committed to Storm Lake, as recent investments in the plant bear out. This commitment is due not to available labor, which increasingly must be imported, but to the availability of cheap corn and the hogs produced with it. Whatever their reasons, IBP is welcomed by city leaders, business owners, and hog producers, who recognize its central place in the local economy.

Bil-Mar Foods will also remain an important employer, although its impact on the regional economy is significantly less than IBP's. But as long as working conditions and benefits remain better than those at IBP, Bil-Mar will hold an important role by increasing the stay of some newcomers who otherwise might move on after leaving IBP.

Given its dependence on imported labor, IBP will continue to shape the processes of transformation already under way in Storm Lake. Thus far, Storm Lake has shown a willingness and ability to confront these changes in positive and constructive ways. But as crime climbs and Storm Lakers find themselves paying for new services to accommodate newcomers, the mood may change. It remains to be seen how much the community will pay for supplementary health services and ESL programs in the schools: 1993 city budgets were cut by 10 percent to pay for a new police officer and the community service officer assigned to the newcomer community.

The key to a constructive encounter with the changing nature of the community will be the continued cooperation of IBP and Bil-Mar administrators. As long as they keep channels of communication open to community leaders and are willing to be involved in mitigating some of the problems associated with their labor forces, Storm Lake has a good chance to avoid unrest and serve as an example to other communities facing rapid social and demographic change.

References

Bauer, T. 1982. Analysis of the Economic Impact on Storm Lake If Iowa Beef Processors Locates in Storm Lake. Typescript/Handwritten, 3 pages. Author's files.

Blundall, J., and P. Brown. 1992. *Recommendations for Unmet Community Needs.* Buena Vista County, Iowa, Joint Task Force on Unmet Community Needs. Storm Lake: Northwest Iowa Mental Health Center.

Broadway, M. J., and D. D. Stull. 1991. Rural Industrialization: The Example of Garden City, Kansas. *Kansas Business Review* 14(4):1–9.

Cullen, A. 1992a. A Revolution in Pork: IBP Led It from Storm Lake, Has More Plans. *Storm Lake Times,* September 25.

———. 1992b. Hospital Battles Decline. *Storm Lake Times,* December 18.

Des Moines Register. 1981. 500 Jobless as Plant Closes at Storm Lake. October 24.

Grey, M. A. 1990. Immigrant Students in the Heartland: Ethnic Relations in Garden City, Kansas, High School. *Urban Anthropology* 19:409–27.

Griffith, D. 1987. Nonmarket Labor Practices in an Advanced Capitalist Economy. *American Anthropologist* 89:838–52.

Iowa Bureau of Refugee Services. 1991. Survey of Refugee Population in Storm Lake, Iowa. Des Moines. Unpublished Mimeograph. Author's files.

IBP. 1990. *Annual Report to the United States Securities and Exchange Commission.* Dakota City, Nebraska.

_____. 1992. *IBP Medical Benefit Plan and Flex Plus Plan.* Storm Lake, Iowa.

Iowa State Department of Education. 1980–81 through 1993–94. *Iowa Educational Directory.* Des Moines: Iowa State Board of Education.

_____. 1980–81 through 1993–94. *Limited English Proficiency Student Count.* Des Moines: Iowa State Board of Education.

Larson, D. 1992. "Let's Get Nosy," Police Tell 55. *Storm Lake Pilot Tribune,* October 24.

Lauria, M., and P. S. Fisher. 1983. *Plant Closings in Iowa: Causes, Consequences and Legislative Options.* Iowa City: University of Iowa: Institute of Urban and Regional Research.

Lippman, T.W. 1982. Iowa Beef Makes Its Move on Anxious Pork Industry. *Washington Post,* April 18.

Mortland, C., and J. Ledgerwood. 1987. Secondary Migration among Southeast Asian Refugees in the United States. *Urban Anthropology* 16(3–4):291–326.

Osterberg, D., and M. Sheehan. 1982. *Jobs, Concessions and the Economy: A Comparative Study of Garden City, Kansas, and Storm Lake, Iowa.* Iowa City: University of Iowa, Department of Urban and Regional Planning.

Pilkington, R., and R. A. Padavich. 1989. *Targeted Industry Analysis and Marketing Program Analysis Prepared for Storm Lake Area Development Corporation.* Cedar Falls: University of Northern Iowa: Institute for Decision Making.

Ryan, V. 1992. *Summary of Storm Lake Community Survey, May 1992.* Ames: Iowa State University, University Extension.

Storm Lake Times. 1992. IBP Crucial to City Infrastructure, Krepps Says. September 25.

Stull, D. D., J. E. Benson, M. J. Broadway, A. L. Campa, K. C. Erickson, and M. A. Grey. 1991. *Changing Relations: Newcomers and Established Residents in Garden City, Kansas.* Report no. 172. Lawrence: Institute for Public Policy and Business Research, University of Kansas.

7 | *Hay Trabajo*

Poultry Processing, Rural Industrialization, and the Latinization of Low-Wage Labor

David Griffith

We were having a difficult time finding labor four, four-and-a-half years ago. We had to get innovative. We sent screeners down to Indiantown, Florida, and began recruiting Guatemalans. They all worked in agriculture. At first we housed them in the old motels along Route 13, but after awhile they matriculated into the community. They help each other out.

—Poultry plant personnel manager in Maryland, October 11, 1993

Recent Trajectories of Industry Growth

When the American electorate sent an Arkansas governor to the White House, it was partially because the governor had overseen the creation of thousands of "new" jobs. Few people looked beyond the quantity to the quality of those jobs, but some news reports pointed out that they were primarily low-paying, hazardous, and fairly undesirable jobs in Arkansas's chicken plants. Arkansas, home to Tyson Foods, produces more processed poultry than any other state in the union (see Table 7.1).

Arkansas is well suited to poultry production. During the presidential campaign, Bush's supporters tirelessly portrayed its people as poor and uneducated and the state as backward and underdeveloped. Ross Perot enhanced this picture during one of the presidential debates, comparing Arkansas to a corner drugstore and the nation to Wal-Mart. Characteristics such as Arkansas's attracted poultry companies into southern locations throughout the 1950s and 1960s so that, today, 10 of the top 14 states producing poultry are in the South.

The movement of the poultry industry toward southern production locations coincided with early industry growth and vertical integration. Drawn by low land and labor costs, by the early 1980s companies based in southern states produced nearly 90 percent of all broilers and 40 per-

TABLE 7.1. Poultry Production by State, 1990
(millions of lbs)

	Broilers	Turkeys
Alabama*	3,642	n.a.
Arkansas*	3,995	453
California	1,109	723
Delaware	1,159	n.a.
Florida*	490	n.a.
Georgia*	3,760	61
Maryland	1,141	2
Minnesota	198	852
Mississippi*	1,693	n.a.
Missouri*	362	360
North Carolina*	2,593	1,160
South Carolina*	343	168
Texas*	1,454	n.a.
Virginia*	882	316

* Southern production location.

Source: *U.S. Statistical Abstract, 1991.* Department of
Commerce, U.S. Bureau of the Census.

cent of all turkeys (see Lasley 1980). The same low-cost environment
that fostered its growth during the 1950s and 1960s continues to keep
poultry production in the South today, yet the terms by which the industry interacts with this environment have undergone qualitative
changes. What drew the poultry industry south was primarily a resident
labor force of African Americans and poorly educated "hillbillies"
from the Appalachians and the Ozarks. Families used to tenant farming, sharecropping, and other low-income and seasonal economic activities provided abundant reliable labor for the plants. Particularly important was the superfluous labor on small farms, primarily women and
older children, who had been crucial to farming operations during
peak labor-demand periods but who were available for poultry work
during the off-seasons (Fite 1984; Schwartz 1945). These families sent
labor into the processing plants and supplied much of the part-time labor on the grow-out farms, often raising birds on contract for the
plants.[1] Evangelical Christianity, racism, white supremacism, antiunion
sentiments, and other ideologies of dominance succeeded in keeping
workers loyal to the plants, relatively docile, and susceptible to authoritarian methods of labor control.

From the late 1960s through the 1980s, several factors combined to cause poultry firms to consider using immigrants as supplemental, complementary, or primary workers in the plants. First, it was during this time that the South emerged as what Robert Marius (1984:145) has termed "the regional incarnation of all that was hateful and decadent and backward about America," stimulating national attention on the South's poverty, racial discrimination, rural character, and uneven development. The civil rights movement, increased educational opportunities, welfare reforms, and other features associated with Lyndon Johnson's Great Society programs constricted labor supplies to the plants while decreasing worker tolerance for authoritarian labor control.

Second, southern chambers of commerce were, by this time, well into their drives for industrial recruitment based on cheap, docile, non-unionized labor (Vass 1979; Cobb 1982). The targets of these drives were usually manufacturing firms that produced their goods in northern locations with unionized labor. Even firms that were unwilling or unable to leave the North could use southern production locations to "out-source" or subcontract the production of portions of their products. The growth of the chemical, textile, auto parts, and other small manufacturing industries competed with poultry-processing labor. A smaller competitor for plant labor was the Vietnam War, whose hunger for warriors drew disproportionately on poor and minority households.

Accompanying these sources of competition for poultry industry labor were changes brought about by nationwide demographic processes. A South transformed into a "Sun Belt" attracted tourists, seasonal residents, and increased in-migration among retirees and other groups who were unlikely to provide labor to the plants. The southern flight of large portions of the U.S. population encouraged suburban development, a boom in house building and infrastructure construction, and the growth of motels, hotels, and restaurants—all industries that have traditionally attracted the same kinds of workers that were drawn into poultry.[2] Despite competition from other industries, by this time the industry was well entrenched in the South.

With more women entering the labor force during this period, the industry might have been able to staff its industry sectors with natural population increases—mothers referring daughters, for instance—if demand for its products had remained stable. But the per capita consumption of red meat in the United States has slowly given way to consumption of poultry products; in 1987, poultry consumption surpassed red-meat consumption. With increased information on the health benefits of white as opposed to red meat, poultry has been particularly well situated to take advantage of shifting consumer concerns. Compared with other white meats (e.g., seafood), most consumers are familiar and comfortable with cooking chicken and turkey. In the decade from 1981 to 1991, poultry consumption grew from 26 percent to 40 percent of total U.S. consumption of all meat products (U.S. Department of Commerce 1991).

Developments in product lines and product marketing created additional labor demand. Responding to consumer demand for more conveniently packaged products, the industry developed a variety of "further-processed" products, such as boned breasts, which added new departments inside processing plants that performed progressively more tasks per bird. Packaging has become particularly advanced, with most of the large firms producing the priced and labeled packages sold to end consumers. As with meat and fish processing, further processing in the poultry industry has enhanced the movement of value-adding from the retail to the processing sector, replacing more highly paid grocery store butchers with low-wage processing-plant workers. Packaging in the plants opened the door for product branding, which drove the continued process of standardizing production practices for birds with uniform textures, sizes, colors, and so forth (Smith and Daniel 1987). Branding also facilitated the expansion of the domestic market and increasing export opportunities. The latter are bound to increase under the North American Free Trade Agreement (NAFTA) and the General Agreement on Tariffs and Trade (GATT).

A growth environment such as this either attracts corporate capital or demands that existing firms, many of which began as family farming enterprises, adopt the typical financial and political strategies of corporate capital. Major poultry firms have become involved in mergers and acquisitions, expanding into new markets, new product lines, and even new meats and other commodities. Historically, the major firms have had access to government commodity subsidy programs through their feed operations, which fueled the growth of the broiler industry in its early years, and they have been careful to maintain this source of funds (Reimund et al. 1981). The industry has enlisted additional public support from land grant colleges in the continuing industrialization of its birds. Further government support has come in the form of the Job

Training Partnership Act (JTPA) and the Targeted Job Tax Credit (TJTC), which were designed to stabilize the incomes of disadvantaged workers and which subsidize poultry firms' production costs with tax credits and assistance in paying wages. To increase productivity, it has engaged in ergonomic and other studies of time and movement in the workplace. New pressures on state and federal legislators have been introduced to streamline U.S. Department of Agriculture inspections and thereby subtract government intervention from the speed of plant disassembly lines. In plants that have been able to maintain high levels of untainted birds, line speeds have increased from 72 to 90 birds per minute (Griffith and Runsten 1988).

These developments have been mixed blessings for the communities, regions, and populations that depend on the industry for jobs, benefits, and revenues. Its increased production demands create greater stresses on workers' muscle tissues and consequent higher rates of injury. Yet the industry has become ever more creative in disguising its high rate of occupational injury. Some of the most tragic industrial accidents and flagrant violations—such as the fire at a processing plant in Hamlet, North Carolina, or the occupational injury suits against Perdue—have caught the attention of the national press, yet many cases go either unreported or misrepresented. New-immigrant workers play an active role in this process while creating additional housing, educational, legal, and other problems for communities that are home to processing plants.

In this chapter, I argue that, with the increases in line speed and other production pressures, the industry needs to engage in ever more comprehensive patterns of labor control. I argue further that this is most efficiently accomplished with immigrant labor, yet it is not restricted to immigrants, since the mere presence of immigrant workers in plants serves as an incentive to native workers to submit to the terms of plant-production regimes.

Methods

This chapter draws on information from poultry-processing regions in North Carolina and northern Georgia, both further developing and adding to the arguments of earlier works (Griffith 1987, 1990, 1993). The research was conducted in three phases. In the first phase, during the spring and summer of 1988, I interviewed poultry-processing plant personnel managers from four major poultry-producing regions of the southeastern and eastern United States (North Carolina, northern Georgia, Texas/Arkansas, and the Delmarva Peninsula), supplementing these interviews with interviews with workers, employment service personnel, union officials, and others knowledgeable about the industry. These interviews were conducted either in person or over the telephone; supplemental data were collected through visits to each of the regions and review of industry publications, newspaper articles, and local government reports. The second phase began in March 1989 and lasted through April 1990. This phase was part of an expanded study that included meatpacking plants in Kansas, Iowa, and Minnesota. In addition to visiting these new regions, I revisited North Carolina and northern Georgia poultry-processing communities, again interviewing personnel managers and others I had interviewed in the previous year. Fourteen plants in Georgia and 17 in North Carolina were included in the study. In the poultry-producing regions, the second-round interviews were more in-depth and detailed than those of the previous year, and I was careful to cross-check them with interviews with workers, union officials or "grassroots" organizers, and local observers of the industry (e.g., JTPA administrators, OSHA inspectors). Finally, I interviewed poultry workers and plant personnel managers in North Carolina and Maryland during the fall of 1993 as part of a research project on the use of temporary "nonimmigrant" alien labor in several low-wage industries of the United States.

General Features of the Poultry Industry in North Carolina and Northern Georgia

Five integrated sectors constitute the poultry industry throughout the United States: breeder/egg farms, hatcheries, feed mills, grow-out farms, and processing plants. In this chapter I focus on the processing plants, since this sector draws the most immigrants and is responsible for the highest occupational injury rates. Processing plants also stand at the heart of the other operations in both a spatial and a temporal sense. As a rule, other facilities lie within 25 miles of the plant, and hatching of eggs and growing of birds is done with processing production schedules in mind.

The processing plants themselves are organized so that birds enter one end of the plant and trucks carrying packaged and priced products leave from the other. In the receiving, or "live-hanging," area, workers wearing paper gas masks pull live birds from plastic crates. The rooms are dimly lit with blue lightbulbs because the dark is thought to calm the birds. From here the birds are mechanically stunned, plucked, killed, and partially eviscerated. Entering the plant floor, workers and USDA inspectors further eviscerate and inspect the birds, usually standing on wet mesh platforms, wearing rubber boots, gloves, layers of clothing, and aprons. From this point on the plants get progressively cooler; the temperature drops from normal room temperature to freezing in the huge walk-in coolers where the birds are stacked for shipping. The floors follow the drop in temperature by becoming wetter and slipperier, coated with chicken fat, and constantly hosed down. As the birds leave the eviscerators and inspectors, they are routed to stations where quality-control personnel check them for imperfections and send the least bruised birds to a station that weighs, packs, and prices whole birds. Imperfect birds then enter the further-processing sections of the plant.

At this phase of production the plants vary considerably. Some perform very few further-processing cuts, while others produce an entire range of boned and fully cooked products. One northern Georgia plant, for example, produces all the cooked marinated breasts for a national fast-food restaurant's chicken sandwich. Others bone, smoke, boil, broil, bread, fry, chop, roll, press, reconstitute, and fully freeze chicken parts. Some produce a pasty gray substance of fat, bone, skin, and other refuse parts for dog food. In any case, most plants have added further-processing sections in the past few years. These sections produce a range of more or less desirable and hazardous tasks. Most common are those that require a single cut or set of cuts on one portion of a bird all day long, creating conditions for repetitive motion injuries. Less hazardous positions include those that involve testing products for internal temperature during or after cooking, mixing vats of marinade, or staffing the pricing or labeling machines. Yet the majority of plant jobs involve repetitive motions. Increased production demands and the continued shift to further processing—which relies on more specialized, more repetitive cutting motions—have led to higher rates of occupational injury. In the northern Georgia plants in this study, 64.8 percent had either added new shifts or changed in response to new

USDA inspector eviscerating chickens in a Carolina plant. (Courtesy of Meat&Poultry)

product lines in recent years; 50 percent of the North Carolina plants had made similar changes.

Higher occupational injury rates not only lead directly to worker turnover, but also create a need for workers to take off work for relief from the stress and anxiety of working in a poultry-processing plant. Such cycles of "injury and therapy" have been noted in other settings that expose low-wage workers to hazardous jobs (Griffith, Valdés Pizzini, and Johnson 1992; Griffith 1993). Among the working poor, these burdens are multiplied through the generations, where the previously injured, elderly kinsmen of workers demand sporadic or constant health care and other attentions associated with being infirm.

Poultry plants are large factory settings that are becoming more and more ethnically diverse with increased recruitment of Latino workers. This is combined with the generally low wages for unskilled workers in the plants; in 1988 they ranged from $4.75 an hour to $5.85 an hour in Georgia and from $3.70 an hour to $6.70 an hour in North Carolina (see Table 7.2). The 1993 data suggest that rates increased by around 7

TABLE 7.2. Selected Characteristics of Sample Plants

	Northern Georgia ($n = 14$)	North Carolina ($n = 17$)
Wages		
Minimum	$4.75	$3.70
Maximum	$5.85	$6.70
Mean	$5.49	$5.36
SD	.338	.794
Number of Workers		
Minimum	258	280
Maximum	3,126	2,000
Mean	797	755
SD	751	549
Gender and Ethnicity (Averages)		
Percent women	50.7	53.8
Percent white	46.9	31.0
Percent black	39.9	61.6
Percent Latino	10.6	4.8

Source: Griffith 1993.

or 8 percent, to a mean of $5.85; weekly earnings averaged around $200 (Griffith, Heppel, and Torres 1994).

The figures on ethnicity show that, at least in 1988, relatively small proportions of plant workforces consisted of Latino workers. These figures tell only part of the story, however. In keeping with the argument developed in this chapter, it is not the number of Latino workers alone that is important. Their presence in poultry plants alters the labor-management relations in ways that continue to favor management, especially in light of network recruiting practices that allow plant personnel managers easy access to new Latino workers.

To understand this apparent paradox of changing labor relations maintaining management's power over workers, we need to consider, briefly, the characteristics of labor control prior to the coming of Latinos. Before the mid-1980s and continuing into the 1990s in some production locations, poultry plant workforces depended heavily on women and African Americans. In this context many labor relations, especially labor-control mechanisms, derived from gender as well as ethnic inequalities and stereotypes. Historically, poultry production emerged from key tasks on farms associated with women and children, such as gathering eggs and raising hens. The development of the processing sector built on this foundation by converting a typically female task—processing food—from home to factory locations. That this process was fueled by the feed mills—centers of the male activity of subsidized grain production—magnified in factory settings the traditional authority of men over women, whites over blacks, and primary over supplementary wage earners.

These relations of dominance may be subtle and unrecognizable when relatively few workers depend on income from the poultry industry as their primary income. During such periods, labor-management relations may be vertical, similar to patron-client ties, and paternalistic. The inequities of these relations become widely recognized only as crises develop—inflationary pressures on households, competitive pressures on firms, recessions. This became clear when a group emerged in a small, eastern North Carolina town to deal with a variety of problems that women experience primarily because they are women: domestic violence, sex discrimination, child-care difficulties, the private or hidden struggles against sexism in the home.[3]

The Center for Women's Economic Alternatives

Initially run out of a trailer, this group became organized explicitly to protest sex discrimination at a hosiery mill, where women received no vacation or sick pay while the male workers received these benefits. Around this dispute the women formed a nonprofit organization in 1984 called United Women Workers that encouraged entrepreneurship among women and encouraged additional protests. In one case, African-American women were forced to clean bathrooms at a garment factory that they themselves could not use; when they went to United Women Workers for organizational support, they were fired for attempting to form a union. Rather than disperse through the labor market, they began their own clothing company.

From early victories this organization eventually branched out, renamed itself the Center for Women's Economic Alternatives, secured grants from the Ms. Foundation, and fought for increased security for night convenience store clerks, shorter shifts at a ham-processing facility, the development of a safe haven for victims of domestic violence, and, more recently, increased occupational safety measures in the poultry industry. "Perdue cripples workers," said the past director of the center, "then calls them shiftless."

Despite these victories, the women of eastern North Carolina couldn't break free of the fear that inhabits the dominance discussed earlier. This emerged from the way the center's leadership characterized labor organizing as though it was distinct from unions. On the one hand, the center's director said, "The biggest obstacle is trying to deal with the fear, the fear of the company, of Perdue closing, the fear of losing one of the only jobs in the community." On the other hand, she spoke against the United Food and Commercial Workers, saying, "Poultry workers aren't ready for a union. Unions have a bad reputation around here. People have the notion that the union only wants membership dues. They will scare some folks away." As a corollary to this idea, she said that people outside of eastern North Carolina, coming from different experiences, would have no idea how to organize or lead these African-American women.

The center's development illustrates, first, that poultry workers have a history of phrasing their struggles in terms drawn from family life and the more general experiences of women, minorities, and the poor: domestic violence, racism, sexism. This is a source of strength, of collective action, yet it confines their struggles to local contexts. It becomes holistic resistance, supplanting, fully or partially, those organizations that might be able to increase their effectiveness in the long term. Labor unions, for example, typically focus on a narrower range of issues yet are national in scope and more effective in keeping management responsive to labor issues. In this sense, embedding struggles in these broader issues can be a source of vulnerability as well as strength. The paradox of holistic resistance is similar to the paradox of paternalism, where employers establish relations with workers that are both benevolent and exploitative.

Latino workers entering the plants exacerbate the vulnerability of African Americans and other domestic workers while following the model of embedding labor relations in broader issues and problems. Yet in the case of immigrants, the basis of coalition becomes questions about legal status, hostility, problems of family and network formation, racism, and educational and other public programs. In Georgia only 2 of 14 plants (14.3 percent) had no Latino workers, and the percentages of Latinos in the others ranged from 1 to 59 percent; in North Carolina only 12.5 percent of the plant personnel managers interviewed reported hiring no Latinos, and in the other plants Latino percentages ranged from 1 to 33 percent.

Two other developments make the entry of Latino workers into the plants all the more significant for industry labor relations. First, these figures were based on a 1988 survey; by 1989 the practice of hiring Latino workers had spread to nearly all plants in the two regions, and the proportions in the plants had increased. By 1993 only 1 of the 17 plant personnel managers in North Carolina and Maryland reported having no immigrant workers; in the other plants, immigrants made up around one-quarter of the workforce. Second, as the quote introducing this chapter indicated, plant personnel managers have been recruiting workers much more aggressively, through network recruiting and locating supplies of workers in distant regions, utilizing bonus programs, providing some (if temporary) housing and transportation, and engaging other strategies to bring them into the plants. It was not uncommon for personnel managers to say things like "We're working with job services in Gainesville where there are lots of Hispanics. The Department of Labor is helping us get organized to recruit them" (see Griffith 1993:166–67).

This occurs at a time of increased Latino and other immigration into both regions, fueled in part by developments in the agricultural labor market (Griffith and Kissam 1994). According to a recent report on students with limited English proficiency (LEP), such students have increased in North Carolina by 258 percent in the past five years (NAPE News 1992). Much of this increase has been due to the almost complete displacement of African-American workers by Mexicans in the apple orchards, tobacco fields, and most other important harvests (Migrant Health Task Force 1991). Some of this has been driven by H-2A visa programs, which import foreign workers to harvest pickle cucumbers and tobacco when the U.S. Department of Labor determines a labor shortage exists. These programs are often accompanied by campaigns to ease the entry of Latino workers into the community, touting Latinos as hardworking and family-oriented—qualities highly desired by the poultry plant personnel managers (see Griffith 1993:156–57).

Occupational Injury and Labor Relations

Under conditions of high occupational injury, comprehensive labor-control mechanisms become critical to plant production regimes.

Maintaining line speeds of 72 to 90 birds per minute hinges on being able to keep the line fully staffed throughout the production shift while keeping injuries at a low level of severity. Two strategies employed by plants facilitate this: the use of workers with extended networks for replenishing injury-riddled workforces, and intimidating workers into tolerating or underreporting their injuries, a practice also reported by Hall in this volume. Both of these strategies are accomplished most effectively in plants employing significant numbers of immigrants.

Network Recruitment

Poultry plants recruit new workers through ties of family and friendship. According to personnel managers, 85.7 percent of plants in Georgia and 100 percent of those in North Carolina recruit new workers through friendship and kinship ties of current workers, recruiting up to 80 to 85 percent of workers in this way. In Georgia, 50 percent of the plants pay bonuses to current workers who bring new workers into the plants, as long as the new employees stay for a designated period (usually 30 to 90 days); in North Carolina, 29.4 percent of the plants pay such bonuses.

While network recruiting is not restricted to Latino or other immigrant workers, these practices are particularly effective among immigrants. Network recruiting is positively correlated with Latino workers in both regions; in the Georgia plants, where recruitment of Latinos has been most pronounced, the correlations are particularly high relative to white and black employees (Griffith 1993:160).

Further, qualitative information about the ways Latino workers have come to the East Coast suggests that their migration has been facilitated by networks. These observations come primarily from studies of the farm labor force. The relationship between the farm labor force and the poultry-processing labor force merits detailed consideration because the former provides the initial "doorway" into the U.S. economy for many Latino workers. As such, it is in the farm labor market that Latino workers first develop their expectations about wages, working conditions, supervisory methods, task assignments, and other attributes of finding and keeping a job.

The most recent observations of farm labor dynamics have emphasized the pervasiveness of network recruiting in farm labor. The Commission on Agricultural Workers found the following:

[F]amily networks play a critical role in labor recruitment across international borders. Finding a job through such networks appears to be especially effective in low-wage occupations with few skill requirements or screening barriers. In seasonal farm work, recruitment is generally the responsibility of the foreman or farm labor contractor—positions which, over the years, have been filled by experienced immigrant farmworkers who have gained legal status. These individuals fill available jobs by turning to their own or their crew members' friends and relatives, many of whom still live in Mexico. (Commission on Agricultural Workers 1993:91–92; cf. Heppel and Amendola 1992; Kissam and Griffith 1991a, 1991b)

In addition to the widespread reliance on networks, other studies have noted the creativity with which workers form and transform networks in relation to one another and to their employers. These processes of network construction and change influence a number of other attributes of the labor process. For example, Kissam and Griffith (1991b), in studies of communities in California, Texas, and Florida that supply farm labor, found that workers commonly formed "artificial" networks, or networks that were based not on friendship, kinship, or village residence but on the availability of transportation, housing, or funds of knowledge. Farm-labor contractors, bringing crews from Florida into Georgia and North Carolina, commonly assemble crews with an eye toward mimicking friendship and kinship networks, providing workers with a wide range of services (e.g., credit, translation services, food and medicine during "wet" times). Workers used to these practices come to expect housing and transportation to be parts of job packages or among the services provided by their employers. Although fewer than 15 percent of the poultry employers interviewed in 1993 provided housing for workers, in some counties plant personnel managers have encouraged the construction of low-cost trailer parks and other housing developments, provided temporary housing, or assisted workers in their housing search. In one of the largest plants in North Carolina, the provision of housing to Latino poultry workers has been viewed with suspicion among native North Carolinians at the same plant (Griffith 1993:190–94). In this case the company purchased 40 acres of land and built a trailer park, reserving the right to place workers in the units with other workers whom they may or may not know. This model of work and housing is identical to that found in the farm labor market in the seasonal labor regions of Georgia and North Carolina (Griffith 1991; Amendola, Griffith, and Gunter 1993; Griffith and

Camposeco 1993). The practice of providing transportation between workers' homes and their plants also has some precedent in the poultry industry. Just over a quarter (28.6 percent) of the Georgia processing plants provide transportation for their workers; 17.6 percent of the North Carolina plants provide this service.

Utilizing networks among Latino workers has helped maintain the flow of workers into and through the plants, especially in the past decade. Recent migration research, especially that conducted in the aftermath of the 1986 Immigration Reform and Control Act and the Immigration Act of 1990, suggests that new immigration laws have facilitated cyclical migration and the development of transnational communities (Papademetriou et al. 1988; Bach et al. 1991; Griffith 1990; Griffith and Kissam 1994). These developments assure the continued replenishment of plant workforces by new immigrants, since they involve the growth of immigrant enclaves and "anchor" households to which and from which immigrant workers attach and detach themselves depending on labor market developments (Griffith, Valdés Pizzini, and Johnson 1992).

Underreporting Injury

It is impossible to study the poultry industry and not at some point learn that plants continually try to keep their reported occupational injury rates low. The two most obvious reasons are to minimize workers' compensation and insurance premiums, and to reduce the amount of attention the government gives to plant production methods and workplace safety. Nearly all workers interviewed reported that plant supervisors would rather pay an injured person to come to work and sit rather than stay home sick, if it meant not reporting the injury. In addition, plant nurses routinely treat repetitive motion disease in a symptomatic manner (with ibuprofen and vitamin B_{12}) and encourage workers to return to the line and tolerate their pain. Plant nurses also routinely question the origin of workers' injuries, suggesting that they are due to causes outside of plant working conditions:

> In one case, a woman who complained to the nurse that her hand needed surgery, because of carpal tunnel syndrome, was told that the condition was probably hereditary. Suspecting the nurse was saying this as a way of putting her off with medical jargon, the woman quickly said that no one else in her

144 | DAVID GRIFFITH

family suffered from such a condition. After this, the nurse claimed that the woman, who was thirty-eight years old, was going through menopause, to which the woman responded, "You better go ask some of those nineteen year olds out there with swollen hands if they are having menopause." (Griffith 1993:174)

In response to allegations that they underreport injury, industry spokespersons often claim they are one of the most inspected industries in the country and that high injury rates could not go unreported or underreported (see Bjerklie, this volume). This is a reference, of course, both to USDA inspectors who work throughout the plants and to state labor department inspectors who occasionally check the plants for injury rates. Unfortunately, USDA inspectors are predisposed to upholding plant appearances of low injury rates, and state labor department or employment security commission personnel occupy ambivalent positions in relation to the industry. USDA inspectors, although paid by the government, are hired from plant labor forces; they can easily be screened for loyalty to the firm. In addition, USDA inspectors are engaged not in workplace safety inspections but in inspections of birds, which require their attention. And they remain in one place throughout the workday.

The role of state labor and employment personnel is more difficult to characterize, given the multifaceted nature of this complex agency's interaction with industry. Some segments within state employment agencies and departments of labor acquire legitimacy from services they provide to poultry managers, while other segments acquire legitimacy from the services they provide to workers. This is further complicated by the fact that local labor department offices often provide training grounds for personnel managers in poultry plants. These offices may rely on the poultry industry for their own legitimacy, since the industry is one of the few to use a variety of the agency's services, including its employee referral service, its document (I-9) validation functions, and its administration of the TJTC and JTPA programs.

Yet there are those among the state labor and employment personnel who act and advocate on behalf of workers. The most vocal workers'-rights advocates within departments of labor are usually in the wage and hour and occupational health and safety divisions. If these individuals are not predisposed to upholding workers' rights when they join these departments, they often become so on the job from encountering, day after day, abuses of workers' rights and clear violations of labor law. Yet, as Hall's contribution to this volume makes clear, these individuals and their offices are often constrained by budget and personnel shortages and by political pressures.

Through network recruiting, the use of new-immigrant labor, and underreporting of injury, the poultry industry has been able to maintain high line speeds and expand methods of labor control among its workers. The additional benefits of increased productivity and reduced complaints among workers also derive from these practices. They are indicative of the overall trajectory of rural industrialization that relies on industries like poultry and on the increasing availability of Latino workers.

The Latino Presence in Poultry-Processing Communities in the Eastern United States

It is impossible to ignore the many Spanish-speaking immigrants who have come to work in the poultry plants via the agricultural labor force. Many were granted work authorization status as seasonal agricultural workers under the 1986 Immigration Reform and Control Act, and they continue rotating among agriculture, food processing, and return migration to Mexico. Yet the context of their entry into cities like Gainesville in Georgia or Mount Olive in North Carolina was framed, initially, by the poultry industry. The initial adaptation of Latinos to Georgia and North Carolina, and of Georgia and North Carolina to Latinos, is one steeped in labor-management relations in the plants. Poultry production in both states, however, is not a new industry. Its history is intertwined with that of the rural communities and people of the area (Saindon 1991). Prior to the mid-1980s, the industry relied on native, local labor. These workers, not the Latinos, laid the social and cultural foundations on which new recruitment strategies, new labor-management relations, and other practices associated with the growing use of immigrants have been erected.

High occupational-injury rates, low wages, and high worker turnover and absenteeism have been central to the landscape of working in poultry processing since the plants opened. These attributes suggest that their workforces are extremely fluid, with workers coming and going as they are injured, as they seek relief from job stress, or as they grow frustrated with their compensation relative to the work they are expected to perform. Yet this fluidity describes only a portion of the poultry workforce. According to plant personnel managers, poultry plants often have "core" workers, who experience lower rates of injury and come to work reliably, working alongside groups of progressively more high-turnover workers. This corresponds, roughly, to the fact that different shifts and positions in the plants stimulate different rates of turnover. The live-hanging, or receiving, area of the plant, where workers pull live chickens from crates and hang them on hooks, has high turnover. Contrasted with these jobs are those of quality-control personnel and the men who drive forklifts at the opposite end of the plant. While there is some rotation among positions inside the plant, there are not enough positions available to rotate everyone between the more and less preferred tasks. Further, "good" workers (as defined by management) can be rewarded with more highly preferred tasks. Also, segmentation inside the plant along ethnic, gender, or other lines may lead to certain groups being "pigeonholed" into less desirable tasks. In a study of a poultry plant in Utah, Walker (1988) found that new-immigrant workers filled the highest-turnover, least-desirable positions. An earlier study found that Latino workers were initially placed on the least desirable second shifts in the plants (Griffith 1993). But this is by no means a straightforward process. In some plants and some industries, it is often the immigrant workers who are given the desirable tasks, in an effort to discourage native workers from coming to work.

These observations suggest that there are both "loyal" and "marginal" components of plant labor forces, and that customs already exist for differential treatment of workers based on factors such as gender and ethnicity. As long as such differential treatment is customary, it becomes relatively easy to incorporate new-immigrant workers into the labor force without seriously disrupting, at least initially, the internal politics of the plant. At the same time, it becomes easy for new workers to establish footholds in plant workforces and, subsequently, to "colonize" them.

Network recruiting facilitates the "colonization" process. From the workers' perspective, network recruiting is beneficial along a number of lines. First, workers are able to bring family and friends into their workplaces, creating a more amenable social environment. Second, they may reap the satisfaction of helping a family member or friend find employment in an area where employment alternatives may be limited or contracting. Third, they improve their positions in relation to plant management by helping plants meet their personnel needs and by having potential companions in any labor disputes or acts of resistance against management. Fourth, among those who engage in generalized reciprocity with family and friends, network recruiting enriches the entire network. Finally, having family and friends in the plant allows workers to help one another in preparing and supporting excuses for missing work.

Through network recruiting, the "colonization" of the poultry labor industry, or of various shifts or tasks within the plants, becomes possible, even probable. Using new-immigrant, primarily Mexican, workers in this context expands on yet another customary practice among poultry workers: "rotating" among different economic activities, multiple jobs, and periods of rest, relief, and work. Among the new-immigrant workers in northern Georgia, most of whom are Latinos from agricultural labor backgrounds, the practice of rotating workers among such activities assumes an international or transnational character, as workers return to Mexico or to communities in Texas, Florida, and California as part of their annual rounds of income-generating, cultural, and social activities. One personnel manager said that the plant had accommodated Latino annual schedules by giving them enough time off at Christmas to visit Mexico. Of course, the plant benefits from this if the workers who return to Mexico (as is common) bring more workers to plants after their time abroad (Griffith 1993).

The practices of rotating and network recruiting, combined with an appreciation of the internal structural features of the labor force, suggest that the colonization of poultry plant labor forces will proceed in a sporadic and piecemeal fashion. It is, in short, an uneven process. We cannot expect that native workers would relinquish their hold over certain positions, shifts, or tasks in the plants simply because of the presence of new immigrants. Even if management's power over the composition of the workforce were absolute (which it isn't), the numbers of Latino workers are not yet sufficient. New immigrants made up less than 10 percent of the total poultry workforce in 1988. Yet by 1993 that figure had risen to 25 percent (Griffith 1989:167; Griffith, Heppel, and Torres 1994).

The presence of new immigrants—especially a continued *flow* of new immigrants—becomes important to plant labor relations not in the sense of completely displacing native workers from the industry but because their presence satisfies a number of management's productivity needs. New immigrants make docile and more eager workers, willing to fill positions that native workers find repugnant. They serve as a constant threat to native workers as well, reminding them of their vulnerability to being replaced by cultural "others." In this way they reduce the propensity among native workers to protest wages and working conditions.

In line with segmented labor-market theory, however, native workers may reap some benefits from the employment of new immigrants. Any savings from hiring new immigrants may be redistributed to "loyal" native workers, at least in part, in the form of pension plan contributions, bonuses, and health and insurance packages. Also, native workers continue to occupy those positions—USDA inspectors, quality-control personnel, and so on—that require basic English skills, and new immigrants complement their jobs and give them the satisfaction of knowing they are not the lowest-paid or lowest-status workers. These "benefits" are being rapidly eroded by the general, natural deterioration of "primary sectors" within workforces and labor markets, as union memberships decline, right-to-work laws flourish, and subcontracting spreads.

Yet the role of new immigrants is a changing one, responsive to shifts in the political climates of communities with poultry plants and to economic cycles. Those practices that facilitate the staffing of the plants are reflected in the communities and their responses to new immigrants. Rotating between work and rest, between Mexico and Georgia, between the apple harvests of North Carolina and eastern Tennessee and the poultry plants of Georgia and the Carolinas—recruiting more new immigrants at every turn—these workers lend poultry-producing communities a fluid, restless character. Groups of three and four young men walk about together around town, carrying small satchels and plastic bags because they live under poorly secured conditions. Supermarkets begin carrying Spanish advertisements and Mexican products. Local employment services advertise English as a second language (ESL) classes, and school systems wrestle with limited English proficiency (LEP) programs. Catholic churches offer Sunday masses in "La Lengua de Los Angeles"—Spanish: the language of angels. Among flyers and posters offering such services to the immigrants are those from the poultry plants, also printed in Spanish, telling of work in Athens, work in Cumming, work in Canton. They read: "Trabajo. Pollo. Llamada 549–7007. $5.50 por hora."

Growing transnational communities have emerged in low-income neighborhoods throughout Georgia and North Carolina. One of these, in Gainesville, Georgia, lies in the shadow of the industry's most symbolic piece of infrastructure: a water tower that reads "Gainesville: Poultry Capital of the World." That neighborhood contributes to the internal differentiation of Gainesville by ethnicity, language, race, nationality, and social class, mirroring the internal labor markets of the plants. That community supports and even enriches those whose incomes depend directly on the poultry industry, while competing for public resources with those whose well-being and future depend on a sound education, a fair legal system, and adequate and accessible health care. Is it mere coincidence that Clinton's signature on the presidency consists of just these sorts of issues, that he has pushed for a more diverse and representative government, justice, and more accessible health care? At the same time, should we be surprised by developments at the other end of the political spectrum, where the presence of growing numbers of Latinos in Gainesville stimulated a Ku Klux Klan march protesting immigration? Somewhere between these extremes, in years to come, we will see allegiances expressed, alliances established, and boundaries strengthened, maintained, or overcome.

Notes

Research for this chapter was supported in part by the U.S. Department of Labor, International Labor Affairs Bureau.

1. This tradition of moving between farms and processing plants on a seasonal basis continues today in a variety of forms. For example, Central American and Mexican immigrants typically work in seasonal fruit and vegetable harvests, moving into the plants when work slows down in the harvest.

2. That these industries all compete for the same workers has been officially recognized by the fact that many receive special access to foreign workers through the H-2B visa and other "nonimmigrant" programs. In selected states, this is true for poultry and seafood workers, quarry workers, stable attendants, fast-food workers, shrimp deckhands, tree planters, and hotel and resort staff (mostly chambermaids). H-2B visas are reserved for temporary legal aliens employed in seasonal nonagricultural jobs for which a worker shortage has been demonstrated.

3. These accounts are based on interviews with Sarah Fields Davis and Donna Basemore of the Center for Women's Economic Opportunities, Ahoskie, North Carolina, spring 1990.

References

Amendola, S., D. Griffith, and L. Gunther. 1993. The Peach Industry in Georgia and South Carolina. In *Report to the Commission on Agricultural Workers, Appendix I: Case Studies and Research Reports*. Washington, D.C.: U.S. Government Printing Office, pp. 445–522.

Bach, R., H. Brill, T. Bailey, N. Chinchilla, D. Griffith, J. Hagan, N. Hamilton, J. Louky, T. Repak, N. Rodriguez, C. Schechter, and R. Waldinger. 1991. *The Impact of IRCA on the U.S. Labor Market and Economy*. Institute for Research on Multiculturalism and International Labor. Binghamton: State University of New York.

Cobb, J. 1982. *The Selling of the South*. Baton Rouge: Louisiana State University Press.

Commission on Agricultural Workers. 1993. *Report of the Commission on Agricultural Workers*. Washington, D.C.: U.S. Government Printing Office.

Fite, G. 1984. *Cotton Fields No More: Agriculture in the U.S. South*. Lexington: University of Kentucky Press.

Griffith, D. 1987. Non-Market Labor Processes in an Advanced Capitalist Economy. *American Anthropologist* 89(4):838–52.

_____. 1990. *The Impact of the Immigration Reform and Control Act's (IRCA) Employer Sanctions on the U.S. Meat and Poultry Processing Industries*. Final report. Institute for Multiculturalism and International Labor. Binghamton: State University of New York.

_____. 1993. *Jones's Minimal: Low-Wage Labor in the United States*. Albany: State University of New York Press.

Griffith, D., and J. Camposeco. 1993. The Winter Vegetable Industry in South Florida. In *Report to the Commission on Agricultural Workers, Appendix I: Case Studies and Research Reports*. Washington, D.C.: U.S. Government Printing Office, pp. 573–634.

Griffith, D., M. Heppel, and L. Torres. 1994. *Labor Certification and Employment Practices in Selected Low-Wage/Low-Skill Occupations: An Analysis from Worker and Employer Perspectives*. Report prepared for the West Virginia Bureau of Employment Programs, Charleston, W.Va.

Griffith, D., and E. Kissam. 1994. *Working Poor: Farmworkers in the United States*. Philadelphia: Temple University Press.

Griffith, D., and D. Runsten. 1988. *The Impact of the 1986 Immigration Reform and Control Act on the Poultry Industry: A Comparative Analysis of the Southeast and California*. Report prepared for the International Labor Affairs Bureau, U.S. Department of Labor, Washington, D.C.

Griffith, D., M. Valdés Pizzini, and J. C. Johnson. 1992. Injury and Therapy: Proletarianization in Puerto Rico's Fisheries. *American Ethnologist* 19:53–74

Heppel, M., and S. Amendola. 1992. Immigration Reform and Perishable Crop

Agriculture: Compliance or Circumvention. New York: University Press of America.

Kissam, E., and D. Griffith. 1991a. *Final Report to the U.S. Department of Labor.* Vol. 1, *Summaries and Conclusions.* Washington, D.C.: Office of the Assistant Secretary of Policy, U.S. Department of Labor.

―――. *Final Report to the U.S. Department of Labor.* Vol. 2, *Case Studies.* Washington, D.C.: Office of the Assistant Secretary of Policy, U.S. Department of Labor.

Lasley, F. 1980. *The U.S. Poultry Industry: Changing Structure and Economics.* Agricultural Economic Report no. 502. Washington, D.C.: U.S. Department of Agriculture.

Maurius, R. 1984. Musings on the Mysteries of the American South. *Daedalus* 113:143–76.

Migrant Health Task Force. 1991. Health Conditions of Migrant Farmworkers in North Carolina. Cooperative Extension Service manuscript. Raleigh: North Carolina State University.

NAPE [National Association for Public Education] News. 1992. *Limited English Proficient Students by State.* Washington, D.C.: NAPE.

Papademetriou, D. G., R. Bach, K. Johnson, R. Kramer, B. L. Lowell, and S. Smith. 1989. *The Effects of Immigration on the U.S. Economy and Labor Market. Immigration Policy and Research Report no. 1.* Washington, D.C.: International Affairs Bureau, U.S. Department of Labor.

Reimund, D., J. Martin, and C. Moore. 1981. *Structural Change in Agriculture: The Experience for Broilers, Fed Cattle, and Processing Vegetables.* Technical Bulletin no. 1648. Washington, D.C.: U.S. Department of Agriculture, Economic Research.

Saindon, J. J. 1991. *Piney Road: Work, Education, and the Re-making of the Southern Family.* Athens: Department of Adult Education, University of Georgia.

Schwartz, H. 1945. *Seasonal Farmworkers in the United States.* New York: Columbia University Press.

Smith, D., and P. Daniel. 1987. *The Chicken Book.* New York: Atheneum.

U.S. Department of Commerce, Bureau of the Census. 1991. *Statistical Abstract of the United States.* Washington, D.C.: U.S. Government Printing Office.

Vass, T. 1979. Low Wages and Industrial Development: North Carolina's Economic Predicament. *Carolina Planner* 5:14–21.

Walker, P. 1988. Stability in Production and the Demand for Mexican Labor: The Case of Turkey Processing in Rural Utah. Ph.D. diss., University of Utah.

8 | New Immigrants in an Old Industry

Blue Crab Processing in Pamlico County, North Carolina

David Griffith

THE SEAFOOD INDUSTRY is one of the most dynamic segments of the nation's food system. In the harvesting sector, increased governmental intervention has created a number of systems allocating fishing stocks that have altered relations between fishers and processing plants. The processing and marketing sectors have pioneered the development of new products, have expanded markets, and have become increasingly involved in interregional and international trade. Seafood market and restaurant owners have experienced the irony of increasing seafood demand, coupled with fears about seafood's safety and pressures for a mandatory seafood inspection program (Anderson and Anderson 1991; *Consumer Reports* 1992).

These changes have caused the reorganization of crews on fishing vessels, changed the ethnic complexion of the processing sector, and created new pressures on others involved in harvesting, processing, distributing, and marketing seafood. The seafood industry is similar to other food production systems in its general approach to labor relations, yet at the same time it offers telling differences. Producing a product from raw marine, lacustrine, or riverine materials involves a series of social ties and ecological arrangements distinct from those used to produce apples, oranges, pork chops, chicken breasts, or boxed New York strips.

In this chapter I examine changing labor relations in the crab-picking and other seafood-processing houses in Pamlico County, North Carolina, placing these changes within the broader context of the seafood industry's harvesting and marketing sectors. After outlining some of the general problems of harvesting and marketing seafood, and presenting a typology of the processing sector, I discuss the industry's role in this rural, coastal North Carolina county.

Pamlico County has depended on commercial fishing and seafood processing for the past century. Beyond this, however, the selection of the county is particularly relevant to the current volume because of a recent influx of immigrants to work in its seafood-processing houses. Imported directly from Mexico under a special (H-2B) class of visa, these new immigrants have replaced and displaced a native labor force composed primarily of African-American women.[1] Their use in the seafood houses both departs from and conforms to the use of immigrants in beef, pork, and poultry processing. On the one hand, as in other food-processing systems, the new seafood workers are new-immigrant Mexican nationals with ties to their home country. Combined with their highly restrictive legal status, their linguistic and cultural backgrounds confine them to sectors of the economy characterized by low wages, authoritarian methods of labor control, and high rates of occupational injury. In this respect they have much in common with many undocumented or recently "employment-authorized" immigrants in meatpacking and poultry processing. On the other hand, the seafood workers in Pamlico County are unique in that they are imported under visa classifications that confine them to specific employers who control not only their labor in the plants but their housing and transportation as well. This constitutes another example of food-processing firms enlisting the aid of the state to solve production problems. The restrictive nature of H-2B visas gives employers a degree of labor control that reflects attempts by employers throughout the food-processing industry to assume authoritarian methods of labor control. Industry-wide labor relations are further reflected in the fact that these new-immigrant workers have contested and resisted—in U.S. courts—the labor practices of the owners of Pamlico County's seafood-processing houses.

General Issues Facing the Seafood Industry

Relations between Harvesting and Processing Sectors in Contrast with the Meat and Poultry Industries

Unlike meat or poultry products, most fish and seafood products are harvested in common property resource settings. Common property resources cannot be privately owned and tend to be managed by the state. This poses a number of problems for the seafood industry that do not exist for the other processing industries discussed in this volume. First, outside of aquaculture operations, fish processors have difficulty achieving the degree of vertical integration found in the poultry industry or the control over feeds and other features of beef and pork production. This affects the quantity and quality of supplies of fish and shellfish to processors, which, in turn, affect labor demand. Most processing operations are highly seasonal, shutting down for anywhere from a few weeks to a few months every year. Second, public stewardship of water resources exposes the industry to government regulation that may threaten raw material supplies. Regulations limiting the entry of fishermen into certain waters or the use of certain gear types may facilitate capital concentration in the harvesting sector, driving smaller vessels out of business or into different fisheries (Sinclair 1983; McCay, Gatewood, and Creed 1989). This affects seafood processors who rely on these smaller vessels, especially when larger vessels are tied to other seafood-processing firms through debt relations or outright vessel ownership.

Problems arising from the harvesting sector pressure seafood processors into developing new products and securing seafood from a wider range of suppliers. These two forms of branching out involve increasingly interregional and international connections, allowing a range of vessel types, fishing gears and styles, and social groups to engage in seafood trade. Standardizing production, as has been accomplished in the meat and poultry industries, is nearly impossible in this kind of setting. Increasing interregional and international ties are also fueled by the high perishability of seafood and its susceptibility to a wide variety of pollutants: having a number of suppliers protects seafood processors from overdependence on a source that may be suddenly cut off due to oil spills or red tide.

Expanding one's supply sources and diversifying into new product lines discourages processors from vessel ownership and harvesting. Although some of the larger firms—those with floating factories capable of hiring crews from countries with low labor standards, roaming the high seas, and processing large amounts of seafood at sea—may maintain and even expand their harvesting operations, smaller processing firms and some larger ones have found it beneficial to cut all but market ties with the harvesting sector. Severing ties between processing and harvesting encourages development of subcontractual relations between these sectors, approaching arrangements commonly found in the poultry industry. This redistributes risk from the processing to the harvesting sector. Private management tools, such as subcontracting, create attractive environments for corporate investment, which emphasizes control over risk in new business ventures (Nash and Fernandez-Kelly 1983; Sassen-Koob 1985). Independent fishers, operating in riskier environments, then become encouraged to migrate for fish or to exploit a wider variety of species in order to stabilize income and keep their fishing capital employed for a greater portion of the year (McCay, Gatewood, and Creed 1989).

These developments have influenced the characteristics of labor in harvesting and processing. Some vessel crews who previously borrowed trip expenses prior to fishing excursions now find themselves unemployed as processors shift from direct employment of fishers to subcontracting (Floyd 1988). Crews on remaining vessels usually undergo reorganization to accommodate new migration schedules, longer stints at sea, increased probabilities of injuries (as fishers enter less familiar environments and use less familiar gear), and increased economic risks.[2]

Recent changes in the processing sector reflect the development of new product lines and increasing per capita consumption of fish products. Adding value by further processing and packaging is less well developed than in poultry or meat processing, yet the industry is moving in this direction (Perkins 1991:45–54). The complexity of packaging extends to the restaurant sector, where packaging includes the service, the restaurant's "ambiance," and condiments and garnishes; ironically, value-adding in this sector sometimes means attempting to reconstitute a food to its previous, seemingly more natural, less-processed condition.

The Raw, the Cooked, the Breaded, and the Canned: A Typology

Seafood processing is far more diverse than meatpacking or poultry processing. The wide variety of fish and shellfish, seafood's high perishability, the range of national and international sources of seafood, the lack of a federal inspection program, and the "commons" status of most fish and shellfish habitats—all allow small processors to take advantage of market niches and remain in business despite the capital concentration and increasing market shares of the larger firms. The following typology builds on observations along two lines: (1) the amount of control that direct producers (i.e., line workers) have over the processed product—that is, over the marketable commodity; and (2) the organization of work in the space of processing (e.g., in the plant, the shucking house, on the vessel). It represents a continuum from full control to no control over the seafood commodity and from informal, family organized work to more formal work organized according to Taylorist principles of factory production.[3]

Family Processing. Many fishing families prepare their catch for immediate sale and consumption. Some perform processing tasks that range from sorting the catch to gutting and freezing species to deheading and deveining shrimp. Other families sell their catch themselves, on street corners, along roadsides, or out of the backs of their trucks to retail outlets. In these contexts the processing tends to be an individual or household operation, rarely involving anyone other than the fisher, his or her spouse, and perhaps their children. The space of processing is generally the household, the boathouse, or some work space attached to the household or launching areas; the timing of the processing is directly determined by the fishing schedule. As such, these tend to be small-scale, flexible organizations, relying on the often-contestable and negotiable authority that rests on cultural traditions of age, gender, and family. Fishers have complete control over the disposition of the product, and some may sell their catch without licenses. Accumulation is directly tied to the household's labor supply, their skills and dispositions, and the household head's control over the total pool of household labor. Simply, the authority figure—wife, husband, grandparent—can work the household members as much or as little as is within his or her power. All value added to the product remains in the household.

Seafood Houses. Expanding family processing is constrained, in part, by the state, which must inspect and certify the cleanliness of a seafood-processing facility. Federal certification, coordinated by the Food and Drug Administration, is necessary to obtain a certificate to ship products across state lines. While some fishing households have obtained certification, it is easier for a number of fishing households to pool their obligation to the state by processing their catch at a state-certified "seafood house." Most commonly, the facility houses wooden tables or booths with some apparatus that aids in moving refuse (e.g., shells, viscera) away from the processing area. Essentially, seafood houses replicate the "family processing" system on a multihousehold scale. Thus, one of the impacts of state intervention in seafood processing has been the consolidation or centralization of small-scale, family processing into certified processing facilities.

The effect of certification has been, first, to criminalize seafood processing conducted outside the umbrella of government scrutiny. Second, certified facilities provide space to families on the condition, usually, that they sell their processed product to the owner of the facility. Both developments influence the complexion of the market and the control fishing families have over the disposition of their catch. Although most fishers process their own catch, these facilities may hire a few employees to prepare the catch that fishers do not wish to handle themselves. Use of the house implies sacrificing some control over the disposition of the catch.

Packer-Shippers. Packer-shippers are similar to packinghouse operations in the fruit and vegetable industry. They are brokers more than processors, simply icing down the fish that comes in off the boats and shipping it to other locations for further processing or sale. Some may grade the fish or shellfish prior to shipment.

Seafood Plants. Seafood plants in North Carolina perform only a few processing functions, most of which involve making marine products ready for end consumers. In contrast to the packer-shippers, who market to intermediate consumers,[4] seafood plants generally employ between 15 and 100 individuals to shuck and pack oysters, behead and devein shrimp, pick and pack cooked crabmeat, and fillet finfish. They may or may not be seasonal operations. Products that leave North Carolina go directly to retail outlets.

These plants differ from seafood houses in that, instead of multiplying the family-based processing enterprise, seafood plants employ workers for wages, usually figured as a piece rate rather than an hourly rate. Relations between workers and their employers are "conventional" employer-employee relationships, although generally much of the workforce within and between plants is related. Seafood plants buy marine products directly from fishermen or from dealers and may also either put boats to sea themselves or control harvesting operations—in whole or in part—through credit relationships with fishing families. Most plants in the coastal zone, from southern Delaware and Maryland to Brownsville, Texas, are based on this model (Paredes, Sabella, and Hepburn 1977; Thomas and Moberg 1990; Thomas and Formichella 1987; Griffith 1993). Plants in inland regions (including the Mississippi

Delta), north of Baltimore, or along the Pacific and Pacific Northwest coasts tend to fall into one of the following, more factory-like, categories (Doeringer, Moss, and Terkla 1988).

Mariculture and Aquaculture Operations. Several species have been developed as maricultured or aquacultured seafood products in recent years (e.g., catfish, striped bass, trout, salmon, shrimp, oysters, crawfish). This is probably the fastest-growing sector of the seafood industry today.[5] Unlike seafood plants, mariculture and aquaculture operations have a steady supply of a product that is consistently of similar size, quality, and other features that allow the development of a streamlined disassembly process. The processing component of the seafood industry is most comparable to poultry processing, where continual systemic links exist among developments in feeds, the character of the product, and extent of further processing and packaging. Also similar to poultry processing is the aquaculture/mariculture processing labor force. Workers are predominantly African-American women and other minorities, earning hourly wages instead of piece rates. Workers at one of the largest producers, Delta Pride of Indianola, Mississippi, are currently represented by the union that also represents poultry workers: the United Food and Commercial Workers (UFCW; Straus 1991a). Union representation in the catfish business is more than coincidental: ConAgra, one of the nation's largest poultry producers, owns Country Skillet Catfish in nearby Isola, Mississippi, and many of its poultry firms have UFCW representation.

Further-Processing Plants. Further processing of seafood products includes canning facilities, breading/freezing plants, "surimi" (fish paste) plants, and those plants that produce the cooked, branded, and other products (e.g., Mrs. Paul's, Starkist) familiar to most of the nation's shoppers. This level of production, yielding sophisticated products for end consumers, is the most attractive to large corporate capital such as General Foods (which owns Red Lobster) and Oscar Mayer (which owns Kemp Seafood).

Relocation and the Use of Immigrant Labor

These sectors of the seafood-processing industry are differentially affected by the pressures mentioned earlier. Among the most pressing problems are (1) state intervention in the form of a mandatory seafood

inspections program; (2) the continuing trend toward capital concentration and competition between firms of various sizes and with various
degrees of access to foreign and domestic capital; and (3) sporadic scar-
cities of low-income, low-skilled workers due to high rates of worker
turnover and absenteeism (Griffith 1987, 1993).

As in other low-wage industries requiring large amounts of unskilled
labor, the industry has also witnessed its share of the two related processes of "capital flight" and an increasing reliance on new-immigrant
labor at home. On the one hand, the major tuna companies moved
their canning facilities to Puerto Rico and Mexico during the 1970s.[6]
Table 8.1 shows that these operations have increased in size since 1977.
It reveals two additional trends: (1) plants have gotten smaller, employing fewer workers, in all but two regions (the Mid-Atlantic and U.S. Ter-
ritories); and (2) they have moved from inland to coastal locations, with
the number of plants increasing most in the Gulf and Pacific states and
decreasing most in inland states. On the other hand, the use of new
immigrants is growing in the industry, as in the case of Asian refugee
workers in Gulf state plants or the recent importation of Mexican workers into seafood-processing plants of North Carolina, Maryland, and
Virginia (Thomas and Moberg 1990; Griffith 1993).

Finally, the flight of capital has contributed to the development of
mariculture and aquaculture throughout the world. Overseas production and processing operations have more than kept pace with the industry's development in the United States. Even a short list of producers of cultured shrimp would include the Philippines, China, Vietnam,
Thailand, Indonesia, India, Bangladesh, Burma, Australia, Ecuador,
Mexico, and Colombia. In many overseas locations mariculture constitutes a growth industry following modernization models pioneered by
agricultural producers during the 1960s and 1970s. During the 1980s,
for example, Ecuador's shrimp growers have "built 100,000 hectares of
ponds and harvests have increased from only 5 metric tons in 1979 to
over 70,000 tons in 1990" (Straus 1991b:64). In many locations, the impacts of mariculture and aquaculture development have paralleled
those of the modernization of agriculture to an almost perverse degree:
the loss of launching and landing centers once used by peasant fishers,
the joint transformation and destruction of estuaries, the reduction of
biodiversity, the conversion of communities into labor forces for the industry, a shrinking subsistence base, and inflation.

Such developments, of course, set standards and establish param-

TABLE 8.1. Changing Locations of Production: Seafood Processing
in 1977 and 1989

Region Year	No. of Plants	EMPLOYMENT		Total Workers	Workers per Plant
		Seasonal	Year-Round		
Northeast					
1977	246	9,942	7,903	17,845	72.5
1989	252	6,364	6,182	12,546	49.8
Mid-Atlantic*					
1977	317	12,514	9,659	19,473	61.4
1989	191	7,887	7,472	15,359	80.4
South Atlantic					
1977	146	5,510	4,266	9,776	66.9
1989	167	4,955	4,746	9,701	58.1
Gulf States					
1977	388	15,481	11,146	26,627	68.6
1989	490	13,549	12,647	26,196	53.5
Pacific (including Alaska)					
1977	432	28,939	19,612	48,551	112.4
1989	556	20,525	16,337	36,862	66.3
Inland States					
1977	107	2,300	1,965	4,265	39.8
1989	39	547	540	1,087	27.9
American Samoa, Guam, Puerto Rico, and other U.S.					
1977	24	8,539	7,346	15,885	661.9
1989	23	12,016	12,013	24,029	1,044.7
Total					
1977	1,660	83,225	61,897	145,122	87.4
1989	1,718	65,843	59,937	125,780	73.2

* Includes North Carolina.
Source: National Marine Fisheries Service, *Fishery Statistics of the United States, 1991.*

eters for seafood processing throughout the United States. Even in
small, sparsely populated Pamlico County, North Carolina, these developments have influenced the place of processing operations in their
communities. As noted earlier, the selection of Pamlico County derives
from the overall importance of seafood processing and fishing in its
economy, and the growing, even pioneering, use of new-immigrant
Mexican workers imported under the H-2B visa classification.

Geography, Population, and Economics of Pamlico County

Looking at a map of Pamlico County, an artistic child might see the profile of an alligator's head as the creature rests, on a hot summer day, with its mouth open a few inches, inviting sandpipers to pick meat from between its teeth. Bay River, flowing almost due west into Pamlico Sound, crossing the Intracoastal Waterway, would constitute most of the alligator's mouth. Goose Creek Island, north of Bay River and Jones Bay, would form the snout, with its four north shore finger creeks of Oyster Creek, James Creek, Clark Creek, and Middle Prong tracing the intricacies of its nasal passages. Beneath its puffed throat, to the south, the Neuse River flows past the mouths of no fewer than 22 creeks, emptying, like Bay River, into Pamlico Sound. In the early evening, almost every evening, old African-American couples fish with bamboo poles along the banks of the river and its creeks. The Neuse is a large river, between three and five miles across from the shores of Pamlico County. It is also one of North Carolina's largest estuaries, separating Pamlico from Craven County and allowing the residents of the riverbank villages of Minnesott Beach and Oriental access to the sound. A 20-minute ferry with a 22-car capacity links the county with the military bases and job opportunities of Cherry Point and Havelock. The county seat of Bayboro sits on the edge of the watershed feeding Bay River, just south and west of where you would expect to find the alligator's eye; this far inland, maybe six miles from the sound, Bay River is fed by a number of creeks and smaller waterways. Along these, sheltered from hurricanes and other storms born at sea, sit some of the county's oldest crab-picking and fish-processing plants and a few fishing vessels.

The county's resemblance to an aquatic reptile runs deeper than mere appearances. The land itself seems indecisive about being land. Wooded, swampy wetlands, known as pocosin, make up a good deal of the land area. The county's population, too, has nurtured a relationship to water that, like the alligator's, is symbiotic, offering security, and amphibious. The principal characteristic giving Pamlico County its pockmarked, wrinkled, alligator-skin appearance is water: creeks, bays, rivers, and the big Pamlico Sound. Not only has such diverse, sheltered access to Pamlico Sound underwritten the growth of the seafood-processing and fishing industries; tourism and real estate development have been among the county's fastest-growing sectors in the past five years.

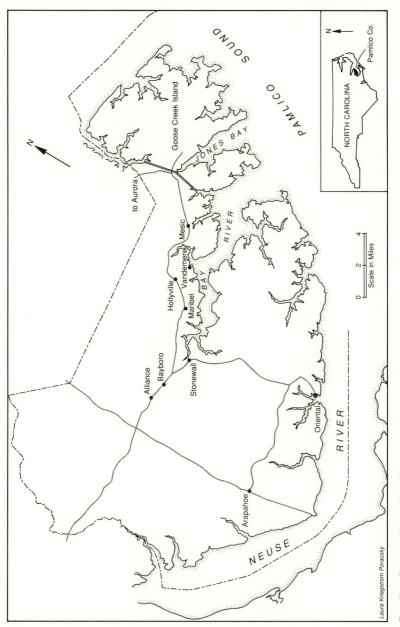

Laura Kriegstrom Poracsky

Pamlico County, North Carolina.

Beyond its dependence on water and wetlands, the county has no conspicuous industrial base. Only 13 of the county's firms bothered to list their names and addresses in the North Carolina Industrial Directory: 10 are seafood processors and shippers; another depends on seafood firms to make animal feeds with crab shells and other fish parts; and the others are a grain elevator and a newspaper. Fewer than 12,000 people live in the county, concentrated along two stretches of road that resemble rural highways all across eastern North Carolina. No town officially boasts a population of 1,000, although the central "metropolis" that runs from Alliance to Bayboro to Stonewall might contain between 10 percent and 12 percent of the population, or between 1,200 and 1,400 people. The county is thus 100 percent rural, and many of its folks depend on seasonal occupations that are tied to agriculture, fishing, or forestry. Through the 1980s, while the population remained relatively stable, the unemployment rate fell from 7.0 percent in 1980 to 5.3 percent in 1985 to the current 4.0 percent. This has caused labor supply problems for the seafood processors, some of whom, within the past three years, have turned to Mexico for their workers. In a county with fewer than 70 resident Hispanics, the 300 or more Mexican migrant workers imported to process seafood seem particularly misplaced.

Whites represent 73.5 percent of the population, and blacks 25.9 percent, leaving only 0.6 percent of the resident population in "other" ethnic categories. Whites and blacks tend to be segregated into different neighborhoods and communities. The small inland towns of Mesic, Maribel, and Hollyville are primarily black settlements, while the town of Vandemere and the community of Goose Creek Island, both enjoying direct access to the sea, are primarily white. Arapahoe (pop. 374), Bayboro (pop. 545), and Oriental (pop. 592), the other towns of any size, include both black and white neighborhoods.

The residential segregation of the population is both contradicted and reinforced in the seafood and fishing industries. On the one hand, blacks and whites work together in the processing houses; on the other, they tend to remain sexually and ethnically segmented into different components of the production process. In the wider community, of course, the chronically ambivalent ethnic relations found throughout the South are similar to those portrayed in Melissa Fay Greene's *Praying for Sheetrock* (1991): symbiotic yet confrontational, easygoing and courteous while suspicious and tense. In the white-owned and operated *Pamlico News,* much of the county's crime—particularly its rising tide of drug abuse in the form of crack cocaine and homegrown marijuana—is portrayed as originating with the black community or from various "out-of-town" sources (e.g., migrant farmworkers or passing motorcyclists). The black communities have not been spared the well-known phenomenon of "drive-by" shootings. Neither are the county's white communities internally harmonious: conflicts arise from land-use issues, particularly marina and other recreational boating developments that threaten water quality and "traditional" access to waterways by commercial fishing interests. Within the county's ethnic relations, the county's disputes over access to water, and the developing practice of using Mexican workers to pick crab, the seafood-processing industry occupies a central position.

Seafood Processing in the County's Industrial Profile

Unlike the meatpacking plant in Garden City, Kansas, or the turkey-processing plant outside Mount Olive, North Carolina, seafood processing in Pamlico County is a "homegrown" enterprise. Local families own and operate the plants. With one exception (an eel and catfish processor from the Netherlands), the county's 15 plants have no connection to corporate capital or financial backing outside that available through local institutions, social relations, or marketing ties. The 11 plants that reported their date of establishment in the North Carolina Industrial Directory listed the following dates: 1945, 1946 (2), 1947 (2), 1948, 1956, 1967, 1969, 1975, and 1979.

This homegrown character implies that the industry has not stimulated major transformations in the county's industrial profile. Just as the industry itself has emerged from the local society, so, too, until recently, had most seafood-processing workers. Although this is changing rapidly with the use of Mexican workers, most processing workers used to be African-American women who were born into resident Pamlico County households. The fact that owners and workers grew up in the county once provided owners with cultural and social mechanisms of labor control, while providing workers with cultural and social mechanisms of resistance. The dynamic between power and resistance played out in the plants and the communities in subtle and complex ways. Historically, for example, African-American workers exercised a great deal of flexibility over their work schedules, coming to work when it was convenient for them and when working didn't conflict with social obligations, home production schedules, or other demands on their time. Their ability to resist the regimen of plant production schedules derived from their having alternative means of support based on social ties, shared consumption practices, and state programs. Processors tolerated this, if grudgingly, in part because they relied on local African-American women to process their seafood and to bring new workers into the plants, train them, discipline them to the extent that was acceptable within workers' parameters of legitimacy, and share in their supervision at work. Processors, simply, relied on them for both production (labor) and reproduction (labor supply). At the same time, processors have been able to exercise control over African-American households by those traditional mechanisms of labor control in the community and within the labor force: extending credit to workers, mediating access to jobs for men in the industry and in related industries (as crew on fishing boats), controlling portions of the market for the catch of African-American crabbers, influencing local politicians and clergy, and drawing on the authority of senior men and women over the younger members of their households and networks.

The balance between labor control and resistance is shifting with the use of Mexican workers. The growing use of Mexican workers has created tensions similar to those in communities hosting large poultry, beef, and pork plants. In the meat and poultry industries, few if any firms rely exclusively on immigrant labor; most have drawn on local labor supplies to meet some or all of their production needs (Griffith 1990a, 1993). The use of new-immigrant labor has been used to either replace or supplement native labor; in either case, immigrant workers, more susceptible to labor control, set the standards for wages and working conditions. In Pamlico County it is exactly the local, homegrown tradition of seafood processing that underlies the current problems the industry faces by importing workers from Mexico. By providing owners with a political method of labor control, processors have been able to reduce the effects of local methods of labor resistance. This has given them more control over the entire workforce. At the same time, however, it has altered the basis for worker resistance,[7] creating other problems for processors in the wider community.

Occupational Health and Safety in the Industry

Public health issues have entered the seafood industry from the same two directions that they have entered the whole of the food industry:

from concerns about the safety and nutritive content of seafood, and from concerns about the occupational health and safety of processing workers and fishers on the job. Historically, the public's outrage has been more vociferous over the former than the latter. As Anderson and Anderson (1991:156) note, following publication of Upton Sinclair's novel *The Jungle*, "Consumers reacted with horror, not to the plight of the dismembered or deceased laborers as Sinclair intended, but with revulsion regarding the quality of the food they were eating."

Seafood inspections constitute one of the principal issues consuming the industry's attention today. Occupational injury and worker safety, by contrast, seem to be of little concern to those who occupy ownership or management positions. The plants themselves boast no signs saying "X Days without an Accident," as is common at the gates of eastern North Carolina manufacturing plants. Nor do plant owners and managers stress safety, as is common among personnel managers of poultry-processing plants.

This lack of concern does not reflect the safety of the plants. Injuries common to food processing in general are also common to seafood processing: cuts, slips on wet floors, cold stress, repetitive motion disease (cumulative trauma disorders), and pulled muscles from heavy lifting all occur in seafood plants (personal communication, Richard Ambrose, North Carolina Occupational Safety and Health Administration). In addition, some women acquire what is known as "crab rash" from handling crab.

Conventional injuries tend to be confounded by those that derive from the "presence" of the industry in its workers' lives. In small communities such as those throughout Pamlico County, the importance of seafood processing presents processors with the opportunity to engage in a variety of labor-control strategies. On top of the subtle powers that derive from class and race in southern communities, employers' strategies include providing workers with transportation to and from work, using kinship and network ties between workers to enhance authority over workers, and, with Mexican employees, providing housing and having a legal basis for keeping workers confined to the job. The effectiveness of labor-control strategies is enhanced by the industry's linkages with the local fishing community, its involvement in gender and ethnic relations, and its homegrown character. Sympathy for plant owners' class position and behavior can be seen in perceptions of the few community organizations oriented toward workers.

Community Services and Grassroots Organizations

The seasonal, hazardous, and low-wage character of seafood processing makes its workers ideal candidates for the services of the state that one associates with low-income populations. Although the Mexican workers have access to few public assistance programs, native workers participate in a variety of social services. They are provided no health insurance through the plants, and so seek coverage under Medicaid or the plant workers' compensation programs. They are laid off periodically due to plant slowdowns, and so seek unemployment insurance. They earn incomes that are below poverty standards, and so seek food stamps, energy assistance, Aid to Families with Dependent Children (AFDC), and USDA-sponsored commodity giveaway programs.

The Pamlico County Department of Social Services (DSS) coordinates most of these services; the department itself is a satellite office of a larger system that includes Craven and Jones Counties. The office also stands on the edge of ethnic or race relations in the county, acting as a buffer between black and white, a position structurally similar to that of the county sheriff's office yet substantively quite different. In the popular view, the DSS administers services to the black and low-income communities with taxes drawn from the higher-income, largely white community members who control most of the county's wealth. The DSS is viewed, at least by seafood processors, as the agency that has been undermining the reliability of the industry's workers by providing the support listed previously. In fact, DSS regulations may contribute to labor problems because some paperwork requirements work against seasonal workers. For example, there is a lag time between monthly earnings and benefit eligibility, so that workers who earn high wages in August, during the peak of the season, may be ineligible to collect benefits two months later, during a slower part of the crab season. Also, those who collect benefits while employed need to complete monthly paperwork (which may involve arranging for transportation and child care and other scheduling problems), while those who are unemployed need to complete paperwork only every six months.

These conditions do not make for friendly relations between DSS employees and owners of the processing plants.

Alice[8] [an eligibility specialist] told me that crab processors were the worst of all employers from whom DSS asked for earnings figures for social service recipients. Of the 300 or so AFDC recipients in the county, she said that crab pickers, fish filleters, and commercial fishermen made up about half. . . . She said that the seafood processors yelled at them over the phone, taking their jobs as social services personnel as personal affronts to their ability to conduct business. Often they refused to cooperate. (Griffith fieldnotes, June 10, 1985)

Today the DSS remains a focal point of dispute in the county. Nearly every issue of the county's main newspaper runs editorials or articles critical of the DSS, usually citing the agency's "fiscal irresponsibility," even pointing fingers at specific employees.

Other than the state-supported community organizations, a variety of churches coordinate support for those in low-income occupations and neighborhoods, as is common among African-American and Latino groups. Church-based forms of support, however, simply build on services provided by the state, generating or organizing community support for the elderly, for example, or for those whose roofs are in need of repair. Churches, like the DSS, tend to deal with the consequences of poverty, without challenging the roots of poverty itself.

Working Conditions and Household Coping Strategies

Seafood Plants, Payment Systems, and Seasonal Schedules

The seafood plants reflect a labor-intensive production process. Usually concrete block buildings painted white, they range in size from around 2,000 square feet to upwards of 10,000 to 20,000 square feet; they may or may not sit on the water. Those on the water tend to be larger plants, with their own vessels, elaborate docking and landing facilities, winches, pulleys, conveyor belts, and forklifts. In the crab plants, live crabs are landed at the back doors from boats or are trucked in from landing centers around the Chesapeake Bay. Once inside, the crabs are steamed and cooled, then loaded into wheelbarrows and distributed with a large scoop shovel. The organization of work is simple: women crab pickers/finfish filleters sit at tables, either cutting finfish or, more commonly, picking the meat out of cooked blue crabs with tools resembling a nutcracker, an oyster knife, and a pair of rubber gloves. Young men roam through the plant, renewing supplies of the unprocessed product.

Blue crab pickers at work. (Photograph by Scott Taylor)

Crab pickers are paid variable rates per pound, depending on the quality of the meat they pick. Typically "jumbo lump" (simply, big pieces rather than flakes of crab) pays around $1.70 to $1.75 per pound, while the flakier meats yield about $.10 per pound less. These rates represent an increase of $.35 to $.50 per pound (28 percent to 40 percent) over the past eight years. Processors claim crab pickers can pick an average of 35 pounds per day and that good pickers can pick as much as 45 pounds per day. According to workers, between 25 to 30 pounds is average and 40 pounds a day is within the capability of a good worker. They point out, as well, that work is seasonal. The main picking season begins in late March or April and lasts, usually, until November. Through the winter some seafood plants cut finfish, but most close. Annual incomes from the industry rarely reach federally established poverty levels, but generally hover around $7,000. A 1993 study of crab pickers in North Carolina, Virginia, and Maryland revealed average weekly earnings of $213.44 (SD = 96.95).[9] Weekly earnings ranged from a low of $17.00 to a high of $441.00, showing the extreme variability that derives from varying qualities of meat, volumes of crab, and abilities of the workers. North Carolina workers' average pay was lower, around $192.00 per week. Among the African-American workers, the low and fluctuating incomes drive household coping strategies that combine multiple economic with multiple social means of support. Most workers must rely on networks of friends and kin to survive, a factor that influences labor recruitment.

Elsewhere I stress the "network" and family bases of recruitment into seafood processing, emphasizing the role of network recruiting in labor control or worker resistance (Griffith 1993, 1990a, 1990b, 1987; Griffith and Runsten 1988, 1992). Expanded economic opportunities, low unemployment rates, and low levels of immigration into a region combine to benefit workers: the networks of workers in the plants may be used as tools of worker empowerment. Simply, related workers agree to behaviors that benefit their positions relative to management. On the other hand, with shortages of economic opportunities, rising unemployment, or high levels of immigration of low-wage workers, workers' networks benefit employers as tools of labor control. Employers can threaten to punish all network members for the misbehavior of a single member.

Under these conditions, workers benefit by expanding their economic opportunities, especially when it is beyond their capacity to restrict immigration or reverse rising unemployment. Conventional methods of this include enrolling in training programs or emigrating into areas with robust economies. A recent study of crab pickers in North Carolina quoted a processor as saying, "The community college system has opened doors for ladies who in the past would have only crab picking or domestic service to look to for income" (Mosher 1993:24).

In Pamlico County—as in many rural areas that host high-turnover, seasonal, hazardous, and unpleasant industries—expanding economic opportunities involve formal employment, informal economic activity, and pooling survival skills to allow movement among different sectors of economic and social support. This includes drawing upon all the skills in the household to secure a number of jobs, as well as working in the informal sector. Most households employ both strategies: in a survey among North Carolina seafood-processing workers conducted in 1985–86, I found that 68.3 percent of workers lived in households that derived income from more than one job in the formal economy. Yet Pamlico County's overall economy provides few job opportunities compared with the economies of bustling urban areas. Forestry, fishing, agriculture, phosphate mining, tourism and real estate, financial and insurance services, retail trades, transportation, public works and services, and seafood processing account for most of the formal economic employment. That many of these operations are seasonal suggests that residents of the county have time to engage in multiple economic pursuits through the year. This predominantly seasonal, relatively undifferentiated economic base conceals a highly differentiated and small-scale informal economy that provides incomes to 1 in every 6 to 10 households. Estimating the importance of this sector on households is difficult. Most of the goods produced, repaired, traded, or absorbed by this sector—as part of its definition—never enter official statistics on employment, income, and retail sales. Despite this, the informal sector builds on and contributes to the formal sector in important ways.

The informal sector in Pamlico County consists of services that range from unskilled (e.g., tree stump removal, maid services) to skilled (e.g., engine repair, cosmetology, painting), as well as a variety of productive and extractive activities, including silk-screening, crafts production, gardening, hunting, dog breeding, fishing, and even the processing of foods for street vending, a favorite throughout the Third World. The estimate of 1 in 6 to 10 households derives from driving along the principal county roads and making counts based on either the litter of industry of the compounds one encounters or the signs telling of the services for sale. The "industrial compounds" are usually composed of two or more dwellings and a work space consisting of the scrap of the productive activity; the services usually boast little more than a sign. Without marshaling a comprehensive investigation, it is impossible to know what percentage are licensed or otherwise counted in the formal sector. Nevertheless, they tell of a population willing to operate small-scale economic enterprises out of their homes (a mark of informal economic activity) and of one used to drawing on multiple paths of survival.

In addition to informal economic activities, Pamlico County's seafood workers pool their survival strategies through what might be called "creative consumption." This takes place, primarily, in the realm of housing. As often as we find households with the cluttered work spaces telling of informal economic activities, we find households and home "compounds" that have been constructed in light of the high costs of housing. Martha Tompkins (pseudonym), a veteran of the processing industry, exemplifies this:

Born in 1940, Martha has lived all her life in the predominantly African-American community of Maribel, North Carolina. For 15 years, on and off, she has found work in the seafood-processing plants; currently she works in a plant in Stonewall, 5 miles southeast of Maribel, but she has also worked in the plants in Lowland, about 15 miles to the north. The only other work she has done is farm labor, picking vegetables for farmers around Pamlico County. She dropped out of school after the ninth grade, and went to work in the crab plant where her mother worked. Her mother, now 70, has retired from crab picking; she keeps house with one of Martha's daughters in their eight-member household. In addition to her mother, she lives with two nieces, aged 28 and 19, two nephews, aged 30 and 9, and a daughter and son, aged 28 and 24, respectively. The two nieces and the elder nephew also work in the crab factories, and her son occupies an unskilled position in a local feed company. (Griffith fieldnotes, summer 1985)

In addition to extended families living together, it is common to find groups of two to four dwellings on a single lot, housing an extended family. While the average number of persons per household among Pamlico County seafood workers is only 3.1 (SD = 2.073), households in the 1985–86 sample ranged from 1 person to 8 persons (Griffith 1993). In the county at large, nearly one-quarter of the population live alone (U.S. Department of Commerce 1991); only around 19 percent of the seafood-processing workers, however, can afford to live by themselves. Ranging in age from 18 to 59, workers have an average of 11 years (SD = 9.317) of experience in seafood processing; for fully half the population, seafood processing is the only job they have ever had.

With other members of their households, however, Pamlico County's seafood workers challenge the conservative stereotype of poverty. It is most common for at least two people in a seafood-processing worker's household to be working in the formal economy, with some households having as many as five individuals working. In the household of Beula Williams (pseudonym), for example, her crab-picking position is but one of four that allow household members to engage in informal activities:

Beula Williams, age 51, lives within walking distance of a seafood-processing facility that sits directly on the water. Her own house, on the same road as the processing facility, allows her and her family access to the water as well. Beula's husband works for a large mining facility in Beaufort County, although they have never hired him as a permanent employee; instead, he works on contract with them as part of a cleaning crew. He also works part-time as a security guard. Beula's son, at 19, occupies what she calls a "little job" at another local crab house, helping to load trucks two nights a week. Her eldest daughter, Angie, 23 years old, works alongside Beula at the crab house. Also living with them are another daughter of 14 and a granddaughter of 10 months. During the off-season, Beula cleans houses for people. Her only other job has been one of planting and digging potatoes for local farmers. (Griffith fieldnotes, 1986)

Within these multiple paths of survival, the seafood plants of Pamlico and nearby counties have, historically, played an important part. The extent to which they will remain cornerstone occupations to struggling households, households whose only hope lies in pooling consumption and income-generating behaviors, is currently under negotiation, as processors, with increasing frequency, turn away from local labor and import workers from over 3,000 miles away.

Future Directions: Imported Labor and the Seafood Labor Process

Seafood processing shares a number of features with other sectors of food processing. Its highly seasonal character differentiates it from poultry processing and meatpacking. Its seasonality underlies similarities between seafood processing and other rural industries involved in food production, handling, and processing and its use of H-2B workers, who are imported on a temporary basis only. At the same time, the organization of work in the seafood plants and the dynamics of recruitment bear striking similarities to those that are found in poultry processing and are becoming more common in meatpacking.

The growing reliance on new-immigrant workers unites the various sectors of food processing. This practice is not new to meatpackers, as Upton Sinclair's work makes clear, despite shifts in labor sources from Eastern Europe to Mexico, Central America, the Caribbean, and Asia. Neither is it new in seafood processing. In addition to the Asian refugees who recently "saved" the seafood industry in Alabama (Moberg and Thomas 1993), seafood processors have used Chinese, Samoan, Italian, and Portuguese immigrants at various times and in various places throughout the industry's history. The use of new immigrants is, however, new in Pamlico County.

The processors' use of the H-2B visa classification to import Mexican women is important in light of current immigration policies and the effects of those policies on labor supplies throughout food processing. This class of visa creates, like no other, a class of workers whose mobility in the U.S. labor market is restricted to an extreme once found among indentured servants. Whatever disadvantages accompany relying on a resident labor force—a labor force with its own sources of resistance and its own patterns of social reproduction and transformation—dissolve under conditions of the immigration of low-wage, unskilled workers into a region. This is particularly so with workers who have been imported specifically to occupy these seafood-processing jobs. The use of Mexican workers has been justified by saying that there are insufficient workers to staff the plants from the local population. This situation, after nearly a half century of using local African-American women, allegedly has developed from demographic and economic roots. Processors point to the aging of the labor force and the fact that younger workers won't do this work. It may be that the local younger African-American workers simply do not accept their subservient status as willingly as did those African-American women whose working lives began prior to the "awakening" of black pride and ethnic/class consciousness that occurred through the 1960s and finally penetrated places like Pamlico County in the 1970s. Nevertheless, plant output has been increasing along with increasing demand for seafood, of which crabmeat is among the top 10 best-sellers, creating an increase in demand for labor.

In any case, the use of the H-2B program has grown considerably since the first plants used Mexicans in 1988. Initially, the program was used by only three or four processors in Virginia, North Carolina, and Maryland, who together imported around 100 workers. Since 1988 it has grown to include between 18 and 21 crab processors in North Carolina, between 7 and 9 in Maryland, and between 7 and 11 in Virginia (the actual number depends on how one counts processors, since some own more than one plant or import workers under the name of more than one company). Together, the North Carolina processors import between 1,100 and 1,200 workers (U.S. Department of Labor certification records put the number at 1,128), or around 10 times the number they imported originally. The Maryland and Virginia processors, together, import only around 200 Mexican workers.

Obviously, North Carolina crab processors have relied on the H-2B

TABLE 8.2. Number of Plants, Employment, and
Pounds in the Blue Crab Processing Industry:
1980–91

Year	Employment	Pounds	Plants
1980	885	8,727,431	32
1981	1,088	9,161,147	33
1982	1,051	10,259,678	34
1983	1,267	10,808,881	33
1984	1,148	10,828,806	37
1985	1,391	11,899,081	39
1986	1,291	10,083,447	39
1987	1,120	11,216,283	37
1988	1,168	9,511,042	37
1989	989	8,900,778	35
1990	n.d.*	9,428,868	44
1991	n.d.	10,818,353	48

* The Division of Marine Fisheries stopped counting
employment in 1989, probably because it was unsure of
how to count H-2B workers, who are often rendered
invisible in census counts.

Source: North Carolina Division of Marine Fisheries, 1992.

program more heavily than processors in any other state. Plant owners
in the program constitute between 50 and 60 percent of the crab-processing plants in the state. They tend to be the larger plants, accounting
for most of crab-processing employment. Those plants that import
Mexicans are concentrated in Pamlico, Beaufort, and Hyde Counties,
although there are plants in the program in Tyrell, Washington, and
Carteret Counties as well. All continue to employ domestic workers, but
the Mexican workers make up at least half or more of their labor forces,
signaling a distinct change in the cultural complexion of the crab-processing labor force that has been accompanied by increased production, turning around the industry trend of falling employment and production (see Table 8.2).

Despite the relatively short history of the program, already they have
begun "inventing tradition" regarding the use of foreign labor, as well
as justifying their use of foreign workers in other ways. Processors who
use H-2 workers are able to achieve higher levels of productivity from
H-2 workers because of their lower rates of absenteeism, the captive na-

ture of their jobs, and various other practices described below. According to a recent report, for example:

> One North Carolina user of the program, Christopher Fulcher, imported about 50 Mexican women in 1991 for two North Carolina plants he owns, in Oriental and in Aurora. Soon, some complained that they were not being credited for all hours worked and were being underpaid by as much as $100 a week. They also said they had to pay for hairnets, knives, and aprons, although they never agreed to such deductions. And Mr. Fulcher had confiscated their papers and refused to give them back. (*Wall Street Journal*, December 28, 1992)

Some residents have expressed fears concerning the Mexicans' arrival in communities as small as Oriental (pop. 522) and Arapahoe (pop. 274). Importing Mexican workers not only involves certification by the local labor department, which must determine that there are no local workers willing to work, but also requires housing the migrants (*Pamlico News* 1990). In April 1991 a resident of Arapahoe complained before a public meeting about a seafood processor building housing for Mexicans. The processor assured him that the 28 women and 6 men would be "escorted most of the time" (*Pamlico News* 1991a). This was the first in a series of expressions of public apprehension about the use of migrants, stimulating reassuring responses by processors and others that the workers posed no problem for the small communities of the county (*Pamlico News* 1991b, 1991c). Among the responses in local newspapers were claims that (1) the Mexicans were not taking jobs away from local workers; (2) the Mexicans had not applied for any assistance from the DSS; (3) the Mexicans had come to work and spend money in the local stores, not to make trouble; and (4) the use of migrant and, by extension, Mexican workers actually has a long history in the county, being used by local farmers for 20 to 25 years (*Pamlico News* 1991d, 1991e).[10]

The use of Mexican workers in Pamlico County raises four issues that may define some of the principal dimensions of the changing labor process in food processing throughout the United States. First, linkages between food-processing and agricultural labor markets (where migrants are likened to H-2 workers) are likely to expand and become more complex in the future, which may lead to changes in recruitment systems, patron-client relationships, and work organization in the processing plants based on models drawn from agricultural labor processes (Griffith and Kissam 1994). In our recent study of the H-2B program, we found that many of the processors had established fictive kin relations with some of the Mexican workers, usually those who have some command of English, and subsequently placed these workers in positions similar to labor contractors, where they performed cultural brokerage and supervisory functions (Griffith, Heppel, and Torres 1994):

> "I consider these people family," said Garson Perkins [pseudonym], adding, "I've been to Mexico, I've eaten in their homes, and I've seen how they live. One of the girls who translates for us had a child here and named it after my wife." This woman also occupied a supervisory or managerial position and, with Garson's wife, established a minority-owned business to handle all the paperwork requirements of the H-2B program, becoming a registered labor contracting firm. Another attribute of Garson's fictive kinship relationship with the H-2B workers was the proximity of his own house to the houses he rents for the Mexican workers. Two of the big houses sit across from the plant, but the others are very near his own home. He made a special effort to point this out to me, showing me his own home, his partner's home, and two of the houses he rents for the Mexican pickers, saying, "See? They're in the same neighborhood." (Griffith fieldnotes, August 27, 1993)

Linkages between agricultural and food-processing labor markets also suggest that meat-, poultry-, and fish-processing operations often form an important occupational bridge for migrant farm workers interested in settling out of the migration stream. This will influence education, social services, and other infrastructure, as well as the quality of the housing stock available in these communities.

The housing issue brings us to the second implication of using new-immigrant workers. In low-income, seasonal occupations, housing and transportation are likely to become increasingly important components of employment. This may be true even where employers do not provide housing and transportation directly but influence the development, say, of trailer parks or other low-income housing alternatives (Benson 1990) that, in turn, become focal points for taxi or minibus systems (Griffith 1986). Tapping into programs such as H-2B, further, may select for single-sex, dormitory-style housing as opposed to family housing, which may influence the structure of low-income households and neighborhoods. Also, the "colonization" of native low-income workers' neighborhoods by new immigrants—combined with a joint process of labor replacement and displacement taking place in low-wage jobs, and the movement of immigrant workers into informal economic activities that compete with those of native workers—may lead to tense interethnic relations. This could reduce the capability of low-wage workers to organize and resist the labor-control mechanisms of their employers.

In our recent study, we found that virtually all H-2B workers live in housing either owned or arranged by their employers, on or near the plant premises. They rarely live with African-American workers or interact with them outside the plants. The proximity of H-2B workers' housing to the plants, coupled with the distance of most plants from large population centers and employers' control over transportation, underlie many of the legal problems experienced by plant owners, particularly accusations of indentured servitude (*News and Observer* 1991a, 1991b).

The housing provided for H-2B workers varies considerably from plant to plant: 24.1 percent live in trailers or mobile homes; 30.4 percent in dormitory-type housing; 4.5 percent in apartments; and 41.1 percent in shared houses. These figures are less telling than descriptions of the housing recorded in fieldnotes, however:

> Both houses are old, two-story farmhouse-type structures, with broad porches across the front, torn screens, sleeping three and four to a bedroom. Twenty workers occupy one of the houses and 26 live in the other. The common areas of the houses consist of kitchens with two to three refrigerators, small living rooms, and dining areas that are mostly tables.
>
> They have two dwellings for the workers: one a fairly comfortable trailer that houses mostly older women. Their visitors are so restricted that they get in trouble, they said, even if there is a strange car in the drive. But this is a peaceful location in a quiet neighborhood, surrounded by large shade trees. Inside there are three bedrooms and a commons area of a kitchen and living room, with a television.
>
> The other location is an active, crowded place, with many younger women and the few Mexican men that work in the plant. It looks like it might have been an old day-care center or lodge of some sort, with dormitory rooms off of two long hallways and a large open kitchen and living area with a television and a few tables. They store their dry food and some cooking utensils in locked cabinets that have been built into the walls. Outside is an expansive yard with a high new privacy fence and picnic tables.

> This is a block house, across from the crab plant. Very new, clean, with air-conditioning and a well-lit kitchen. Two televisions, washer, dryer. . . . Eight young women live here, the eldest only 23. All of the appliances seem new, and include a refrigerator, stove, hot water heater, and toaster oven. (Griffith fieldnotes, selected passages, August–October 1993)

As these brief descriptions indicate, the housing varies from crowded and mildly dilapidated to clean, new, and well equipped with appliances and air-conditioning. Workers have almost no opportunity to select their housing: 92.2 percent of those surveyed said it was simply assigned (see note 9). In Fishing Creek, Maryland, however, plant managers told us they gave workers a choice of three or four homes to rent. By contrast, in one case in North Carolina, workers desiring to relocate to housing on their own were told they could not by plant owners. These behaviors have led to lawsuits claiming that processors use the program as a tool of excessive labor control that borders on indentured servitude. For example, a recent judgment against two processors—one based in Maryland and one in North Carolina—found as follows:

> On May 18, 1991, plaintiffs [Mexican crab pickers] were given a tour of PJH [the crab plant] by Harrington [the owner], who showed them where the boundaries of the plant property were. . . . Harrington told the women that they were free to walk around the plant grounds, but not necessarily around the nearby areas not owned by PJH. Harrington also warned them not to walk around town at night and told them to remain near the PJH plant during the first week of their stay. . . . On May 19, 1991, Harrington told plaintiffs to relinquish their passports, visas, and work permits to him so that the papers could be placed in the office safe for safekeeping. (*Silvia Marquez Arreola v. Philip J. Harrington & Son* 1992:9)

Rural communities in coastal Virginia, Maryland, and North Carolina often are suspicious of outsiders, let alone those incapable of speaking English. The claims of plant owners that they are protecting workers by arranging their housing or even building housing for them on plant premises are understandable in this light. Yet in some cases the isolation and confinement go beyond protection, and the potential for housing to become a tool of labor control is great. This is especially true in the extremely isolated locations where workers live at the plant, as is the case for 39.1 percent of the workers. Other indications of owners' excesses in protection of workers are that 15.6 percent of the workers have fences around where they live, and 70 percent have restrictions on visitors at workers' homes. In most cases, plants with fences around them also post No Trespassing signs to deter contact between the H-2B workers and others who do not work for the plant, including the young Mexican farmworkers who migrate up and down the eastern seaboard through the summer growing season.

Virtually all plant owners compensate for the isolation of the plants by providing free transportation to workers, both for shopping on weekends and for occasional outings. The most progressive employers give workers access to vans or trucks, even providing them with credit at local gas stations. More commonly, plant owners take weekly or biweekly trips to towns where workers can buy groceries and other goods. While providing transportation compensates for the physical isolation of the workers to some degree, it is this controlled isolation from the wider community, including other Mexicans, that makes it easy for plant employers to dictate H-2B workers' schedules of work and leisure. Our recent study found, in fact, that H-2B employees work more days per week than domestic workers. They believe they have fewer options regarding missing a day of work now and then, leaving the plant early, or taking the same liberties that domestic workers have taken with the industry. The ''casual'' and unreliable approach to work in the plants on the part of domestic workers, and the stark contrast of H-2B workers' eagerness to work, is what has made the H-2B program so attractive to crab processors (Griffith, Heppel, and Torres 1994).

In addition to the growing importance of housing and transportation in jobs of this character, the use of labor intermediaries (crew leaders, labor contractors, ethnic foremen) is likely to increase with the growth of foreign-born, immigrant workers, especially those drawn from agriculture. In the crab industry, recruitment techniques reveal that blend of labor contracting and network recruiting so common among foreign-born workers in agriculture (Griffith and Kissam 1994; Vandemann 1988). In 1993, 21.4 percent of the H-2B workers had been contacted about their U.S. jobs by labor contractors, while 63.1 percent had been contacted by friends or relatives. Typically, labor contractors recruit using network ties, which would yield proportions such as these. Once workers are recruited, however, labor contractors usually assume more active roles in their performance on the job. As evidence of this, we found that labor contractors arranged for the visas and traveling arrangements of 67 percent of H-2B workers coming to the Mid-Atlantic crab-picking plants.

With the growing use of labor intermediaries, more components of the recruitment, production, and reproductive processes associated with food-processing jobs may be subcontracted out as these labor intermediaries become subcontractors, taking advantage of illegal immigrants via their own personal, ethnic, and home-village networks. The benefits of subcontracting are not limited to the transfers of risk noted earlier. Under most subcontracting arrangements, food-processing firms are not responsible for complying with labor standards, paying unemployment or workers' compensation insurance for workers, or paying into their social security funds.

Finally, we can expect to see an overall "Latinization" of food processing and the neighborhoods of food-processing workers. While this is an uneven process, it is clear that Latin workers are rapidly becoming the preferred labor force among food processors. As Mexican and other Latin American workers, overwhelmingly, define the character of the food-processing labor force, it will be necessary to understand in more detail the cultural history of Latin America and the place of labor within those societies.

Notes

This chapter is based on research supported in part by grants from the National Office of Sea Grants, NOAA, to the University of North Carolina Sea Grant College Program and the North Carolina Department of Administration; and by the U.S. Department of Labor, Employment and Training Administration.

1. The use of the H-2 class of visa has been controversial ever since the end of the bracero guest-worker program in the mid-1960s. Briefly, the H-2 visa is a "nonimmigrant" class of visa, allowing its holder severely restricted access to the U.S. labor market: workers are certified to work for a single employer and cannot move on to other employers without either a legal struggle or their current employer's permission. Currently, workers are imported under this visa classification to work in seafood plants, as shrimp deckhands in Texas, as ornamental stone quarry workers in Idaho, as stable attendants at racetracks in Arizona and California, as tree planters in a number of states, and as chamber-

maids and waiters in exclusive hotels and resorts. The program has been likened to indentured servitude on a number of occasions and has been the target of litigation on the behalf of workers on and off over the past 30 years. Recently, the American Civil Liberties Union, in conjunction with legal aid offices in North Carolina, Maryland, and Virginia, filed suit against seafood processors who use H-2B workers, charging that workers lived in servitude, were overcharged for housing, and—due to piece rates—were underpaid for the actual hours worked.

2. Longer periods at sea, in particular, have come about because of the introduction of freezers on shrimp boats in the Gulf of Mexico, lengthening trips from 10 or 14 days to the current 50 to 60 days. This, in turn, has caused many local workers who used to hire on as "headers" (deheading shrimp) to reject these jobs, leading owners of shrimp boats or shrimping fleets to turn to the H-2B program for shrimp deckhands (Griffith, Heppel, and Torres 1994).

3. Taylorism refers to an approach to management of shop floors in which the management assumes as much control as possible over the speed and character of the production line, usually through a combination of authoritarian methods of supervision and mechanization. This approach to factory production, still widely taught in U.S. business schools, is based on F. W. Taylor's *Principles of Scientific Management,* which was itself based largely on Taylor's own experience working in a factory.

4. The practice of performing minimal "dressing" functions on fish and then shipping them to fish markets, supermarkets, and restaurants for further processing is similar to the old system of meat and poultry processing, where butchers cut up large portions of beef and pork, sometimes made sausages and other cooked products, as well as received and processed whole birds. I would predict that the industry will follow the lead of boxed beef, canned cooked ham, and the further-processing poultry plant, with larger firms buying fish and shellfish wholesale, and producing products more useful to end consumers. As this occurs, smaller firms will either convert to packing-shipping (as appears to be occurring in North Carolina), be forced out of business, or exploit small market niches in the same way some specialty plants have emerged on the margins of beef and pork processing (e.g., producers of pickled pigs' feet).

5. Part of the reason for the growth of this sector is that most natural stocks of fish and shellfish have been discovered. Thus, to keep up with growing consumer demand, new stocks need to be developed artificially.

6. Puerto Rico, while not offering the same labor savings as Mexico, provides seafood processors with tax breaks through section 936 of the Internal Revenue Service Code, and assures the big tuna companies an adequate, docile labor force through continued threats that they will move to the Dominican Republic in the event of worker unrest.

7. In particular, instead of subtle methods of resistance, or those based on social and cultural processes, new-immigrant Mexican workers have to rely on formal methods of resistance such as the American Civil Liberties Union or the various offices of the U.S. Department of Labor, particularly those investigating wage and hour violations (see Griffith, Heppel, and Torres 1994).

8. Although using pseudonyms, these cases describe real individuals, not "composites."

9. This survey was conducted between August and November 1993 and used a sampling strategy similar to that used in the 1985–86 study (Griffith 1993:9–10), visiting every plant that used Mexican workers and other plants in the same regions or communities that did not, for a total sample of 34 plants and 133 workers.

10. In this last case, the association between "migrant" and "Mexican" is implied throughout the article, without explicitly stating that the use of Mexican migrants is in fact quite recent, dating back to the early 1980s; prior to that, most of the migrant farmworkers in eastern North Carolina were African American.

References

Anderson, J. G., and J. L. Anderson. 1991. Seafood Quality: Issues for Consumer Researchers. *Journal of Consumer Affairs* 25:144–63.

Benson, J. 1990. Good Neighbors: Ethnic Relations in Garden City Trailer Courts. *Urban Anthropology* 19(4):361–86.

Consumer Reports. 1992. Is Our Fish Fit to Eat? February issue, 57(2):103–20.

Doeringer, P., P. Moss, and D. Terkla. 1988. *The New England Fishing Economy: Jobs, Income, and Kinship.* Amherst: University of Massachusetts Press.

Floyd, J. 1988. Recent Development of International Tuna Industries and the Asian Pacific Trade. In *Proceedings of the Symposium of Markets for Seafood and Aquacultured Products,* edited by D. Liao. Charleston, S.C.: International Institute of Fisheries Economics and Trade and the South Carolina Wildlife and Marine Resources Department, pp. 214–32.

Greene, M. F. 1991. *Praying for Sheetrock.* New York: Addison-Wesley.

Griffith, D. 1986. Social Structural Obstacles to Capital Accumulation Among Returning Migrants: The British West Indies Temporary Alien Labor Program. *Human Organization* 46:34–42.

———. 1987. Non-Market Labor Processes in an Advanced Capitalist Economy. *American Anthropologist* 89:838–52.

———. 1990a. *The Impact of the Immigration Reform and Control Act's (IRCA) Employer Sanctions on the U.S. Meat and Poultry Processing Industries.* Report prepared for the International Bureau of Labor Affairs, U.S. Department of Labor, Washington, D.C.

_____. 1990b. *Consequences of Immigration Reform for Low-Wage Workers in the Southeastern U.S.: The Case of the Poultry Industry. Urban Anthropology* 19:155–84.

_____. 1993. *Jones's Minimal: Low-Wage Labor in the United States.* Albany: State University of New York Press.

Griffith, D., M. Heppel, and L. Torres. 1994. *Labor Certification and Employment Practices in Selected Low-Wage/Low-Skill Occupations: An Analysis from Worker and Employer Perspectives.* Report prepared for the West Virginia Bureau of Employment Programs, Charleston, W.Va.

Griffith, D., and E. Kissam. 1994. *Working Poor: Farmworkers in the United States.* Philadelphia: Temple University Press.

Griffith, D., and D. Runsten. 1988. *The Impact of the Immigration Reform and Control Act on the U.S. Poultry Industry.* Report prepared for the International Bureau of Labor Affairs, U.S. Department of Labor, Washington, D.C.

_____. 1992. The Impact of the 1986 Immigration Reform and Control Act on the U.S. Poultry Industry: A Comparative Analysis. *Policy Studies Review.* 11:118–30.

McCay, B., J. Gatewood, and C. Creed. 1989. Labor and the Labor Process in a Limited Entry Fishery. *Marine Resource Economics* 6:311–30.

Moberg, M., and J. S. Thomas. 1993. Class Segmentation and Divided Labor: Asian Workers in the Gulf of Mexico Seafood Industry. *Ethnology* 32(1):87–99.

Mosher, K. 1993. Delicate Work, Low Pay: The Legacy of Crab Pickers in North Carolina. Master's thesis, North Carolina State University.

Nash, J., and M. P. Fernandez-Kelley. 1983. Introduction. In *Women, Men, and the International Division of Labor,* edited by J. Nash and M. P. Fernandez-Kelly. Albany: State University of New York Press, pp. vii–xv.

National Marine Fisheries Service. 1991. *Fisheries of the United States, 1990.* Washington, D.C.: U.S. Department of Commerce, National Oceanic and Atmospheric Administration.

News and Observer [Raleigh, N.C.]. 1991a. Mexican Workers at Crab Plant Decry "Virtual Servitude." August 8.

_____. 1991b. Mexicans Say Crab Houses Violated Rights: Guest Workers Contend N.C. Recruiter Threatened to Abandon Them at the Border. August 8.

North Carolina Division of Marine Fisheries. 1992. *Seafood Dealers List 1991.* Morehead City: North Carolina Division of Marine Fisheries.

Pamlico News [Oriental, N.C.]. 1990. Looking South (of the Border) for Workers. August 15.

_____. 1991a. Arapahoe Resident Complains about Influx of Migrant Workers. April 10.

_____. 1991b. Mexican Workers Not Filling Local Jobs. July 24.

_____. 1991c. Crab Pickers Come Here for Money. July 31.

_____. 1991d. St. Thomas Episcopal Church Hosts Spanish Language Service. August 7.

_____. 1991e. Pamlico Farms Have a Long History of Using Migrant Workers. August 14.

Paredes, A., J. Sabella, and M. Hepburn. 1977. *Human Factors in the Economic Development of a Northwest Florida Gulf Coast Fishing Community.* Final Report. University of Florida Sea Grant College Program, project R/AS-1. Tallahassee: Department of Anthropology, Florida State University.

Perkins, W. 1991. Adding Value to Seafood. *Seafood Business* 10(3):45–54.

Sassen-Koob, S. 1985. Capital Mobility and Labor Migration. In *The Americas in the New International Division of Labor,* edited by S. Sanderson. New York: Holmes and Meier, pp. 226–52.

Segal, W., and P. Philips. 1990. *The Effect of Immigration Reform on Collective Bargaining in the California Fruit and Vegetable Processing Industry.* Immigration Policy and Research Working Paper no. 5. Washington, D.C.: U.S. Department of Labor, Bureau of International Labor Affairs.

Silvia Marquez Arreola v. Philip J. Harrington & Son. 1992. Memorandum Opinion. United States District Court, District of Maryland, Civil no. L-91-1934, July 6–14.

Sinclair, P. 1983. Fishermen Divided: The Impact of Limited Entry Licensing in Northwest Newfoundland. *Human Organization* 42:307–13.

Straus, K. 1991a. Delta Pride Strike and Boycott End with New Contract. *Seafood Business* 10(1):30–31.

_____. 1991b. Shrimp Supplies: An International Update. *Seafood Business* 10(6):60–70.

Taylor, F. W. 1911. *Principles of Scientific Management.* Norwood, Mass.: Plimpton Press.

Thomas, J. S., and C. M. Formichella. 1987. *The Shrimp Processing Industry in Bayou La Batre, Alabama.* Research report no. 11. Mobile: Center for Business and Economic Research, University of South Alabama.

Thomas, J. S., and M. Moberg. 1990. Labor Recruitment in the Seafood Industry: A Test of the Class Segmentation Hypothesis. Paper presented at the annual meeting of the American Anthropological Association, New Orleans, November 1990.

U.S. Department of Commerce, Bureau of the Census. 1991. *North Carolina Census of Population and Housing.* Washington, D.C.: U.S. Government Printing Office.

Vandemann, A. 1988. Labor Contracting in California. Ph.D. diss, University of California.

Wall Street Journal. 1992. Hard Labor: Mexicans Recruited for Nonfarm Work Describe Mistreatment. December 28.

9 | Industries, Immigrants, and Illness in the New Midwest

Robert A. Hackenberg
Gary Kukulka

Industrial Nomads: New Factory Workers in Old Farming Towns

This chapter is concerned with the Midwestern states that are the locus of the restructured meatpacking industry.[1] Once considered the stronghold of the self-sufficient family farmer, they now provide homes for giant food factories. ConAgra, IBP, and Excel—packers of more than 70 percent of this country's beef consumption—operate in or adjacent to farm towns and modest-size cities. The world's largest beef plant began operation in Holcomb, Kansas (pop. 1,400), in 1980. And white meat is following red meat. One of the world's largest pork-packing plants opened in 1995 in Guymon, Oklahoma (pop. 8,400), 90 miles to the south.

Elsewhere in this volume Broadway and Bjerklie focus on the reconstruction and relocation of the meat industries. They confirm that these highly competitive, vertically integrated corporate systems operate on paper-thin profit margins based on maximizing the volume of output and minimizing the costs of production. Labor is a major cost, and survival requires that it be minimized. And who will perform the most dangerous work in the United States, under some of the most disagreeable working conditions in industry, for an entry-level wage of $7.00 per hour?

As noted by Stull and Broadway (this volume), this industry has *always* offered the least attractive employment in the country to the most recent arrivals. The places on the packing plant's disassembly line are filled by Hispanic and Asian immigrants. Recent arrivals, numbering in the thousands, bring to host communities different languages and cultures, and a pervasive set of poverty-related problems.

The high turnover in employment, low wages and minimum benefits, and opposition to organized labor for which the industry is notorious have brought a new marginal working class to the heartland host communities. The process of "creating a disposable labor force" has been described by Hackenberg et al (1993).

This new class is the source of stresses and strains on housing, schools, social services, and law enforcement wherever it appears. These are described by others in these pages and in two companion volumes (Lamphere 1992; Lamphere, Stepick, and Grenier 1994). The nature of the work determines that employees sustain the highest rate of industrial injury recorded in the United States, and generate the most claims for workers' compensation. As a result, the industry has paid some of the largest fines ever levied by the Occupational Safety and Health Administration (OSHA).

This occupational health issue, its consequences for the victims, and the inadequacy of the resources available to deal with it are given comprehensive treatment elsewhere in this volume (Stull and Broadway 1995). The present essay is concerned with broader issues of community health created by the presence of an influx of medically indigent households of younger workers in locations whose minimal health resources have been steadily shifting toward providing limited care for the elderly (Kukulka, Van Hook, and Muchow 1991).

The core of our argument here is that a newly designed industry and a class of workers with unique characteristics have combined within a set of rural communities to define a unique and distinct client population for which there is a critical shortage of primary care. Because of their pattern of intermittent employment and semimigratory behavior, these workers have become *industrial nomads* in the U.S. labor force.

Our argument offers observations in descending order about delivery of health care services to this population:

1. The five-state region that includes Iowa, Nebraska, Colorado, Kansas, and Oklahoma contains sites at which restructured industries are locating and bottom-rung employment is exploding; but the region also reveals a countertrend in a multiplication of small-scale, white-collar enterprises offering middle-class wages and lifestyles to increasing numbers of residents. Between them, these intruders have redefined, and in fact polarized, the traditional class structure. We will distinguish between the permanent residents who have access to a full range of preventive and curative services, and retain those services within the region through their use, and the industrial

nomads who have neither insurance nor access to anything other than emergency care.

2. A four-county area in southwest Kansas, which contains the nation's densest concentration of rural meat industries. We will find within them substantial countertrends in population processes (an upsurge) and community health indicators (a downturn). The consequences incurred by the community from maintenance of a health system intended for the insured and financially responsible will become clear.

3. The factors that contribute to industrial nomadism. Embedded in this description will be the circumstances that, aside from their economic position, define them as a particularly difficult population to bring within the scope of community-oriented primary health care.

4. A particular community, Garden City, Kansas (pop. 24,097), where a primary-care clinic struggles to cope with the health burden imposed by an industrial labor force representing an estimated 25 percent of its residents. We will conclude with some observations on the elements of a more effective primary care program for meeting the health needs of the industrial labor force.

The Heartland as a Region of Contrasts

This is Willa Cather country—better known to today's audience from Roger Welch's "Postcards from Nebraska" on *CBS Sunday Morning,* or from Robert Waller's *Bridges of Madison County,* set in Iowa farm country. But the illusion purveyed by these sources is deceptive. The five states to which these statements apply represented only 5.3 percent of the U.S. population in 1990.[2] They are to be found among the 19 states whose population was more than 40 percent nonmetropolitan.

The image of sturdy, self-sufficient midwestern farm households of north European immigrant stock persists and is reinforced by the media. More perceptive observers in recent years have seen it as a region in decline. The evening news of the 1980s frequently dramatized foreclosures and auctions, watched dejectedly by families sustaining the loss of lifetime investments of work and worry.

This is the region that Frank and Deborah Popper, Rutgers University regional planners, advocated converting to a federally managed "commons" on which (joining with writers of movie scripts about mythical Indians) they proposed to "bring back the buffalo." Notions of this sort gain some support from the identification of 110 heartland counties that have lost population in every census year since 1960 (Frazier 1991).

These states today are more accurately portrayed by the publications of Denver's Center for the New West (1992). As owner-operated farms, which were the bulwark of an agrarian middle class, fade before the advance of agribusiness, the center notes two important countertrends: rural industrialization and information-based commercial enterprises.

Small midwestern towns, where property values have fallen for decades, are linked to the financial and population centers on the Atlantic, Pacific, and Gulf coasts by communications technology. Creative work, clerical operations, billing and marketing, sales promotions, and consulting services can all be economically provided from these accessible points on the information highway.

Entrepreneurship is the key ingredient in these new enterprises, unobtrusively housed in existing structures that previously served as banks, hotels/motels, or chain-store outlets. These small businesses, which typically hire fewer than 25 persons, are welcome sources of white-collar employment. With salaries well above local living costs, and with a sprinkling of professional and technical employees, they represent the basis of a new nonagricultural middle class. Superior, Nebraska; Brush, Colorado; and Oberlin, Kansas, provide typical examples (Luther and Wall 1991; Murphy 1992).

Rural industries associated with meat production and processing represent the other component of the midwestern economic renaissance. There is nothing unobtrusive about these vertically integrated food factories, each representing an investment of tens of millions of dollars and a labor force numbered in the thousands. In 1991, Nebraska companies added 5.31 percent more nonagricultural jobs, the highest growth rate in the nation (Center for the New West 1992:19). These jobs were concentrated in the two leading industries just described: information-based services and food processing.

The polarized nature of the class structure emerging in the same or adjacent towns in which *both* high-growth information-based and food-processing industries appear has escaped much comment. However, it is hard to ignore the contrast between income levels and lifestyles of educated white-collar households of middle-class second- or third-gen-

The region's contrasts are nowhere more apparent than in Garden City, where shops of new-immigrant entrepreneurs open under the watchful eye of an "old American" economy. (Courtesy of Donald D. Stull)

eration "old American" stock and the near-illiterate non-English-speaking households of minimum wage arrivals from Mexico and Southeast Asia. The contrast tends to explain regional asymmetry in the distribution of health resources and access to health care. The usual clichés and shibboleths about rural health care affirm the ubiquitous nature of hospital closings, elimination of categories of acute care, and flight of practitioners from the region (Kukulka, Van Hook, and Muchow 1991). But this is overgeneralized.

There is a murky macropicture and a somewhat brighter micropicture. The bleak macropicture of rural health in the heartland is exemplified by the situation in Colorado:

> In Colorado, rural health care is sliding slowly but surely from crisis to catastrophe. . . . Half of Colorado now has a federally designated health-care shortage. Six rural counties have no physician and at least 37 are severely underserved. Meanwhile, rural doctors are retiring in record numbers. Officials predict that by the year 2000, rural counties will need 335 new physicians just to maintain already dangerous doctor/patient ratios. Colorado lost nearly 1,000 active physicians from 1986 to 1990. (Booth 1992)

The worst disparities are found in provisions for maternal and child health. Where metropolitan areas have 61 obstetricians and 70 pediatricians per 100,000 women of childbearing age, rural areas have 24.5 and 22.3, respectively (Booth 1992). Causal factors in the exodus of these specialists are inadequate Medicaid compensation and increasing frequency of malpractice suits. The overall picture in Nebraska is similarly bleak: "The population of rural Nebraska is small, getting smaller, and disproportionately elderly. . . . Since 1986, seven rural hospitals have closed . . . all in counties with populations under 8,000" (Nebraska Rural Health Advisory Commission 1992:6–7).

The proportion of total active physicians located in rural counties declined by 36 percent between 1972 and 1990. The decline was even greater in frontier counties (47.2 percent) and small trade center counties (40.9 percent). But the bright spots appear in those rural counties designated as "large trade centers." Between 1972 and 1990 they attracted 135 active physicians, increasing the total from 237 to 372 (Nebraska Rural Development Commission 1992).

The southwest Kansas packing communities with which the remainder of this essay is concerned qualify as "large trade centers." Like their counterparts in Nebraska, they remain adequately equipped with viable hospital and clinic facilities and sufficient medical personnel to operate them. However, the polarized class structure determines that meat-industry workers and their families, because of medical indigence and practitioners' refusal to accept Medicaid as payment, are effectively excluded from service.

Asymmetry in health status results from circumstances in which the burden of illness in the community is concentrated among those least likely to be served. Despite the media attention drawn to industrial injury on the disassembly line, it is women and children who are most likely to suffer unattended. This is a function of *indigence* rather than *injury*. We will test this assertion by examining the following propositions:

1. The dismal occupational health record of the industry, especially as it relates to injury to workers, may act to produce intermittent employment and significant intervals of unemployment. The most important health consequences befall household members and result from inadequate insurance coverage, indigence, and lack of access to care.
2. Exclusion of workers' families from maternal and child health services, routine primary care, and especially preventive intervention is the primary cause of health-problem indicators found in industry communities.

Health Conditions in the Inland Empire of Southwest Kansas

Three counties in southwest Kansas—Finney, Ford, and Seward—are home to five major packing plants, employing more than 9,500 persons, most of whom claim Hispanic or Asian ancestry.[3] Each county is also the location of a moderate-size market town (Garden City, Dodge City, and Liberal) ranging in size from 16,000 to 25,000 (see Table 9.1). Cattle production in these and the adjacent counties of Scott and Grant leads the state and contributed to its third place in the nation in 1991.

Finney, Ford, and Seward Counties have other atypical characteristics. In a thinly populated region, their levels of urbanization (73 to 88 percent) were higher than that of the state (69 percent) in 1990. In a state where four out of five counties sustained 1980–90 population loss, they registered growth of 10 to 39 percent. Where the proportion of Asians and Hispanics in Kansas is an insignificant 5 percent, these minorities in the three counties range from 17.3 to 28.9 percent of the total population. Their presence determines other deviations from statewide norms. The lowest median age (27.2) and the highest number of persons per household (3.03) were both in Finney County, which contains Garden City.

These counties rank among the highest in mobile-home occupancy,

TABLE 9.1. Four Counties in Southwest Kansas: Population,
Factory Labor Force, and Minority Data

County Pop.	Major City Pop.	Factory Name/ No. of Employees	Hispanics Pop.	Asians Pop.
Finney 33,070	Garden City 24,097	IBP 2,900	8,353	1,203
		Monfort 1,500		
Ford 27,463	Dodge City 21,129	Excel 2,340	4,083	663
		HyPlains 900		
Seward 18,743	Liberal 16,573	National 2,100	3,660	449
Grant 7,159	Ulysses 4,653	None	1,543	41

Source: 1990 population data are from *Kansas Statistical Abstract, 1991–92*. Institute for Public Policy and Business Research. Lawrence: University of Kansas. Employment data were provided in October 1994 by local chambers of commerce or employers.

and also in median rentals charged for housing units ($263 to $300 per month) among nonmetropolitan counties in Kansas. The highest teacher-pupil ratio in Kansas is found, once again, in Finney County. Per capita personal income in these three counties (1990) was the lowest ($15,300 to $17,300) in southwest Kansas, which otherwise posted the highest nonmetropolitan personal incomes in the state.

The emerging picture is one of regional economic growth, population gains, and high personal income for which the expanding meat industry is responsible. But there is also a "down side" found in the counties where this factory labor force is concentrated. Here incomes are atypically low, the population is young, and high rents are correlated with low-cost housing units (mobile homes).

The highest values of adverse indicators appear in Finney County, where Garden City, with two large packing plants, contains the largest numbers of Hispanic and Asian minorities. It follows, unfortunately, that Garden City features adverse health characteristics that might be predicted by its socioeconomic and demographic indicators.

The Kansas *Primary Care Status Index* (Kansas Department of Health and Environment [KDHE] 1992) placed Finney County in the 8th, 9th, or 10th (poorest) decile among all 105 counties of the state on each of the following community health-status variables:

Health Indicator	Decile Rank
Percent of all births to single teens	10
Percent of births lacking early prenatal care	10
Percent of children lacking adequate immunization	10
Percent of births to mothers lacking high school degree	10
Juvenile arrest rate per 1,000 persons under age 18	10
Reported child abuse/neglect (children under age 18)	9
Percent low-birth-weight babies	8
Percent of children receiving economic assistance	8

The same source discloses that the violent death rate among teens (aged 15–19) in the county was 1.9 times the state average.

Further documentation is contained in the Kansas *Primary Care County Analysis* (KDHE 1993). Among specific concerns identified for Finney County were the highest rate of sexually transmitted diseases in the Southwest region and rates of hepatitis B and tuberculosis that were significantly higher than those of the state as a whole.

Two composite indices prepared for statewide comparisons are a maternal and child health index and an overall primary-care index. Both of these placed Finney County in the high-risk category. A significant contributor was the finding that in 1990, 42 percent of women giving birth were judged to have received inadequate prenatal care.

These disturbing figures are partly explained by circumstances surrounding access to and availability of health resources for the low-income minority households responsible for a large proportion of the problems reported here. The *Primary Care County Analysis* identifies Seward, Ford, and Finney Counties as first, second, and third within the 19-county Southwest region in terms of "Medicaid eligibles" (medically indigent) within their populations.

The severity of this circumstance becomes clear when we add the following from Garden City's application of February 1, 1994, for designation as a "medically underserved" community. Garden City has 15.8 full-time equivalent primary-care physicians; however, only 2.96 of that number will accept Medicaid patients! The application concludes:

The demographic challenges are made worse by Garden City's shortage of primary care physicians accepting Medicaid patients or offering sliding fee schedules to low income persons . . . from a total of 15.8 FTE, only 2.96 FTE is available for persons at or below 200 percent of the poverty level. . . . The non-Medicaid/low income population of the city enjoys a physician to patient ratio of 1:1,251. The Medicaid/low income population's physician to patient ratio is twice that, at 1:2,695. (Kansas Department of Social and Rehabilitation Services 1993:3)

The insights contained in this section confirm the advancing polarization of medical care corresponding to earlier remarks about an emergent two-tier class structure in the region. The community health conditions identified in Table 9.2 are those associated with low income and medical indigence. Access to care appears to be concentrated among the upper tier, where these conditions seldom appear.

Industrial Nomads and Community Health

temporary workers in dead-end jobs

sum

Meatpacking workers in southwest Kansas are largely male and Hispanic, and are recent arrivals to the United States. Most have little education and minimum skill levels. In the majority of disassembly-related jobs they will fill, the maintenance of line speeds transporting five or more carcasses *per minute* past each workstation is critical to the achievement of production quotas and the maintenance of the profit margins on which the industry operates. Although some training is provided for new employees, it is minimal (Erickson 1994).

Occupational psychologists would be quick to observe that survival in this type of employment requires superior perceptual skills, reaction time, and manual dexterity (eye-hand coordination). Each of these variables is normally distributed in the general population across a wide range of competence. This would also be true of job applicants in the meat industry unless pretesting is used to eliminate applicants at the lower end of each distribution, that is, the 16 percent who would fall more than one standard deviation below the mean in a typical normal distribution.

At a more sophisticated level, stress-tolerance testing could be used to determine the applicant's capacity to withstand the tension and pressure associated with time constraints and the repetitive nature of tasks.

In the absence of aptitude testing (which, to our knowledge, is not used by any employer in the industry), selective pressures on the kill floor and the disassembly line are permitted to weed out the physically and mentally less fit among accepted job applicants.

Removal from employment temporarily or permanently due to a work-related health condition may result from three types of risk associated with this work: death, dismemberment, and disability. Death is infrequent and actual dismemberment (severance of limbs) is rare, though lacerations account for one-third of injuries and illnesses reported to OSHA, according to Stull and Broadway in this volume.

This leaves disability, primarily by *ergonomic disorders,* a broad category of neural and muscular complaints resulting from excessive manual operations performed at high speed. Severity of injury can range from intense pain to functional impairment, either temporary or permanent. Ergonomic disorders are associated with a broad range of occupations, only recently recognized by OSHA. They include computer operators, supermarket checkout clerks, and a variety of factory workers.

On September 8, 1991, the Denver-based regional OSHA administrator observed that "ergonomics is *the* issue of the '90s with regard to workplace safety." He added that ergonomic complaints are the top safety violations reported to OSHA. "There are very few segments of modern industry . . . where we aren't seeing the potential for ergonomic problems" (Bronikowski 1991).

The nature of the work (Stull and Broadway, this volume; Stull 1994a; Erickson 1994) determines that "repetitive motion disorder," technically referred to as carpal tunnel syndrome (CTS), should be the most frequent form of injury occurring among meat industry employees. Stull and Broadway (this volume) affirm a rate of 134 per 1,000 workers for 1992, the highest of any industry in the United States. One packing plant in southwest Kansas produced more workers' compensation claims involving attorneys in 1992 than any other employer in the state (Shields 1993).

Without discounting the severity of the problem, or its tragic consequences for those affected, our focus is community health rather than industrial accidents. We turn, then, to how attrition in the workforce, produced by a combination of injury, fatigue, stress, and symptoms of depression resulting from the environment and the nature of employment, leads to occupational turnover and residential discontinuity, which dramatically affect community health and provision of primary care.

The circumstances defining industrial nomadism also serve to create the health conditions described in the previous section. To examine the underlying issues, we will create a pseudonymous packing plant, QXR Industries, in the mythical small city of Valley View, Kansas (pop. 22,500 in 1990). The data on QXR are a blend of information from several similar facilities.

QXR has a slaughter capacity of 5,000 animals per day and employs some 2,150 persons. The stratification of employment within the company is heavily biased toward hourly workers, who constitute about 90 percent of the workforce. Of the remainder, 5 percent are classified as management and 3 percent as clerical. Hourly employees are 83 percent male and 17 percent female. Hourly wages range from about $7.00 to $10.50 per hour, but the vast majority cluster in a narrow interval around $8.50 per hour. Five of six hourly workers are Hispanic.

Assuming a 40-hour week and 52-week year, $8.50 per hour yields an annual gross salary of $17,680. The descent below the poverty line and into the category of "Medicaid eligible" results from the impact of several variables: number of dependents per worker and factors determining the intermittent nature of employment: fluctuating hours, occasional shutdowns, immigration status, and turnover rates.

Employment records for QXR reveal the number of tax exemptions (dependents) claimed per hourly worker. The actual number ranges from zero through 8, but the composite data for both sexes yields a figure of 2.7 exemptions per hourly worker, of which 1,935 are currently employed. This suggests that the QXR plant adds 5,224 persons to the population of Valley View, Kansas—a number equal to one-fourth of the community.

There is a significant sex difference in dependency. The average figure for male workers is 3.1 exemptions, but for females the figure drops to 1.8. However, one-fourth of male workers claimed *five or more exemptions*. The health implications of these numbers will be considered in the next section from the perspective of the Garden City Clinic, which serves a similar population.

There are several dimensions to the intermittent nature of employment. The first of these arises from the management policy of controlling supply, and maintaining price levels for products, by periodic shutdowns of the disassembly line. Since management is paid a monthly wage, the financial burden is borne by the hourly workers. Examples are numerous but infrequently reported. However, in 1991 a major meat-processing "slowdown" spread across three states. On March 23, Monfort of Colorado (a ConAgra subsidiary) announced a halt to beef slaughter and fabrication at plants in Texas, Iowa, and Colorado, idling 4,500 workers. Within the same week, the Kansas-based Excel Corporation (owned by Cargill) announced a shutdown at Sterling, Colorado, and IBP, with headquarters at Dakota City, Nebraska, closed its plant at Denison, Iowa (Leib 1991).

[handwritten margin note: industry control of price thru control of product supply]

A seldom-considered dimension of the industrial labor force, despite its predominant Hispanic composition, is its immigration status. The implications of the 1986 Immigration Reform and Control Act (IRCA), which legalized the status of a number of undocumented workers while imposing penalties on employers who hired future arrivals, remains unclear (Griffith 1992). Immigration and Naturalization Service surveillance continues, however, and prompt action is taken where violations are discovered. On September 4, 1993, Monfort was fined $103,000 in connection with a raid the previous year at its plant in Grand Island, Nebraska, which identified 300 "illegals" in a workforce of 1,900. Of these, 250 accepted immediate deportation to Mexico (Rebchook 1993).

But the most substantial contributor to the intermittent character of work in the meatpacking industry is the rate of turnover. The QXR plant sustained turnover of 5.5 percent of the workforce in a typical month in 1994. This rate is equal to an annual rate of 66 percent. For an industry in which monthly turnover is more frequently calculated at 6 to 8 percent (Stull, Broadway, and Erickson 1992), the QXR workforce is relatively stable.

However, detailed information on length of employment provides a more disturbing picture. Duration of employment for all hourly workers at QXR averages 4 years; a hypothetical labor force, in which each worker served for 4 years, would have been totally replaced *four and one-half times* in the 18 years of QXR's operation in Valley View. Actual beginning, termination, and reemployment dates for each employee in the current labor force permit us to dispense with hypotheses. The record is distinctly bimodal: *slightly more than half of hourly workers were added to the labor force since 1990 and average two years of service;* the other half have worked at QXR for various periods, with an average seven years of employment. Non-Hispanic employees appear disproportionately among those workers averaging seven years of service. Inspection

[handwritten margin note: worker turnover]

of occupational titles for hourly workers discloses that employees with longer terms of service hold positions demanding less stamina and physical exertion.

Until proved otherwise, we conclude that Hispanics among hourly workers at QXR are most likely to experience shorter lengths of employment, resulting from assignments to more physically demanding tasks with a higher probability of disabling injury, exhaustion, and/or depression. However, after intervals of rest and rehabilitation, the absence of employment alternatives may force them to return to their former jobs. One-fourth of the short-term employees (those averaging two years of service) were *rehires!*

This section is offered in support of the premise that QXR Industries creates industrial nomads–temporary employees in dead-end jobs. The 6 out of 10 hourly workers who average little more than a year at work came from similar short terms of employment, alternating or mixed with welfare support, elsewhere. Nomadism is reinforced by (1) availability of temporary residences—trailer park rental units—containing utilities and basic appliances; (2) availability of similar employment in another packing plant in a nearby town; (3) and access to federal assistance programs in any of the moderate-size communities of southwest Kansas and adjacent "industry" states.

Community-Based Primary Care for Industry Households

The state health department laments the absence of primary care throughout southwest Kansas: "In ten of the counties in this region less than 25% of the physicians surveyed . . . were able to accept new obstetrical or Medicaid patients into their practices. These counties include . . . Finney, . . . Grant, . . . and Seward" (KDHE 1993: 71).[4] However, the same source also notes that: "a state funded community based primary care clinic is located in Finney County with satellite clinics in Ford, Haskell, Seward and Grant Counties. This clinic is a major provider for prenatal care to Medicaid and uninsured clients who reside in the area" (KDHE 1993:72).

The primary-care facility referred to above is the United Methodist Western Kansas Mexican-American Ministries Care Centers and Clinics (hereafter, Methodist Clinic) with headquarters in Garden City. The Kansas Department of Health and Environment accurately reports that the Methodist Clinic is the primary-care facility for *all* meatpacking

*The sign in front of the United Methodist Care Center in
Garden City reflects the growing ethnic and linguistic diversity
of southwest Kansas. (Photograph by Donald D. Stull)*

communities and their employee households. However, it is only partially state-supported.

The Methodist Clinic

From its base in Garden City, a network of full-time primary-care centers operates in nearby Dodge City, Liberal, and Ulysses, each with large
Hispanic, industry-based populations (see Table 9.1). Part-time care is

provided at several smaller sites. Staff for the entire complex consists of one physician, two nurse-practitioners, three registered nurses, four community development technicians, and a social worker. There are also three nursing interns, management, business office, and clerical personnel, making a total of 24 employees, 13 of whom are full-time.

Services are intended for the unemployed, the uninsured or under-insured, the indigent, the undocumented, and others unable to access medical care. Services provided include (1) treatment of illness and injury; (2) health education; (3) preventive care; (4) prenatal and post-natal care; (5) laboratory tests; (6) prescription assistance; (7) referrals; (8) management of chronic conditions; (9) and physical examinations and health screening. A comprehensive schedule of social services embodies the concept of the clinic as family resource center and provides for "one-stop shopping."

Client Population

In 1990 the potential client population consisted of the 17,639 Hispanics and 2,356 Asians (see Table 9.1) who make up the service area in which major facilities are located: Finney, Ford, Grant, and Seward Counties. This population (total of 19,995) compares with an industrial labor force estimated at 8,500, or 2.4 minority residents per employee. This figure is comparable with the 2.7 exemptions per worker reported for the QXR plant.

In Garden City the registered social service population (24,097) included the following in 1992 (Kansas Department of Social and Rehabilitation Services 1993):

Program	Average Monthly Case Load
Aid to Families with Dependent Children	1,028 persons
Low-Income Energy Assistance	1,505
Food stamps	2,475
Medicaid eligible	4,519

The food stamp and Medicaid figures are equal to 30 percent and 54 percent of the county's Hispanic population, respectively.

The emphasis on medical indigence in a population that is at least intermittently employed in a major industry raises the question of health insurance coverage. The largest industry employer in the five-state area covered by this discussion is IBP. It offers substantially the same policy to all its hourly employees, and this plan is similar to others throughout the industry.

Two important features of the plan (described earlier in this volume by Grey [see pp. 122–23]), given the high turnover and short duration of employment for most workers, are the absence of any coverage during the first six months and the exclusion of pregnancy-related care for a conception occurring before the date at which coverage became effective. The combination of substantial medical indigence and limited access to health care underscores the critical position occupied by the Methodist Clinic as the sole source for most minority households.

Utilization Pattern

The single most significant observation concerning the Methodist Clinic is the explosive growth in demand for its services, as the following figures confirm:

	Patients	*Prenatal Visits*	*Total Visits*
1990	4,617	345	6,000
1991	6,128	311	7,500
1992	8,741	484	13,865

Both patients and total visits have doubled from 1990 to 1992. An increment of this magnitude has not been matched by expansion in either staff or financial support. Of the total visits in 1992, 9,837 were received at Garden City; other sites served 3,468 resident clients and 560 migrants.

The second critical observation concerns the composition of the 1992 client population. The 8,741 patients were 81 percent female. This is almost the mirror image of the employee sex breakdown in area packing plants: 83 percent are male at QXR and 74 percent are male at IBP-Finney County (Stull 1994b:114). These facts underscore two significant conclusions: clinic patients consist of women in workers' households rather than male employees, and the expanding demand for care is unrelated to injuries sustained on the factory floor.

The clinic director affirms that 85 percent of her patients are "industry related," yet less than 10 percent of her caseload is associated with occupational injuries sustained in the plant. In 1992, for example, adolescent girls and young women (aged 13–34) made up close to two-thirds of the Methodist Clinic caseload, and their complaints are mostly related to reproductive performance. A three-month (July–September) sample of 1993 records reviewed by a University of Kansas Medical Center epidemiologist revealed the following: 83 percent of patients were female; 66 percent of the caseload consisted of pregnancy-related complaints of women between the ages of 15 and 45; 86 percent of patients were without insurance coverage; and 85 percent of the patients had Spanish surnames, and most of these required translator services.

Among older adults the most frequent complaints reported by the clinic executive director for 1992 arise from diabetes and hypertension. As the population ages, these conditions, which are both expensive and difficult to treat, will gain in importance. Infectious diseases of children are the most frequent occasions for pediatric care.

The public's knowledge of health problems associated with industry employment is one-dimensional: it has been focused exclusively on injuries sustained on the disassembly line. Sharply rising workers' compensation claims have received increasing publicity, reinforcing this impression. But clinic records confirm that maternal and child health prevails in defining demand for care. And poverty-related welfare services were provided *three times* as often as medical treatment during 1992.

During 1992 the Methodist Clinic, through its social service program, completed 32,000 contacts with clients for a variety of purposes. These range from provision of food and clothing to consultation on immigration status, citizenship and taxes, social security, and job referrals. The largest number of contacts, ominously, were for withdrawals from the food bank and commodities (12,300). The next most frequent, predictably, were for clothing (7,160). In third place were requests for "baby bundles"—diapers and formula (1,615). A separately administered Child and Adult Care Food Program distributed 96,000 meal units.

Despite its importance as the sole source for health care for more than one-fourth of Garden City's population, the funding of the Methodist Clinic is uncertain. Its operating budget for 1992 was $301,000, of which only $20,000 was obtained from fees. Patients are asked to pay $5 per visit, but no one is turned away (Hope 1993). Other sources in the patchwork financial structure include the United Methodist Church, the Kansas Health Foundation, and the local United Way.

Polarization, Population, and Primary Care

The three southwest Kansas counties that contain the five packing plants increased in population by 21.6 percent between 1980 and 1990. Factors compounding the growth rate are concentrated among economically marginal, intermittently employed, medically indigent Hispanic working-class households. Time series data from a packing plant in the Garden City area indicate that the number of individuals performing unskilled or semiskilled labor increased from 1,830 to 2,460 (34.4 percent) between 1984 and 1992. Within this category, the proportion of Hispanics increased from 29.7 percent to 68.7 percent; the proportion of Anglos decreased from 40.7 percent to 10.0 percent; the proportion of Asians decreased from 27.0 percent to 20.0 percent; and the proportion of females increased from 19.9 percent to 25.6 percent.

The Hispanic increment to the lower tier of the polarized class structure, based on the QXR Industries data, expands by a factor of 3.1 household members for every new hire. But, in the Garden City area, minority households grow by *reproduction* as well as by gains in factory production. The Methodist Clinic data confirm that 1,140 women were provided with prenatal care between 1990 and 1992. Births supported in the year 1992 alone reached a total of 484.

While the labor force expands and new births to household members multiply, the concentration of short-term hourly workers—the half or so averaging 1.21 years of service at QXR Industries—remains the same. Elsewhere, Hackenberg et al. (1993) argue that, intentionally or not, the personnel policy of the industry favors *replacement* of workers rather than *retention* of workers making up the labor force on the disassembly line. The data reviewed here appear to confirm this proposition.

The buildup of the Hispanic residential population is coupled with rapid turnover in the primary occupational niche available to them. This supports the conclusion, confirmed by the Methodist Clinic 1990–92 utilization data, that demand for primary care is increasing geometrically while the number of jobs advances arithmetically (further reduced by the turnover rate). And the client population served by the clinic is medically indigent—a condition for admission.

The pattern of primary care provided by the Methodist Clinic to the largely Hispanic minority in the three-county area is a response to demand originating among young married couples. Thus far, that demand is concentrated in the area of maternal and child health—prenatal care and well-baby clinics. This care requires little in terms of technology and specialized expertise. It is cheap to provide and extends across a rather brief and self-limiting interval of 18 months (second and third trimesters prenatal and 0–12 months postnatal).

More ominous health care problems loom on the horizon, concentrated among two demographic sectors not yet present in substantial proportions in the Methodist Clinic caseload: adolescents and mature adults. Finney County ranks in the 9th decile among Kansas counties in prevalence of abuse and neglect of children under the age of 18, and in the 10th (highest) decile in arrests of juveniles in the same age group.

The epidemiologist who conducted the 1993 Methodist Clinic record search noted earlier reports as follows:

> Of special concern are the high rates of sexually transmitted diseases. A review of 1993 Kansas Department of Health and Environment records showed high rates of gonorrhea and chlamydia in all three counties. . . . The presence of STDs . . . suggests that HIV may soon enter the Hispanic community. Another infectious disease concern has been the rise of antibiotic-sensitive tuberculosis. The November 1993 Finney County Health Department records of TB testing were reviewed. . . . of 396 PPD tests given during the three weeks November 1 through December 23, 315 PPD's were read and 77 (24 percent) were positive. Of the 77 positives, 81 percent were among Hispanic workers or family members related to workers in the packing plants and feedlots. (Frederickson 1993)

The high prevalence of STDs and the related menace of AIDS, like the juvenile delinquency and teenage pregnancy that are concomitant behaviors, are community health problems of adolescence. Their causes and cures, like those of gang behavior, now making its appearance in the region, lie beyond the reach of a primary-care clinic.

As the medically indigent Hispanic population in southwest Kansas expands and ages, its health status profile will give diminished importance to conditions associated with childbirth, infant care, and infectious disease. Tuberculosis is the concern of the moment, but another health threat looms larger in the near future. The transition to chronic ailments, and explosive outbreaks of diabetes and associated cardiovascular complaints, can occur within a single decade among adults in early middle age.

Non-insulin-dependent (type II) diabetes, or NIDDM, which is now familiar among Native Americans in the Southwest who share genetic ancestry with Hispanics in the Midwest, is already under treatment in San Antonio (Weiss, Ferrell, and Hanis 1984; Urdaneta 1993). Case management is within the range of services that can be provided from a primary-care facility like the Methodist Clinic. But the delivery of primary care for the management of diabetes makes assumptions about the intended beneficiaries that are in sharp conflict with the lifestyles of industrial nomads.

The key requirement for the treatment of adult-onset diabetes is *surveillance.* Measurement of blood sugar, blood pressure, circulation, kidney function, and ophthalmological testing must be continuously performed if severe complications requiring dialysis, kidney transplants, and amputation are to be avoided or deferred. Case management aimed at prolonging useful life and deflecting the high-cost procedures for patients who are already functionally impaired requires, at minimum, *residential stability.*

Since behavior modification based on health education, weight control, diet management, and avoidance of alcohol is the key to success in treating diabetes, care must be both comprehensive and continuous. All community-oriented primary-care models assume that caregivers are dealing with a circumscribed (closed) population in which membership extends over decades.

The objective of primary care is *preventive intervention,* not episodic treatment for illnesses already present. To be effective, family case management is the essential instrument. Knowledge of the family members, their health histories, and their genetic and environmental susceptibilities is an essential ingredient in a health promotion/disease prevention program.

It is difficult to visualize an effective prevention plan targeting tuberculosis and diabetes within the framework of industrial nomadism. Among the Hispanic households described here and elsewhere in this volume, continuous employment and permanent residence are undermined by the consequences of injury, fatigue and physical stress, and

[handwritten margin note: their nomad status would be resolved thru unionization → high minimum wage]

seasonal variations in hours worked. Rising costs of more complex care contrast with a diminished capacity to pay for services received.

Polarization (distance between upper and lower levels of income and concomitant lifestyles) advances as the meat-processing industries tighten their grip on the economy of southwest Kansas and analogous locations in the adjacent states. Accelerated population growth is projected into the next century, expanding the importance of a culturally distinct minority with limited living and working skills.

Conclusion

Like a breakwater holding back a heavy sea, the Methodist Clinic guards southwest Kansas against the social and economic consequences of a flood of chronic disease. Industrial employers are unlikely to increase their contributions to avoid disaster. Now is the time to search for and install more effective community-health measures for disease control among industrial nomads.

National health insurance, if and when enacted, even with "universal coverage," is unlikely to solve the problem. The national program may improve on availability of care and extend the range of conditions for which payment will be provided. And present discussion maintains that coverage will include preventive services as well as treatment. But it is the lifestyle of the industry labor force, defined by interacting elements of residential and occupational impermanence, rather than its impoverishment, that places it beyond the reach of conventional disease-prevention strategies. Additional insurance coverage, even if portable, will not solve the problem of temporal surveillance and continuous support required for effective behavior modification in a population of industrial nomads.

The peculiar characteristics, growing numbers, and desperate need of this unique Hispanic addition to the American underclass are gaining recognition. Research is urgently needed to design and test a new service-delivery model for chronic disease prevention directed at the human foundation of rural industrialization in the new Midwest.

Notes

1. The authors have been engaged in rural community-based primary-care research since they were brought together in 1989 by a Kellogg Foundation

grant to the National Rural Health Association. They designed a component to address health care needs of the new minority labor force at the national conference on New Factory Workers in Old Farming Communities, under the auspices of the Rural Economic Policy Program of the Aspen Institute. The conference was held at Queenstown, Maryland, on April 12–14, 1992. This essay presents the results.

2. This section draws heavily upon reports and publications of the Center for the New West, Denver, Colorado, provided by Colleen Boggs Murphy, senior fellow in rural policy studies. The research behind these reports was also supported by a grant from the Aspen Institute. Additional material shaping our perspective on the issues of polarization of the Midwest class structure and redistribution of rural medical resources was provided by Don Macke, director, Nebraska Rural Development Commission, who was a participant in the Aspen Institute conference.

3. Primary sources for this section were the *Kansas Statistical Abstract 1991–92*, issued by the Institute for Public Policy and Business Research, University of Kansas, Lawrence, and various reports of the Kansas Department of Health and Environment. See references under KDHE.

4. Source material on the United Methodist Western Kansas Mexican-American Ministries Care Centers and Clinics was provided by Penney Schwab, executive director. Her permission to publish is gratefully acknowledged. Ms. Schwab was also a participant in the Aspen Institute conference.

Doren Frederickson of the Department of Preventive Medicine, Kansas University School of Medicine, provided unpublished data from a 1993 survey of health records at the Methodist Clinic, Garden City, and additional 1993 reports from the Kansas Department of Health and Environment. His permission to use this material is acknowledged with thanks.

References

Booth, M. 1992. Second-Rate Care Plagues Rural Towns. *Denver Post,* January 5.

Bronikowski, L. 1991. Companies Hit for Repetitive Stress Injuries. *Rocky Mountain News,* September 8.

———. 1994. Beef Cattle Count Hits 20-Year High. *Rocky Mountain News,* March 17.

Center for the New West. 1992. *The Great Plains in Transition: Overview.* A report to the Ford Foundation and the Aspen Institute. Denver.

Erickson, K. C. 1994. Guys in White Hats: Short-Term Participant Observation among Beef-Processing Workers and Managers. In *Newcomers in the Workplace: Immigrants and the Restructuring of the U.S. Economy,* edited by L. Lamphere, A. Stepick, and G. Grenier. Philadelphia: Temple University Press, pp. 78–98.

Frazier, D. 1991. Sanctuary Plan for Buffalo Kicks Up Dust. *Rocky Mountain News,* May 5.

Frederickson, D. 1993. Hispanic Maternal and Child Health Study. Unpublished manuscript, Department of Epidemiology, University of Kansas School of Medicine. Wichita.

Griffith, D. 1992. U.S. Immigration Policy and Food Processing Industries. Unpublished memorandum, March 31. East Carolina University. Greenville.

Hackenberg, R., D. Griffith, D. Stull, and L. Gouveia. 1993. Creating a Disposable Labor Force. *Aspen Institute Quarterly* 5(2):78–101.

Hope, D. 1993. United Way a Shot in Arm for Clinic. *Garden City Telegram,* October 23.

Kansas Department of Health and Environment. 1992. *Primary Care Status Index.* Kansas Department of Health and Environment. Topeka.

_____. 1993. *Primary Care County Analysis.* Kansas Department of Health and Environment. Topeka.

Kansas Department of Social and Rehabilitation Services. 1993. *Application for Medically Underserved Population Designation.* Finney County Health Department. Garden City, Kansas. February 1.

Kukulka, G., R. Van Hook, and J. Muchow. 1991. Adapting Health Care Policies to Meet Rural Realities. *Midwest Medical Ethics,* Spring/Summer: 22–27.

Lamphere, L., ed. 1992. *Structuring Diversity: Ethnographic Perspectives on the New Immigration.* Chicago: University of Chicago Press.

Lamphere, L., A. Stepick, and G. Grenier, eds. 1994. *Newcomers in the Workplace: Immigrants and the Restructuring of the U.S. Economy.* Philadelphia: Temple University Press.

Leib, J. 1991. Monfort Forced to Idle Three Beef Plants. *Denver Post,* March 23.

Luther, V., and M. Wall. 1991. *A Case Study of Superior, Nebraska.* Part 1. Lincoln, Neb.: Heartland Center for Leadership Development.

Murphy, C. B. 1992. *A Case Study of Brush, Colorado.* Part 1. Denver: Center for the New West.

Nebraska Rural Development Commission. 1992. *Access to Primary Health Care in Rural Nebraska.* Rural Health Care Task Force. Lincoln.

Nebraska Rural Health Advisory Commission. 1992. *Rural Health in Nebraska: Rural Health Policies and Action Plan Recommendations.* Lincoln.

Rebchook, J. 1993. Monfort Pays $103,000 in Immigration Case. *Rocky Mountain News,* September 4.

Rocky Mountain News. 1994. Health: Stress Injuries Costly. March 31.

Shields, M. 1993. Slaughterhouse Workers Say Medical Complaints Often Ignored by Management. *Topeka Metro News,* March 17.

Stull, D. D. 1994a. Knock 'em Dead: Work on the Killfloor of a Modern Beefpacking Plant. In *Newcomers in the Workplace: Immigrants and the Restructuring of the U.S. Economy,* edited by L. Lamphere, A. Stepick, and G. Grenier. Philadelphia: Temple University Press, pp. 44–77.

———. 1994b. Of Meat and (Wo)Men. *Kansas Journal of Law and Public Policy* 3(3):112–18.

Stull, D., M. J. Broadway, and K. C. Erickson. 1992. The Price of a Good Steak: Beef Packing and Its Consequences for Garden City, Kansas. In *Structuring Diversity: Ethnographic Perspectives on the New Immigration,* edited by L. Lamphere. Chicago: University of Chicago Press, pp. 35–64.

Urdaneta, M. L. 1993. Health Care Implications of the Mexican-American Minority. Paper presented at the annual meeting of the Society for Applied Anthropology, San Antonio, March 10–14.

Weiss, K., R. E. Ferrell, and C. L. Hanis. 1984. A New World Syndrome of Metabolic Diseases with a Genetic and Evolutionary Basis. *Yearbook of Physical Anthropology* 27:153–78.

10 | The Kill Line

Facts of Life, Proposals for Change

Bob Hall

Mary Robinson of Leland, Mississippi, remembers her first day on the kill line at Delta Pride, the world's largest processor of farm-raised catfish. "I was shocked," she says. "I was scared of those big old live catfish. It was a stinking scent there, made my stomach sick. Eventually I just got used to it." After a few years of cutting and gutting catfish for Delta Pride, Robinson's hand began going numb. In early 1991, her doctor cut open her wrist to release the pressure on the median nerve, but the surgery didn't work. Two months later, her supervisor fired her. "It makes me mad," she says. "I did all that work, ripping, ripping, ripping those big fishes with those dull knives from eight in the morning until nine at night. And now I be hurt the rest of my life—*the rest of my life*. Ain't nobody else going to want to hire me, with the condition my arm's in. THAT'S A FACT." (Bates 1991)

Rose Ross, another victim of carpal tunnel syndrome, says, "Delta Pride is just like in slavery time. Somebody always standing over you, telling you what to do. To them, we're just here today and gone tomorrow. What do they care? If you get hurt, that's just one more black nigger gone and another one coming to get crippled." (Bates 1991)

THE EXPERIENCES OF WOMEN like Rose Ross and Mary Robinson are as much a part of modern food processing as profit margins and production trends, and far more relevant in considering food processing as a foundation of a community's or a region's economic development. Two decades ago, catfish was heralded as the economic salvation of the Mississippi Delta. But how does a region or town benefit from the investment of a new factory if the workers inside are routinely crippled?

The paradox of economic development based on the routine crippling of workers is the subject of this chapter. After describing the tensions that exist between labor and management in catfish, crab, and poultry processing, it presents the main foundations for these tensions, including the willingness of state and local government personnel to sacrifice not only workers but water quality and revenues to these hazardous industries. Following this assessment, worker, community, and industry avenues for change are suggested.

Injury and Illness, Anger and Fear: Industrial Profiles

The official work-related injury rate in the catfish industry is 21 percent—meaning 21 of every 100 full-time workers are hurt on the job annually. Most suffer from cumulative trauma disorders, a repetitive motion illness that is devastating for workers who must use their hands to earn a living for themselves and their families. The high injury rate in catfish plants stimulated Mississippi Delta workers to organize unions, solicit help, and counteract the abuse resulting from a lopsided power structure that reminded them of the plantation system their forebears had endured.

The testimony of Rose Ross and Mary Robinson at the beginning of this chapter comes from interviews conducted by the Institute for Southern Studies, an independent nonprofit organization located in Durham, North Carolina. Although these testimonies come from the catfish industry, our work actually began in 1987 when Cindy Arnold, then director of the Center for Women's Economic Alternatives (CWEA) in Ahoskie, North Carolina, asked us to examine the poultry industry's rapid expansion across the South and its impact on workers. She and her colleagues at the center bore witness to dozens of women from poultry plants with work-related health problems. They wondered what could be done, how widespread the problems were, who might be allies in a campaign to find solutions, and why the poultry industry was crippling so many people. Taking up the CWEA's challenge, we began plowing through government reports and industry trade journals; interviewing workers, farmers, occupational health specialists, and food safety experts; and analyzing data related to every aspect of the poultry industry.

When we released the results of our work at a press conference in Washington, D.C., they generated a wave of public attention and subsequent media reports. We continued our research, drawing parallels with other parts of the food-processing industry and publishing additional reports on the catfish and blue crab industries. Yet despite increased public concern, three congressional hearings, and new legislation, the problems chronicled by Rose and Mary remain.

In early 1991, Georgina Ramirez left Mexico and came to coastal North Carolina to work in a crabhouse under the federal H-2B program. She was promised $1.30 per pound of meat picked, but after her first 60-hour week, she received only $30. Her boss, who took her papers and discouraged her from leaving the dormitory above the crabhouse, had deducted the cost of food, rent, toilet paper, three knives, and a pair of gloves from her paycheck. (Windham and Bates 1992)

The H-2B program allows people to enter the United States temporarily to work for a specific employer. "These workers are at the total mercy of their employers," says Pam DiStefano, an attorney with Farm Workers Legal Services of North Carolina. "The H-2B program enables seafood owners to displace local workers with people from Mexico who are desperate for any kind of work. It is a prescription for abuse."

When Ramirez's boss applied for H-2B certification, the Employment Security Commission office in Hyde County sent a letter verifying that there was "very little in the way of labor for industry needs." In fact, the unemployment rate in Hyde County is 13.5 percent (Windham and Bates 1992). "It's not a matter of a labor shortage," points out Dr. David Cecelski, a researcher familiar with the crab industry. "It's a desire for a workforce that can be controlled. The local black crab pickers have too much leverage, too much freedom from the point of view of some employers" (Hall interview, March 1992).

"One week we worked from 3:30 A.M. until 6:00 P.M., four days in a row," recalls Ramirez. "We told Carl [Doerter] we were tired. We couldn't keep working these hours. He said from then on we'd stop between 2:30 and 3:30." But soon after that he fired Ramirez and Brenda Cota for protesting the long hours and low pay. The two filed suit against Carl Doerter with the help of legal services attorneys. "I am afraid of him," Ramirez says. "My mother told me he might hire someone to hurt me. Brenda tells me to forget about it, but I cannot."

Along with a Maryland processor named Philip Harrington, Doerter was also sued in Maryland by the American Civil Liberties Union for recruiting women to work in Maryland crabhouses. The suit, filed in July 1991, charged that workers were subjected to "sub-minimum wages, substandard living conditions, racial discrimination, and were held in virtual involuntary servitude." In October 1992 Doerter's North Carolina case was settled, with the company agreeing to pay $25,000 in back wages and another $100,000 in damages to the workers. As a result of the suit, Harrington has quit the crab business, although Doerter continues to operate out of Scranton, North Carolina.

Finally, there is the case of Perdue Farms, the original focus of our food-processing research. After years of complaints from workers, Perdue was fined $39,690 in October 1989 by the North Carolina Department of Labor for violating the Occupational Safety and Health Act (OSHA). Specifically, the citation alleged that Perdue routinely exposed its workers to hazards that cause cumulative trauma disorders (CTDs) and, further, that the company "willfully" underreported the incidence of those injuries on its safety logs. (Elsewhere in this volume, Griffith discusses the underreporting of injury within the framework of labor-control strategies, arguing that plants encourage workers to tolerate and underreport injuries.)

Delta Pride, the catfish giant, along with Cargill, ConAgra, Sara Lee, and several other food processors, have received similar citations. All of them came about because of pressure on government inspectors to investigate the plants. In most cases, organized labor has initiated the complaints that triggered OSHA fines against processing plants.

The Perdue case illustrates how the government rarely acts on its own. North Carolina's commissioner of labor had classified poultry as a "high-hazard industry," but two years *after* the Perdue citation, the majority of North Carolina poultry plants had still never been inspected during OSHA's 20-year history. Yet poultry workers have for decades suffered from skin diseases, repetitive trauma disorders (carpal tunnel syndrome, tendinitis, white finger, etc.), ammonia exposure, infections from toxins, chronic stress, and back problems. The annual industry injury/illness rate hit 23.1 incidents per 100 full-time workers in 1991, down from the 1990 peak (26.9) but higher than all other years. The 1991 rate is almost twice the average for all manufacturers (12.7; see Table 2.1 in Broadway, this volume).

These numbers are based on reported injuries, but OSHA has repeatedly cited poultry firms for willfully undercounting injuries. In 1989 Frank Perdue told the *Washington Post* that the rate of cumulative trauma disorders in his plants was under 1 percent. But doctors from the National Institute for Occupational Safety and Health (NIOSH) found the rate was 18 percent in the two plants where they conducted examinations. NIOSH doctors learned that nearly one in four (23 percent) workers with neck, arm, wrist, or hand problems in the two Perdue plants said their supervisor or foreman "did not let them leave [the line] to see the plant nurse" (NIOSH 1990). An internal Perdue memo says it's normal for "about 60 percent of the work force to visit the nurse every morning for Advils, Vitamin B-6 treatment, and hand wraps." Workers repeatedly complained to us about company doctors misdiagnosing their symptoms, not authorizing light duty or workers' compensation, and allowing the CTD to worsen until they recommended surgery (Goldoftas 1989).

Unfortunately, enforcement of OSHA regulations is difficult under existing manpower constraints. This fact came to the attention of the public in a tragic way following a deadly fire in Hamlet, North Carolina. The state labor commissioner admitted that a majority of North Carolina poultry plants had never been inspected. In 1991 North Carolina had only a third of the safety and health inspectors required by OSHA; an employer could expect an inspection once every 75 years. Serious fines in the state averaged $350 per incident, and the governor's safety and health review board reduces or dismisses about half of those appealed.

When Perdue appealed its citation to the review board, the North Carolina Department of Labor dropped its inspectors' recommendation that the company slow its production lines. "We can't demonstrate what speed will reduce the CTD incidence," said Dr. James Oppold, then state OSHA director. "It would also be unfair to make Perdue slow its production when the rest of the industry doesn't change. The best we can do is insist on a medical monitoring program" (Hall fieldnotes, March 1990).

"You gave away the only thing we wanted," countered Chavuletta Jones, a disabled Perdue worker. Two years after Perdue installed its medical monitoring program, line speeds have not declined. Workers still contract cumulative trauma disorders. The firm hired by Perdue, Health & Hygiene, was founded by Dr. Harold Imbus, the retired medical director of Burlington Industries. In the 1970s Imbus vigorously fought stricter regulations against federal cotton-dust limits for his textile mills, and for several years he refused to tell workers that breathing tests showed they were suffering from brown lung symptoms.

In July 1993 Perdue wrote letters to many of the North Carolina workers it had injured and transferred to "light duty" jobs at the re-

Working on the line in a chicken plant. (Courtesy of Meat&Poultry)

quest of their doctors. The letter warned them that they would be fired within 90 days if other employment could not be found. But firing and hiring workers is typical in this industry. According to the U.S. Department of Labor, poultry workers are five times more likely to quit their jobs than other manufacturing workers. The NIOSH study of Perdue learned that its annual turnover rate was 50 percent in one plant and 70 percent in the other.

High turnover is a reflection of the industry's management focus.

Poultry's chief executives mostly come from an agricultural background, from managing commodities, not people. Most of the companies developed as farm product managers (Tyson, Cargill, ConAgra, Gold Kist, Perdue). Some have hired antiunion law firms and management consultants, but their labor-management relations are generally primitive. Their investment in workers is short-term. By contrast, the Poultry Science Association says private industry and government agencies spend $50 to $100 million each year on poultry science, aimed at reducing "chicken stress" while speeding up the bird's life cycle and feed-to-meat conversion ratio (Hall 1989). Less than one-tenth of that amount is spent on reducing "worker stress" through the science of ergonomics—adjusting job design to minimize the stress of repeated, forceful motions made by poultry workers.

What the industry saves on ergonomics, its managers, executives, and owners gain. Between 1984 and 1990, processors earned an average of $1 billion in annual profits. *Forbes* (1993) now estimates Frank Perdue's worth at $450 million and puts Don and Barbara Tyson's at $1.46 billion. The industry has cycles of overproduction and profit declines, but concentration of ownership and consumer demand are decreasing the dips. In 1960, the top 20 firms produced 47 percent of industry output; in 1990, the top four (Tyson, ConAgra, Gold Kist, Perdue) produced 41 percent.

Profits and concentration of ownership reflect the fact that poultry workers are among the most productive workers in the United States. Between 1960 and 1987 their productivity, measured in pounds of poultry output per hour, increased 176 percent. Poultry productivity has increased 50 percent faster than productivity in all U.S. manufacturing plants. Line speeds have roughly doubled since the mid-1970s to 91 birds per minute on the eviscerating line. The typical worker performs one discrete motion over and over, from 10,000 to 30,000 times a day. Despite high productivity rates, poultry-processing workers' wages are the lowest tracked by the Department of Labor in the food-manufacturing industry. In May 1993 they averaged $7.40 per hour, compared with $10.46 for all food-manufacturing workers and $11.72 for production workers in all manufacturing.

How were workers repaid for high productivity and their evident willingness to work for relatively low wages? At Perdue, injured workers who couldn't be reassigned were given their walking papers in the July 1993 company letter. The letter sent a shock wave through the workforce, says Donna Bazemore, the first Perdue employee to receive workers' compensation for CTD in North Carolina. "One of the things this letter has done is make women shut up from even talking about 'I hurt,' " says Bazemore, who now counsels injured workers in the area. "It's given them [Perdue workers] a sense of the fear of God. Women have said, 'I'm going back on the line and work no matter how I hurt,' because they know they're not going to find employment anywhere else. No one wants someone else's worn-out stuff" (Quillan 1993).

Fear is hard to quantify, but it is a driving force behind many workers' decisions to remain in the poultry and other meatpacking industries in spite of the hazardous nature of their jobs. When coupled with the lack of sustained government or other institutional intervention to help workers, fear becomes a critical factor in why change has not come. The fear of losing a job causes people to censor themselves. Poultry workers generally don't complain about safety violations (even when they know where to report them); they may not seek medical help; they may not even vote or show an interest in community affairs for fear of being viewed as "troublemakers."

Some of this derives, surely, from their already disadvantaged political positions. Nearly half of all employees in poultry processing are women. By contrast, only 18 percent in the meatpacking industry are women. Meatpackers made an average of $9.18 per hour in May 1993, or 24 percent more than poultry workers. The "high-hazard" jobs in poultry are disproportionately held by people of color, mostly black women and Latino men. These individuals desperately want that paycheck from the local slaughterhouse; it offers more than what they'd get elsewhere. It allows them to buy a car or mobile home on credit, and then they can't afford to risk getting fired.

Some exceptional people risk losing their jobs or being ostracized by organizing coworkers or soliciting aid from government and the press. The lesson their neighbors and coworkers learn is that speaking out, organizing, or challenging the boss brings trouble. If people received sustained support from the larger community, and if other workers learned that such support was available, change in the industry might become a reality. Hope would work against rejection, support would counter isolation, achievement and positive feedback would neutralize fear.

These stories are told not to make the discussion about meatpacking communities overly emotional. They are, simply, the realities that ordinary people encounter every day. They describe what happens in communities where an imbalance of power allows food processors to dominate decision making, define the limits of acceptable behavior, circumscribe the options people face. The influence of the poultry industry is not restricted to the relatively uneducated line workers but also affects people with skills and financial resources, even those who, in other contexts, are counted among the industry's business partners: university personnel and poultry farmers who grow birds for the processing plants on contract.

Under the contract system, companies provide the birds, feed, and medicine to growers who furnish the chicken house, water, electricity, and labor necessary to bring the birds to market weight. While farmers typically go in debt for 5 to 20 years to finance a chicken house, the contracts may last only 7 weeks. Some farmers complain of being pressured to accept diseased birds, buy new equipment, or settle for lower payments just to renew their contracts. Does the contract system provide stability and shield farmers from market risks, as the industry and its ag-school apologists claim? Or does it make farmers "serfs on their own land," as some growers charge?

When university personnel and poultry farmers attempted to address questions such as these, they, too, like line workers at Perdue, met with the industry's power. First, two sociologists received approval to conduct research on the contract system by a state-funded agency charged with enhancing rural economic development. However, the agency's advisory board—including representatives from the North Carolina Department of Agriculture and the poultry science department at North Carolina State University—objected. An economist reviewing the decision-making process explained, "Our research depends on gaining access to data and people that the industry controls. We can't afford to alienate the integrators in our state."

Then John Wright (not his real name), who grows chickens for Tyson Foods in eastern Texas, joined several hundred growers to organize a national association of poultry growers. Tobacco growers, cotton farmers, ranchers, and grain farmers all have their groups, but Wright's was the first national organization for this commodity; it incorporated as a cooperative under Arkansas law in March 1992.

About the time of the incorporation, a Tyson field representative went to Wright's farm with a sheaf of papers from company headquarters. They declared: "The drive to organize poultry growers is being funded and led by a network of shady characters and organizations who have a much broader agenda than simply helping growers." The cover letter went on to accuse the ringleaders of "encouraging people to stop eating chicken . . . trying to unionize poultry workers, advancing civil rights, animal rights, and . . . they really don't care about the growers." One page lists several key groups, including the Institute for Southern Studies, and incorrectly describes them as "socialist," "quasi-union," and for "animal rights" (Jaycox 1992).

Poultry farmers, who collectively contribute over half the capital investment involved in the industry, continue to organize despite Tyson's memo. A turning point in their effort to form a national organization came when a series of state and federal cases upheld their right to organize and ordered poultry integrators to pay multimillion-dollar settlements and/or return chickens to the farms of the association members who had been harassed or cheated. "There's still a great deal of fear out there," says former grower Mary Clouse, who was an early association organizer and founding editor of *Poultry Grower News*. "But the growers feel like they've had a breakthrough and can't be picked off as easily, one by one. They've seen the results of getting organized and winning changes that the industry could have done long ago" (Hall interview 1992).

Views of the Labor Problem

Given these conditions, it's not difficult to understand why poultry integrators find themselves constantly in need of new workers. While they recognize that there is a "labor problem" in the meat-processing industry, they will not acknowledge that the "problem" results from specific conditions created through executive decision and action. From their point of view, addressing the labor problem means finding new workers or new machines to meet production demands, a perspective endorsed by some social scientists, particularly agricultural economists, and business schools. Yet from a worker's point of view, addressing the labor problem means changing the workplace (not the workers) so people don't find it so intolerable. The question becomes: What working conditions best sustain a productive workforce as well as serve the community's larger economic and social interests?

One approach assumes the industry's survival is paramount, taking precedent over occupational health; the other assumes the worker's welfare is the central measure of success or failure. I can't think of a better way to illustrate the dichotomy in priorities shaping the debate over the future of meat processing in rural communities. For one side, "competitive pressure" is a sufficient basis to displace whole populations, who then become the subject of welfare studies and a marginalized subeconomy. For the other side, there is no useful reason to encourage a plant to locate in the community unless it offers long-term benefits to the valuable resources already there—namely, the local people and environment. What good is an economic development strategy that succeeds in attracting new investment but slowly overwhelms a community with environmental waste, crippled workers, and disenfranchised farmers?

The poultry industry's disregard for the environment and consumer health has been the subject of numerous articles, including major exposés in the *Atlanta Constitution* and the *Arkansas Democrat*. During the Bush-Clinton campaign, media attention focused on Clinton's reluctance to regulate poultry operations in Arkansas, the nation's leading broiler producer, and the campaign contributions from Tyson and other industry leaders. In sparsely populated Arkansas, the poultry industry accounts for 1 of every 12 jobs. In 1986 Arkansas's congressional leadership campaigned to win a $500 million tax break for Tyson Foods, Perdue Farms, and other family-held processors. In the Arkansas legislature, the poultry industry is "second to none in political clout," says the *Arkansas Democrat*. In 1991 the chicken lobby teamed up with the Farm Bureau to defeat a proposal backed by then-Governor Clinton to strengthen the state's Pollution Control and Ecology Commission, the agency most responsible for Arkansas's last-place finish in environmental policy in a national study. Frustrated by corporate and governmental delay, citizen groups in Arkansas have successfully sued Tyson to curtail its pollution of groundwater and streams.

Similar lawsuits and citizen pressure across the poultry belt have forced industry leaders to devote considerable attention to the management of their waste—more than 7 billion pounds of chicken manure and 14 billion pounds of wastewater each year. More threatening are press reports of salmonella contamination, which are damaging poultry's image as the healthy meat alternative. A roving "media relations" workshop, teaching poultry executives how to "take charge," has become a standard feature at state, regional, and national poultry association conventions. And poultry magazines are now peppered with articles about composting dead birds, land application of wastewater, and other pollution-control strategies. By contrast, little discussion of worker health appears in the trade literature. Instead of acknowledging its weaknesses, the industry issues denials, minimizes problems, and attacks those who force increased public scrutiny of its practices.

This hostility to public accountability coincides with the industry's fear of its farmers or workers organizing and poisons the prospect of a meaningful partnership between the various interests in a community with a large poultry facility. The failure of government to even the balance of power, to intervene aggressively on the side of the abused while supporting the industry with tax concessions and state-funded poultry research, severely limits the prospects of serious change. Policy reforms could significantly improve the poultry- and other meat-processing industries, but reforms often evaporate in their implementation or fall short of their stated mission.

Consider the reforms passed after the poultry plant fire in Hamlet, North Carolina. Under the scrutiny of the national media and an unprecedented public outcry for reform, state legislators passed a dozen bills in 1992 to change everything from fire-code inspections to whistle-blower protection for workers who suffer retaliation for reporting employers' hazardous or illegal practices. However, because the overall political climate in North Carolina strongly favors business and opposes workers' rights, many loopholes or compromises included in the reforms render them less threatening to the balance of power. For example, one law requires that employers must establish worker-management safety committees if the company has over 50 employees and a significantly higher-than-average history of job injury. The indicator chosen to measure a company's injury history is its insurance rating for buying a workers' compensation policy. However, nearly all poultry processors, and nearly all the state's largest employers (from utilities to manufacturers to banks), are now self-insured for workers' compensation. Consequently, they have *no* rating and therefore fall outside the purview of the safety committee law.

Any policy initiative can be subverted, overruled, delayed, or changed back when new political leaders win office, yet changes that expand the capacity of citizens to organize themselves into their own watchdogs and protectors have much more lasting impact. The South, which is today's poultry heartland, suffers from a lack of democratic traditions and a dearth of democratic institutions precisely because it blocked the capacity of ordinary people to organize themselves into self-respecting agents of their own destiny. In one way or another, the region's elite held onto the master-slave model well beyond its legal demise. Alternative models were shunned, belittled, crushed. Empowering bureaucrats and intermediating agencies has done little but expand the influence of politically dominant interests. Empowering people at the grassroots, as in the case of the CWEA or a labor union, nurtures a democratic movement that can articulate public goals and hold economic institutions accountable. It is in the spirit of grassroots organizing that we present the following advocacy positions.

Courses of Action

Worker Health, Safety, and Ability to Organize

Slow down the line speed of the processing plants. Study after study has shown that the current line speed produces high rates of CTDs for workers and increased product contamination for consumers. Reduce the speed and workload on individual workers by at least 30 percent (64 chickens per minute on an eviscerating line, rather than 91) until studies show what speed is safer.

Redesign tools so they, rather than the workers' forceful motions, do the job. Automate or restructure especially hazardous jobs. Increase the number of breaks, and rotate workers to jobs that require less stress on their bodies. Expand the diversity of motions and range of muscles used in each person's job rather than segmenting each job into one or two identical motions repeated over and over. The variety of motions performed, the speed with which they are done, and the associated stress on the body should be tracked and correlated with injury/illnesses—and, if need be, radically changed.

Establish standards for CTDs in the same way there are standards for cotton dust or benzene exposure. Vigorously enforce OSHA's existing "general duty clause," which requires employers to provide safe workplaces; this is the section under which companies are now cited for hazardous conditions that cause high rates of CTD. Enact tougher penalties on violations; mandate more frequent, thorough, and unannounced plant inspections; allow worker representatives to go on site inspections and help identify problem areas; and enforce existing provisions requiring complete reporting of injuries and illnesses.

Reform the Occupational Safety and Health Act of 1970, as detailed in Senate Bill 575 (1993). Require processors to establish health and safety committees that give workers a say in workplace safety issues. The workers on the committee should be elected, not appointed by management, and the committees should have access to all records and the authority to halt production temporarily to prevent imminent danger. All workers should receive continuous training about their rights and the hazards in their workplace.

Establish a supportive political context for worker organization. Encourage workers to organize themselves, refine their leadership skills, and develop strategies for long-range empowerment. Build local associations, unions, shop floor caucuses, and injured-workers associations to provide vehicles for concerted activity and support for individual initiative. Implement the workers' right to bargain collectively for fair work rules, a grievance and seniority system, an end to harassment, and adequate pay. Repeal "right-to-work" laws that allow nonmembers to get the benefits of union members without paying any dues.

Enact laws that allow employees applying for workers' compensation to choose their own physicians. Determine disability settlements based on the income capacity workers actually lose from their injuries and illnesses. Apply reasonable standards of proof in compensation cases involving cumulative trauma. Outlaw the harassment by the employer's agents (or its insurer) that forces people to quit or go back to work before they recover.

Provide whistle-blower protection to workers and inspectors for "committing the truth" of reporting violations of USDA or OSHA standards, incidents of gross negligence, and practices that threaten the worker's or consumer's health. Attorneys' fees, full back pay, and triple damages should be awarded plaintiffs who are victims of retaliation, and their cases should receive rapid hearings.

Equity for Farmers

Establish state oversight of the contracts between processors and farmers to ensure their uniformity and fair standards. Set fair standards for contracts so processors cannot arbitrarily terminate or change their terms after farmers invest huge sums in chicken and turkey houses based on industry promises. Expand the federal Packers and Stockyards Act to include full protection of poultry growers.

Put working farmers on industry and government advisory and policymaking bodies that establish or monitor standards for poultry science, poultry raising, and other aspects of the business that affect growers.

Channel existing federal and state rural economic development funds—and devote new monies—to provide low-cost credit, research, and technical support for growing and processing of healthful, free-range chickens under management control of independent farmers.

Stop the spread of the monopoly control of vertically integrated feed suppliers/commodity buyers/processors who lock out competitors and turn farmers into "serfs on their own land." Use tax, antitrust, and supply-side quotas to diversify ownership and control of commodities.

Publicize the National Contract Poultry Growers Association as a self-help cooperative through the county agricultural extension and other networks (rather than spreading hostility toward it), and encourage farmers to join. Use the NCPGA to get basic information on what farmers should do before signing a poultry contract. Encourage poultry growers to communicate directly with one another, and to the public, rather than let the industry speak for them.

Community Initiatives

Organize "workplace safety patrols" that present themselves to plant managers on an unannounced basis and request a tour of the complete facility. The patrol might be composed of a minister, public-housing leader, retired police officer, disabled worker, teacher, and journalist. If the plant refuses a "community inspection," that fact should be publicized; positive achievements by companies should also be well publicized.

Churches could adopt a workplace or become engaged in an ongoing program that provides a service to workers—sponsoring basic health screening clinics, offering a home for a monthly legal clinic on workers' rights, organizing transportation, developing a housing program, operating a community center. Churches could pool resources to create an emergency loan fund, with worker representatives on its board; the fund could help bridge financial needs of workers receiving medical care, waiting for a workers' compensation determination, or improperly fired. In many rural areas, churches are at the hub of community leadership, cultural activities, and survival strategies.

Monitor county economic development initiatives (sponsored by chambers of commerce, local government, or state agencies), attend all meetings where industrial revenue bonds and other subsidies are handed out, and develop new criteria for such subsidies. The criteria should promote long-term investment in the community and its people. Developing those criteria—a checklist for positive economic development—should be a major objective for concerned community groups; the list could include impact on the environment, local businesses, area wage and benefits levels, affirmative action, workplace health, taxes, and public infrastructure.

Create an alternative economic development strategy, linked to basic community organizing. Promote indigenous economic efforts, including small-scale activities such as gardening, crafts, fishing, home repair, and tailgate marketing. Launch community development corporations (CDCs) for housing, jobs, services, credit, land trusts, and leadership opportunities. Strengthen marketing of locally produced goods and community-based businesses. Microenterprise development, peer group lending and accountability practices, resource networking, and pooling of small business services all should be encouraged.

Sponsor educational forums and cross-cultural events that enable the larger community to understand what life in the meatpacking industry is like. Increasingly, that also means understanding what life for a non–English speaker is like. Include testimony of workers (or former workers if fear among current workers is too high) at events, and hold "speak-outs" with workers from other industries in the area on working conditions. Programs that bridge racial and cultural barriers should be encouraged—gospel sings, soccer games, community picnics, festivals honoring a Latin American country, and so forth.

Monitor the environmental impact of poultry operations. Pressure government authorities to strengthen laws to protect groundwater, control runoff, and promote pollution prevention. Support organizing in neighborhoods near poultry operations to monitor environmental damage, gain access to needed records, and correct problems they find.

Industry Philosophy

Invest in the people who produce the product, not just in the product itself. This begins by treating people with respect and dignity. It includes training, fostering upward mobility, maintaining a complete medical program, and disciplining line supervisors who violate company policy. The payoff includes lower turnover, improved morale, better production, and savings on health costs (although most companies push the health costs onto society by forcing workers to quit and seek Medicaid or Social Security disability).

Invest in the communities where plants are located. Cooperate with the press and community groups. Provide access to the plant and to records concerning worker health and safety, pollution management, product safety, political contributions, and economic impact. Invest in pollution prevention practices, recycling, composting, and systems that generate less pollution as by-products. Invest in community-based CDCs, service providers, credit unions, and organizing projects, including those providing housing, health care, and social services for poultry workers. Pay taxes, support public education, and adopt the corporate responsibility philosophy and techniques of companies as diverse as Cummins Engine and Ben & Jerry's.

Invest in consumers' confidence by improving product safety. For example, change to air cooling of processed birds (as done in much of Europe) and abandon the "fecal soup" chill tanks that spread contamination and add weight (salmonella-laced water) to consumer's bills. Slow down the lines to allow adequate inspection of carcasses. Reject irradiation as an alternative to sight and microbiological inspection and improved management of sanitation, from feed to final product.

Invest in your business. Rather than focusing on mergers and buying out the competition, the industry needs to raise standards and thereby isolate poor producers. Use Don Tyson's "price courage" strategy to raise the prices of poultry products to consumers, but plow the money back into workers, farmers, communities, and consumer safety. Adding four cents a pound would produce over a billion dollars extra each year.

The poultry industry is making huge profits and has a rich future. The wealth of the industry means it has no excuse for avoiding the reforms that could make it more responsive to the people whose lives it influences. But the reforms involve a radical rethinking of the industry's commodity-driven, cutthroat philosophy that uses fear to protect itself. Change is needed in nearly every phase of the business. Whatever the focus, the work will be slow.

References

Bates, E. 1991. The Kill Line. *Southern Exposure* 19(3):22–29.
Forbes. 1993. The Richest People in America. October 18:178, 220.

Goldoftas, B. 1989. Inside the Slaughterhouse. *Southern Exposure* 17(2):25–29.

Hall, B. 1989. Chicken Empires. *Southern Exposure* 17(2):12–17.

Jaycox, B. 1992. Memo to Tyson Foods division managers and complex managers. February 26. Author's files.

National Institute for Occupational Safety and Health (NIOSH). 1990. Health Hazard Evaluation Report: Perdue Farms (HETA 89-307-2009). National Institute for Occupational Safety and Health, Centers for Disease Control, U.S. Department of Health and Human Services. February. Washington, D.C.: U.S. Government Printing Office.

Quillan, M. 1993. Poultry Workers Face Job Loss. *News and Observer*, August 5.

Windham, L., and E. Bates. 1992. H-2B. *Southern Exposure* 20(1):57–60.

11 | Conclusion: Joe Hill Died for Your Sins

Empowering Minority Workers in the New Industrial Labor Force

Robert A. Hackenberg

> A Swedish immigrant named Hillstrom worked his way to America on a freighter, took up the cause of organized labor, became "Joe Hill," and joined the Industrial Workers of the World. He . . . "read Marx and the I.W.W. Preamble and dreamed about forming the structure of the new society within the shell of the old. . . .
>
> "At Bingham, Utah, Joe Hill organized the workers of the Utah Construction Company in the One Big Union, won a new wagescale, shorter hours, better grub. . . . The angel Moroni moved the hearts of the Mormons to decide it was Joe Hill shot a grocer named Morrison. . . . In November 1915 he was stood up against the wall in the jail yard in Salt Lake City.
>
> " 'Don't mourn for me. Organize!' was the last word he sent out to the workingstiffs of the I.W.W."
>
> —John Dos Passos, *Nineteen Nineteen*

Evolving Corporations, Dissolving Unions

Near the beginning of this century, two titans of economic theory exchanged fusillades on issues that recent events, and the conditions described in the preceding chapters, have brought forward once again. In 1917 and 1919, V. I. Lenin and Joseph Schumpeter published works entitled *Imperialism,* with sharply conflicting predictions.

Lenin took the position that leading Western national economies, having reached the highest stage of capitalism (monopolistic control within single industries), would now expand overseas using finance capital to command cheap labor abroad and to invade foreign markets in less developed countries. At the same time, Lenin predicted that migrant labor would penetrate the European and American factory system, reducing both indigenous workers and immigrants to the status of proletarians. *Lenin foresaw the multinational corporation as a voracious instrument for concentrating financial resources, monopolizing production, and accumulating profits in an ever-tightening circle of investors.* His example was General Electric.

Schumpeter argued that expansion of monopoly capitalism was outmoded and would wither and disappear. It could not survive if confronted with universal reduction of tariffs and commitment to free trade sponsored by multiple competing proprietors. Unless impeded by militaristic colonial adventures physically capturing and combining resources, workers, and markets, entrepreneurship and free trade would lead to much more significant economic advances for both industrial powers and less-developed nations. *Schumpeter foresaw the global marketplace as the best (and perhaps last) hope for economic growth and wider distribution of an expanding variety of goods and services to members of all social classes.* His illustrative beneficiary was the industrial worker in the United States.

Joe Hill was a world figure of a different sort. He and his mentor, "Big Bill" Haywood, founded the Industrial Workers of the World (IWW) in Chicago in 1905. Their premises were that production had become international, using cheap foreign labor, and that machines were replacing workmen at home. Only industry-wide unions, extending across national boundaries to enforce equal pay for equal work in similar jobs, wherever they were located, could prevent the continual downgrading of living standards. *The IWW saw the adverse consequences for labor of competing against either unlimited supplies of immigrant workers at home or relocated factories overseas. The union proposed to organize the working class into global unions by industry to prevent this* (Kornbluh 1969).

Could all three, despite apparent conflicts in their arguments, have been right? Ghosts of these positions and their advocates echo across the twentieth century and overshadow the contributions to this volume.

Imperialism. The international extension of oligopolies, which Lenin designated as imperialism, is taking place in three of the four food industries considered in this volume: beef, pork, and poultry, and in "most of the leading 500 industries in the US" (Barnet and Muller 1974:217). Two examples will suffice. In 1992 ConAgra was the world's largest meat company, with $12.5 billion in business. It was represented in 26 countries. It operated beef-processing plants in Australia, Thailand, Spain, and France. It produced poultry in Portugal and Puerto

Rico. In the same year, Cargill earned $5.5 billion from its meat operations and maintained 800 offices in 55 countries with 36 separate meat- and poultry-processing plants around the world (Kay 1992).

Free Trade. With the implementation of the North American Free Trade Agreement (NAFTA) on January 1, 1994, new opportunities were opened up for unrestricted exchange of goods between Canada, the United States, and Mexico. The fear that jobs would move south while "10 million migrants" moved north was also pervasive in the United States (Mead 1994). Companies already dispersing across national boundaries seemed certain to continue to do so. Encouragement is provided by continuing "privatization" in all countries from Mexico to the Straits of Magellan (James and Ludwig 1994).

From the standpoint of food production and processing, the removal of the 20 percent tariff imposed by Mexico on imported beef has had substantial impact. Monfort in Greely, Colorado, doubled its shipment of 525 tons per week to 1,050 tons by May 1994 (Robinson 1994). State development agencies identified north-south U.S. Route 83, linking Regina, Saskatchewan, with Monterrey, Nuevo Leon, for trade development. They proposed a superhighway from Canada to Mexico, which would traverse major U.S. beef-production areas in Nebraska, Kansas, and Texas. The proposal is under congressional review (Unruh 1994).

On the heels of NAFTA, the signing of the General Agreement on Tariffs and Trade (GATT) by 109 nations in Marrakech was announced on April 16, 1994. The accord, which ends the Uruguay round of negotiations begun in 1986, reduces overall import duties by 40 percent and will add $200 billion to the world economy over the next 10 years. The 26,000-page agreement is expected to boost U.S. agricultural exports (Knox 1994). It took effect January 1, 1995.

Labor Organization and Membership. Only old news is good news. Though the IWW and its offshoots (it was prone to fission) expanded to include as many as 4 million members in the peak year of 1919, it was found guilty by association with the American Communist Party, also organized in the same year. It was soon reduced by confrontation with capitalist militancy and widespread prosecution for "un-American activities." Nonetheless, its principles were incorporated into the Congress of Industrial Organizations a quarter century later (Kornbluh 1969).

Union membership, collective bargaining, and labor legislation flourished again during the New Deal years of the Roosevelt administration. In 1955, the year of the merger of the American Federation of Labor and the Congress of Industrial Organizations, membership topped 16 million and included 40 percent of nonagricultural workers. The One Big Union envisioned by the IWW appeared to be a reality. Worker empowerment included purchasing power. Levittown opened in 1958, with homes priced from $11,500 to $14,500.

Reversal in the status of labor began with the Taft-Hartley Act of 1947 and state "right-to-work" (anti–closed shop) laws. Union-busting tactics reached their peak after 1970 when the mergers and acquisitions craze (from which today's major meat and poultry companies emerged) had the side effect of negating labor contracts and decertifying unions. Membership steadily declined from 22 million in 1975 to 16.4 million in 1992 (Judis 1994:25). What remained of the labor movement became more of an extension of management than a bargaining agent representing workers (Mills 1963; Burawoy 1983).

Becoming a Proletarian. Labor finds itself in the decades of deindustrialization and downsizing (Bluestone and Harrison 1982). At the end of the 1950s, 31 percent of private-sector workers were in manufacturing industries. By 1987 this proportion had shrunk to 17 percent. Barry Bluestone reported that 900,000 manufacturing jobs were erased each year between 1978 and 1982 (Beatty 1994:65). Living standards experienced parallel attrition as workers' wages were reduced. "According to Lester Thurow, from 1973 to 1992 average wages for the bottom 60% of male workers fell 20%" (Beatty 1994:66).

Katherine Newman, who has become the spokesperson for the downwardly mobile generation of the 1970s, expresses it this way:

> My own research indicated that there is a growing tendency to see a two tier work force, with a small group of creative people at the top and a large aggregate of people needing relatively low job skills and being paid correspondingly low wages. . . .
>
> Recent evidence underscores the importance of the polarization thesis. Between 1979 and 1984, the middle income share of job growth dropped by almost 20%, while the low income share skyrocketed. More than half of the eight million (net) new jobs created in the US paid less than $7,000 per year. . . .

Organized labor is on the run. As plants move overseas, and as imports increase their market share, wage concessions roll in. Indeed the 1980s have witnessed a remarkable reversal in the fortunes of union labor . . . and "givebacks" have become widespread. (1988:30–33)

A recent publication of the federal Commission on the Future of Worker-Management Relations points to the "increasing hire of more temporary and part time workers to reduce labor costs" and continues:

About 18 percent of the nation's year-around full time workers earned less than $13,091 in 1992—a 50 percent increase over the 12 percent who had low earnings in 1979. . . . These workers consist disproportionately of women, young workers, blacks, Hispanics and the less educated. . . .

The number of bargaining rights elections and the number of labor union victories have diminished sharply over several decades . . . with increasing probability that workers will be fired for pro-union activity. (Eaton 1994)

Evidence of the stratospheric ascent of top management earnings at the upper end of the scale is not hard to find and confirms frequent and recent references to *polarization*. "Colorado CEOs Reap Millions: Average pay for the first 100 executives in state tops $1 million for the first time," screams the Sunday front page of the *Rocky Mountain News,* June 5, 1994.

In more measured tones, Jack Beatty observes in the May 1994 *Atlantic Monthly:* "During the 1980s . . . the number of Americans earning $500,000 or more a year increased by 985 percent. . . . More and richer rich, more poor, fewer in the middle: the pattern is clear, and it is a Latin American, not a North American, pattern." Haynes Johnson's new book, *Divided We Fall,* based on two years (1991–93) of interviews across the country, is "a haunting chronicle of broken promises, deferred dreams, communities scattered, faith crushed" (Loth 1994).

Conscripting the Reserve Army of the Unemployed. Bonacich (1976:47) concludes that management countered the gains of labor, from 1940 to 1960, with three responses that accelerated the descent into proletarian status: (1) relocation overseas, (2) internal relocation to right-to-work (usually rural) environments, and (3) mechanization, displacing highly paid skilled workers. Meat and poultry producers combined all three of these and added a fourth: recruitment of immigrant (primarily Mexican) labor.

Hispanics, first admitted under the bracero program as farm labor (1942–65), numbered 400,000 to 500,000 per year. Those who remained, and family members who joined them since the 1960s, have moved into food processing, restaurant work, and services (Papademetriou and Bach 1989). Currently, legal immigration is in excess of 1 million per year, augmented by an additional quarter-million illegals who are unapprehended (Copeland 1994).

The Logic of Worker Disempowerment

Disassembling the Industries: Axioms and Inferences

This discussion seeks to extract unity from diversity, if not order from chaos. Despite the welter of differences between environments, industries, and minority workers, our search for a common theme disclosed local, small-scale reproduction of processes presented in the introduction as national trends:

1. Management and labor within each industry tend toward *polarization,* as corporate units expand, administrative centers become more remote from factory sites, employment becomes impermanent, and labor becomes a "commodity" to be secured at market rates.
2. *Internationalization* advances as corporate producers decentralize investments by shifting production abroad, meanwhile recruiting labor for plants in the United States from Mexico, Central America, and Southeast Asia.
3. *Disempowerment* advances as immigrant labor pools, whose members are linguistically and culturally disadvantaged, displace indigenous workers with a tradition of collective bargaining. Unions decline in influence as their membership decreases.

Toward the end of this essay I will argue that steps now in progress to (1) regain control of U.S. borders, (2) promote more effective labor organization, and (3) upgrade the quality of the immigrant labor force may lead us to modify the implications of these recently established trends.

Let us start with a set of axioms that apply to the 1990s but were anticipated in the nineteenth century:

AXIOM: Each of these industries advances toward concentration of greater financial and productive power within a contracting number of competitive units. The key to this advance is maximizing output and reducing costs through new technology, which replaces skilled workers with machines. This process is called restructuring. (Broadway, this volume)

Increasing competitiveness through restructuring was described with prescience by Marx and Engels (1932:15–16) in *The Communist Manifesto* in 1848:

Owing to the extensive use of machinery and to the division of labor, the work of the proletarians has lost all individual character, and consequently, all charm for the workman. He becomes an appendage of the machine, and it is only the most simple, most monotonous and most easily acquired knack that is required of him. . . .

In proportion, therefore, as the repulsiveness of the work increases, the wage decreases. Nay more, in proportion as the use of machinery and division of labor increases, in the same proportion the burden of toil increases, whether by prolongation of the working hours, by increase in the work exacted in a given time, or by increased speed of machinery.

Food processors from Canada (Novek 1989) and across several regions of the United States (Stull 1994; Griffith, this volume; Hall, this volume) have confirmed the impotence of organized labor by increasing speed of disassembly lines without regard for increased rates of injury.

AXIOM: Each of these industries advances toward increasing reliance on a labor force of minimal skills, flexible work schedules, and low wages. This prescription for recruitment is best filled by creating a segmented labor market catering to recruited immigrants.

Increased reliance on a substratum of underpaid (by domestic standards) international labor migrants to perform the increasing volume of unskilled tasks in restructured industries was identified in 1917 by Lenin in his essay entitled *Imperialism: The Highest Stage of Capitalism:*

Another special feature of imperialism . . . is the increase in immigration into these countries from the backward countries where lower wages are paid. . . . In the US, immigrants from Eastern and Southern Europe are engaged in the most poorly paid occupations, while American workers provide the highest percentage of overseers or of the better paid workers. Imperialism has the tendency to create privileged sections even among the workers, and to detach them from the main proletarian masses. (1939:106)

In these early times the value of labor migration as a mechanism for reducing wages and factory working conditions to lowest terms was recognized, and the role of native-born workers in supervisor/foremen positions as a force to destroy worker solidarity within the industry was also perceived. The linkage between Lenin's comment on "immigrants from Eastern and Southern Europe" and Stull's (1994) quotes from *The Jungle* by Upton Sinclair in 1906 describing working conditions in the Chicago stockyards hardly require underlining.

We offer two inferences. First, there should be a dialectical relationship between them such that increasing restructuring of the industry becomes interdependent with expanding reliance on immigrant labor. Second, the more concentrated the industry, the larger investment it represents. To ensure adequate returns while operating on slim profit margins (Bjerklie, this volume), it must minimize transaction costs (procurement of animals, utilities, transportation), reduce the wage bill, and externalize indirect labor costs (primarily housing, health care, language instruction, skills training, and other human services).

Transaction costs are controlled by relocating the investment site to a rural environment near a source of supply (Broadway, this volume). Wage bills are reduced by eliminating higher pay grades for degrees of skill, that is, deskilling operations on the factory floor (Novek 1989). Labor costs are externalized by inviting competing communities to provide infrastructure and worker-related facilities as part of an incentive package and by choosing smaller towns to maximize political and economic leverage (Hackenberg et al. 1993).

Can we find empirical support for this chain of suppositions? The red-meat (beef) industry represents the greatest degree of concentration, with 70 to 80 percent of production controlled by IBP, ConAgra, and Excel corporations. It should follow that its plants (1) should be most recently relocated; (2) should be found in the most thinly populated rural areas; (3) represent the highest investment per plant; (4)

have the largest proportion of immigrants workers; and (5) choose to locate near the smallest towns.

The answer is affirmative. The two newest beef plants, opened in 1980 and 1990, are among the largest in the industry with the latest technology (Stull 1994:45). They are located near Holcomb, Kansas (pop. 1,400), and Lexington, Nebraska (pop. 6,601). Each employs more than 2,000 workers. Recently recruited Hispanic immigrants represent the majority of workers in each plant. Both plants are in the remote western regions of their respective states, equidistant from Kansas City, Denver, and Omaha (Gouveia and Stull, this volume). This argument is strengthened by the recent decision of Seaboard Corporation to construct one of the world's largest pork-processing plants at Guymon (pop. 8,400), a similar site in western Oklahoma.

Deconstructing the Labor Force: The Path to Disempowerment

Linkage between trends in the organization of production and worker participation can be better understood by a comparative approach to the four industry groups being examined. They are quite dissimilar across a number of dimensions.

> AXIOM: The four industries considered represent progressive stages in the movement toward concentration and a segmented labor market. There is an incremental advance from seafood through poultry to pork and beef fabrication.

As we move from stage to stage, the pattern of internal organization tends to shift from *periphery* to *core*, as these terms are used by industrial economists. The basic distinction was offered by Bluestone, Murphy, and Stevenson:

> The core economy includes those industries that comprise the muscle of American economic and political power. . . . Entrenched in durable manufacturing, the construction trades and to a lesser extent the extraction industries, the firms in the core economy are noted for high productivity, high profits, intensive utilization of capital, high incidence of monopoly elements, and a high degree of unionization. What follows . . . normally from such characteristics are high wages. . . .
>
> Beyond the fringes of the core economy lies a set of industries that lack

almost all the advantages normally found in center firms. Concentrated in agriculture, non-durable manufacturing, retail trade and subprofessional services, the peripheral industries are noted for their small firm size, labor intensity, low profits, low productivity, intensive product market competition, lack of unionization and low wages. (1973:28–29)

The core-periphery distinction among industries has been matched by partitioning the labor market into complementary components: the core industries utilize the primary labor market and the peripheral industries draw upon the secondary labor market, as noted by Hodson and Kaufman (1982:729). Corresponding to the core and periphery sectors, respectively, are separate labor markets: a primary labor market and a secondary labor market.

A key distinction between them is recorded by Tolbert, Horan, and Beck: "The organization of work in the secondary sector is characterized by low skill jobs and employment instability, whereas the organization of work in the primary sector provides job ladders, on-the-job training and a differentiated wage structure" (1980:1096).

The work environment in the primary sector has often been designated an *internal labor market* in which workers can compete, qualify for advancement to higher skills levels, and bid on better jobs as firm expansion makes them available. This "increases the cost of labor turnover since workers are no longer close substitutes for one another. . . . The rational, profit maximizing solution for core firms is to promote less turnover by providing job security" (Hodson and Kaufman 1982:730–31).

Table 11.1 presents a staging model built around the descriptions of the four food-processing components in terms of the concepts just reviewed: core and periphery industries and primary and secondary labor markets. Fish and poultry are still, to a considerable extent, peripheral industries, departing from the competitive starting point in the drive toward oligopoly. Beef and pork are core industries, moving beyond national oligopoly into the international arena of imperialistic expansion.

There is a glaring anomaly in Table 11.1, which appears when the data on the four components are compared with the definitions provided earlier. The concepts predict that *as peripheral enterprises evolve into core industries, their secondary labor markets should become primary.* Indeed food industries were first classified as peripheral by industrial sociologists (Beck, Horan, and Tolbert 1978) and later reassigned to core sta-

TABLE 11.1. Food Industry and Labor Force Components:
A Sequential Stage Model

1. Competition

Component	Type of Industry	Type of Labor Force	Size of Labor Force*	Ethnicity of Labor[†]	Community Base
Fish[‡]	Peripheral	Secondary	25–50	Native black, some Hispanic	Isolated rural[§]
Poultry	Peripheral becoming core	Secondary	250–500	Native black, some white, some Hispanic	Isolated rural[§]
Pork	Expanding core	Secondary	500–1,000	Native white, some Hispanic, some Asian	Factory town
Beef	Developed core	Secondary	1,000–2,500	Hispanic, some Asian, some white	Factory town

2. Oligopoly:
Concentration of production in United States within a few companies

3. Imperialism:
Multi-industry Concentration
Multinational Expansion

* Size of labor force per site. Numbers are illustrative rather than definitive.
[†] Top line is the predominant ethnic group in each labor force.
[‡] Does not include aquaculture/mariculture.
[§] Transportation to the plant provided.

tus (Tolbert, Horan, and Beck 1980). However, *there has been no parallel shift in upgrading the food industry labor market.*

On the contrary, the meat and poultry industries appear to be prime examples of intentional reduction of dependence on primary labor:

> The new technology has permitted a substantial amount of *deskilling*. In the years following World War II, inside the factory and later the office, managers were introducing new machinery and radically reorganizing work tasks in ways that reduced their dependence on high priced skilled labor. . . .
>
> The creation of these new technologies, and the work reorganizations to implement them, made it easier for managers to take advantage of new sources of cheap and . . . tractable labor in peripheral locations, both within the country and beyond its borders. (Bluestone and Harrison 1982:117)

Novek identifies the source of deskilling in meat industries as the dismantling of the master contracts previously negotiated by unions:

> The shopfloor organization of labor was highly fragmented and a complex system of job classifications, work rules and labor grades evolved through the process of collective bargaining. One midsize packing plant with about 600 employees . . . had 26 major job classifications, 406 subclassifications and 41 pay scale related labor grades in its collective agreement. Other regulations govern work rules and hours of work.
>
> The key to disestablishing meat packing as a core labor market lay in the master agreements which had controlled wages and working conditions across 80 percent of the industry since 1946. In 1984 the pattern of industry wide collective bargaining came unglued. (1989:165–68)

Master contracts such as this, with built-in pay differentials and grades of advancement for which workers could bid (Burawoy 1983), constructed a stepladder of upward mobility, that is, the internal labor market. Such contracts have been replaced, industry-wide, with terms of employment dictated by individual firms. Deskilling converts most workers to perform tasks "which are machine-paced, repetitive and technically controlled" (Novek 1989:168). With little differentiation between job descriptions, there is neither advancement nor salary increments.

Burawoy (1983) adds that avoidance of differential skill levels and refined division of labor in the secondary labor market provides for management's encouragement of turnover and frequent replacement without worker protest or resentment. If there is no loss of seniority or privileged position, the revolving door of alternating employment and idleness involves loss of neither position nor status.

Other dimensions of Table 11.1 are worthy of comment. The advance from early to later stages discloses a progressive tendency to reduce the representation of the native-born, both blacks and whites. In their places we find a small proportion of refugee Asians and an increasing and predominant number of immigrant Hispanics.

Another uniformity is the increasing size of the workforce as we move from stage to stage in the table. One dimension of labor organization is the union—a large contractual structure based on secondary relationships. Another dimension of labor organization is the small face-to-face task force (or work circle) of persons forming a primary group. The primary group, but not the union, may be found among fisherfolk. *Neither* the primary group *nor* effective union organization may be found among the Hispanics on many of the packing-plant disassembly lines.

In each of the industries considered here, formidable concentrations of financial power and intricate corporate raiding have created oligopoly—production of a key commodity controlled by a few giants. The power represented has been used to break labor contracts, dictate terms to state governments, and create bidding contests between communities competing to become plant sites.

And each monolithic enterprise is complemented by its polar opposite: a supine and docile labor force consisting of one or another of the recent migrant streams of political and economic refugees managing to find their way here from Mexico, Central America, Southeast Asia, or the Caribbean. While these groups represent a variety of cultures, languages, and nationalities, they are united by their socioeconomic circumstances.

We find them everywhere, submerged below the poverty line by near-minimum wages, living in substandard housing, medically indigent, and, because of intermittent unemployment, a burden on social services. Their helplessness in dealing with employers is matched by the impotence of the small towns where they have taken up residence. Neither labor nor community is in a position to bargain.

Ironies abound in this situation. Within this decade, the shibboleths of "empowerment" and its companion, "revitalizing local democracy," echo endlessly through the rhetoric of political soothsayers and development planners. At the same time, union membership has shrunk to 12 percent of the nonagricultural labor force, and small communities confront the loss of banks, hospitals, and public transportation as their populations age and diminish.

Disempowerment is multidimensional, as the international, national, and industrial data considered to this point disclose. At a minimum, it consists of the following:

1. Demise and fragmentation of union representation.
2. Disappearance of the internal labor markets with stratified occupational hierarchies within established industries.
3. Unlimited supplies of labor resulting from migration and refugee policies.
4. Lack of political leverage as a result of immigration status, language and cultural barriers, and relatively high spatial mobility.

Is this condition "terminal"? The balance of this essay will consider the possibility that disempowerment may not be a permanent condition for the new proletariat.

Quitting the Plant

Catalysts for Immigrant Achievement

Hispanics constitute the most recent tide of migration to sweep across the United States. From an adaptive standpoint, they are linguistically handicapped and have few transferable skills. But earlier in this century they were preceded by an inundation of migrants from peasant origins whose disadvantages were similar, and whose immediate fate was the packing plants of Upton Sinclair's *Jungle*. Like today's Hispanics, the major asset of the eastern and southern Europeans was motivation; unlike the Hispanics, their ascent from poverty was rapid and permanent. Their progress has recently been examined for the lessons it may hold for today's arrivals.

In his seminal essay entitled *A Piece of the Pie: Blacks and White Immigrants Since 1880*, published in 1981, Stanley Lieberson examines the conditions that enabled eastern and southern European immigrants to both survive and succeed in northern industrial cities, while black labor migrants from the South remained an urban underclass without the comparable capacity to compete (Wilson 1987; MacLeod 1987).

The descendants of European immigrants benefited to a greater degree than African Americans, though both shared substantial improvements in living standards. In examining the contrast between them, Lieberson invokes determinants that identify a powerful corollary to events and groups described by the authors in the present volume.

On a playing field leveled by government intervention and labor organization, asks Lieberson, why did African Americans fare much worse than descendants of the European migration stream? First, the ethnic tide from southern and eastern Europe represented concentrated settlement in major industrial cities of the Northeast, where they were registered as voters and organized into political machines. They acquired political leverage and could command patronage and favors from elected officials.

Second, as they acquired skills that qualified them for the better jobs in the factory system (arc welder, riveter, sheet-metal fitter, die maker), their wages and benefits improved. And since the gate was closed on further immigration from their points of origin in 1924, there were no followers who could bid down wage rates. Skilled labor acquired scarcity value.

With electoral participation and job security, the Europeans and their descendants actually achieved in the early postwar decades the nebulous goal held out to minorities in the 1990s. They were *empowered*. Lieberson (1981) found the sources of successful adjustment and upward mobility to be (1) the use of political instruments by organized voters; (2) access to (and graduation from) good secondary schools; (3) differential job skills; and (4) the exclusion of subsequent (competitive) immigrants of the same background.

African Americans in the northern industrial cities were politically inactive, unlikely to finish secondary school, and constantly challenged by migrants who came after them—Marx's "reserve army of the unemployed"–which made it possible for industries to obtain unskilled African-American labor at entry-level wages that were well below subsistence requirements (Sullivan 1985).

Bonacich (1976:48) adds another factor, more frequently cited today than 20 years ago: access to welfare makes African Americans less inclined to accept the most disagreeable and underpaid employment. As a consequence, 70 percent of migrant farmworkers are now Hispanic instead of African American (Mines 1992). Auletta (1983) and Wilson (1987) base the definition of the underclass on persistent unemployment associated with pervasive residence in poverty. They identify 70 percent of the membership in this category as nonwhite. For a spirited counterargument, however, see Jones (1993).

Can we apply Lieberson's formula to today's immigrant workers, largely Hispanic in origin, and largely isolated within small communities where their work sites are located? What are the essentials to be transferred from the experience of previous migrants? Each of the following seems necessary:

1. An internal labor market within a field of employment, or a comparable ladder of sequenced positions providing for opportunity and competitive placement, e.g., civil service.
2. Skills training and language instruction clearly related to the preceding. Training should be done with a job placement in sight.
3. Socialization of members into political action coalitions so that they may acquire leverage with federal, state, and local representatives.

4. Exclusion of further immigration by prospective competitors so that the labor pool remains limited to present members.

None of these conditions can be met at present by a substantial number of Hispanic households arriving as labor immigrants. We must determine what is necessary to enable them to do so.

It is more than coincidental that three waves of migrants have traversed parts of the United States in the past century: eastern and southern Europeans, southern African Americans, and Hispanics. Substantial proportions of each wave found initial employment in the packing plants of major meat companies in the cities and towns of the Midwest, and now the Southeast.

For the Poles and Italians, it was *up and out*. For a significant minority of blacks, it was *down and out*. For the Hispanics in all of our target industries, to many observers, it appears to be *in and out*. Informed commentary often continues the impression that, despite their increasing penetration of a wider range of employment sectors, Hispanics are either temporary or cyclical migrants and, as individuals, "they will soon be gone" (to be replaced, of course, by others).

This predisposition readily translates, either consciously or not, into a convenient denial of responsibility (1) for job continuity; (2) for language instruction; (3) for quality education; (4) for health care; (5) for child care; and (6) for retirement benefits. It also rationalizes the "revolving door" concept of transient employment at entry level wages, because "they will soon be gone."

This is the point at which we must attack the problem.

Getting Started: From Labor Migrant to Labor Activist

Little Mexicos—usually nothing more colorful than rental trailer courts—are mushrooming across the Midwest and Southeast. They cause more trouble to school principals because of arrivals and departures of children than to anyone else, at least at first. Temporary housing is appropriate for temporary residents. But are these temporary residents?

The most authoritative research on Hispanic movement out of Mexico and into the United States has been conducted by Douglas Massey and associates (Massey et al. 1988), based on a retrospective inquiry completed in 1982–83 on four communities in Jalisco and Michoacán. In a summary article he reported as follows:

A prominent view is that Mexican migrants are temporary rather than permanent immigrants to the United States. Cornelius . . . argues that Mexican migrants are "sojourners" rather than "settlers" and that their long-term impact on the nation will be much less than their large numbers now suggest. . . . However, as temporary migrants make repeated trips northward and accumulate time in the United States, many can be expected to settle. . . . After accumulating 10 years of migrant experience, 42% of rural migrants and 53% of urban migrants have settled in the United States. (Massey 1987:1389–90)

Massey proposes a four-stage model of the migration experience, extending over a decade for most migrant households. Across this interval he affirms that the pull factor is "a class of unstable, poorly paid jobs with limited opportunities for advancement. Since natives shun these jobs, employers turn to foreign workers and typically initiate migration through recruitment" (Massey 1987:1373).

The four stages identified by Massey are:

1. *Departure,* usually of a young father who is a landless farmworker with a few years of schooling.
2. *Repeat migration,* now with wife and children; after three trips the probability of continued migration and settlement increases.
3. *Settlement,* which is most likely to occur for a migrant household when the head has reached age 30, or when he has acquired legal status.
4. *Return,* which is most probable among persons who own property or have invested in a business at their place of origin. As length of stay increases and wages accumulate, probability of return diminishes.

Massey has identified a continuum describing the increasing probability of permanent settlement, *if migrants are followed longitudinally either prospectively or retrospectively.* However, a crosscut at any single point in time would identify many present and prospective settlers as sojourners. A constraint on accepting Massey's data for purposes of broader generalization is that most of his sample had been engaged in agriculture in California under the bracero program.

Leo Chavez (1988) published results from a survey of 2,103 Mexican adults interviewed in San Diego and Dallas. They were nonagricultural workers, employed primarily in services and secondarily in manufacturing. Chavez confirmed most of Massey's conclusions, including the following:

1. Family formation within the United States or movement to the United States with spouse leads to permanent settlement.
2. A shift from seasonal farm work to 12-month urban-based employment promotes permanent settlement.
3. The traditional return migrant leaves family members in Mexico. The permanent settler brings family to the United States.
4. Two-thirds of family households (68 percent) said their permanent residence was in the United States.

In a follow-up study, Chavez (1990) replicated many of these conclusions, adding that five years of residence was a threshold beyond which three-fourths of his sample did not intend to return to Mexico.

The sojourner versus settler question is of profound significance to the concerns of this book and, more pragmatically, to the communities hosting Hispanic households employed by any of the four industries. It is linked with another question of equal impact: Should the employer strategy regarding the recruited Hispanic households be regarded as retention or replacement?

In one of the most-cited works in this field, Burawoy (1976) considers the reliance on migrant labor as most advantageous to employer and host community when workers are frequently replaced sojourners. In addition to minimizing the wage bill to the industry, the costs of reproducing the labor force are fully externalized, being borne by the source locations in Mexico. The argument is more fully developed by Meillassoux (1981). It was demonstrated with data from the QXR plant (Hackenberg and Kukulka, this volume) that slightly more than half of the hourly Hispanic workers have averaged 1.21 years on the factory floor. QXR practices replacement. But if dismissed workers remain in Valley View, Kansas, they have become settlers, even though they may circulate to adjacent communities for alternative income sources (the industrial nomad pattern). It appears that the QXR plant has indeed externalized the cost of reproducing its labor force, but to Kansas instead of Michoacán! The data presented on births to Hispanic households from the Methodist Clinic in Garden City can leave little doubt as to who bears the reproductive expenses.

In the beefpacking plants of the Midwest, Hispanic settlers, despite their nomadic style of intermittent employment in a variety of enterprises, tend to remain within the region. This inference is based on the continuity of clinic records maintained in Garden City and the data on reemployment at the QXR plant. It is tentative but indicative.

These settlers will be either a backbreaking burden on small communities with limited income sources, further reduced by incentive payments to packing-plant operators, or a population increment that could become a valuable political resource. To explore the latter position, we must turn to an argument advanced by Teresa Sullivan (1986).

Sullivan assumes that Hispanic migration moves along a temporal continuum of repeated and lengthening visits, transforming sojourners to settlers, as described by Massey. However, she adds a third category: *activists*. These Hispanic households are long-term residents, are invested in the United States (house and/or insurance payments, possible purchase of income-generating property, credit union or savings association membership), are fluent in English, reside with family, and are present or prospective voters.

If their numbers are sufficient and if intragroup contact is continuous, they may pursue an economic strategy, a political strategy, or both. The economic strategy is based on the *enclave* (Portes and Stepick 1985). It assumes that it is possible for Hispanics to direct a number of their purchases, rent payments, and the like *inside* their own community. Accumulated purchasing power within the community can be translated into Hispanic-operated enterprises, which generate employment as well as profits, savings, and further investment.

The political strategy may be pursued with or without capital formation within the group. Activists, says Sullivan, are

> self-conscious (perhaps class-conscious) political and economic actors. If they are native born or naturalized, they vote. They follow community affairs, and they have widespread networks of friends and relatives. Their political leverage can potentially improve the competitive position of Chicanos/Mexicans vis-à-vis other ethnic groups. Their time and money are fully invested within the U.S. community. . . . The existence of activists is a necessary, though insufficient, condition for the existence of a labor market enclave. Sojourners or settlers are likely employees for an activist employer. (1986:65–66)

Both Lieberson (1981) and Sullivan (1986) are aware of the significance of numbers and ethnic density for the pursuit of activist strategies. However, it is the *proportion* of Hispanics in the community and their citizenship status, rather than absolute numbers, that create the opportunity for activism. In the small towns adjacent to packing plants in the Midwest, Hispanics may represent one-fourth or more of the population. But, as Sullivan points out, they are likely, at least in the early years of settlement, to be distributed across sojourner and settler categories. Activism is a product of length of residence, in addition to ethnic population size and density.

Capitalists and Communities

The Bourgeoisie on the Buffalo Commons

The prospects for activism as a path to minority self-improvement, and escape from disempowerment, depend on community resources. The community cannot be pressured or persuaded to share or dispense what it does not have. To complete the review of the issues raised by the contributors to this volume, we must acknowledge the distorted relationship evolving between corporations and the communities selected for plant sites, for this relationship provides the context for prospective improvement in the status of minority workers.

Griffith, in his discussion of sites for poultry plants in the Southeast in this volume, mentions the expressed desire of managers to choose declining communities at some distance from a thriving city that would offer competitive job opportunities. In the Midwest, the massive investments of packing-plant operators in new high technology contrast sharply with the occasional ill-informed suggestion from environmentalists that the region be returned to a vast "commons" for grazing buffalo.

But, upon closer examination, at least three ominous trends can be discerned for communities intending to profit from investments in "meat-fabrication" facilities.

The Anomaly of Scale. The tendency of ever-larger plants to be placed next to ever-smaller communities has escaped comment. In an earlier decade, the choice of plant sites fell among small cities of 20,000 or so population. In Kansas, for example, Dodge City, Garden City, and Emporia were all selected. During the past 15 years, however, massive beef- and pork-processing facilities have been sited at Holcomb, Kansas (pop. 1,400), Lexington, Nebraska (pop. 6,601), and Guymon, Oklahoma (pop. 8,400).

Each new site was chosen after competitive bidding that involved the assembly of incentive packages: utilities investments, provision of plant sites, tax holidays, and the like. The provision of incentives was justified by the expectation that local residents would be employed and that substantial stimuli would be provided to local business.

Instead, the recruited labor force consisted of "outsiders" and the advantages enjoyed by local business have been minimal (Gouveia and Stull, this volume; Stull, Broadway, and Erickson 1992). These newly opened facilities are all examples of absentee management from remote business centers; IBP plants in Kansas, for example, are administered from Dakota City, Nebraska.

Because of commitments to incentives, local communities will sustain losses for a period of years following the opening of these new plants. Because management is remote, corporations cannot be expected to become "good citizens" of the population centers in which their workers reside. Because of the disproportion in scale, it appears unlikely that the towns will be able to exercise much political leverage to secure advantages in the near term.

Company-Based Contract Networks. Companies pursue procurement strategies that assure them of substantial political influence within the small community adjacent to the plant site. The fabrication plant, for either poultry or beef and pork, has an insatiable capacity for raw materials, that is, animals. On-time delivery is essential to profitable operation.

The mechanism of choice is grower contracts. Heffernan provides an elaborate description of terms for poultry producers:

> Today, if farmers wish to produce poultry commercially, they must sign a contract with an integrating firm. . . . By 1981, little opportunity existed for the limited resource farmer. . . . [A]n adequately constructed and equipped poultry building cost over $80,000. The grower is responsible for the cost. . . . [W]ith the requirement of two or three buildings per grower . . . the capital required is over a quarter of a million dollars [and] they borrow the necessary funds. This sets the stage for a tremendous power inequality between integrating firm and grower. In 1981, 87 of 90 growers interviewed still had debt on their buildings. (1984:247–48)

Heffernan continues with the observation that integrating firms usually require contract growers to modify structures before initial loans are repaid. Firms advance feed on account, weigh birds, and deduct costs before net returns to growers are calculated. The firms keep the books.

Networks of contract growers are well established among pork producers. In 1991, 78 percent of slaughter hogs were raised by large producers marketing more than 1,000 head per year (Rhodes 1993). Over 10 percent of hog production is in the hands of "superproducers" who market more than 50,000 head per year. Three-fourths of these are contract growers.

A case study of the community, corporation, and contractor relationship is provided by the 1992 decision of Seaboard Corporation to locate a mammoth pork plant in Guymon, Oklahoma. Seaboard's investment will be more than $50 million, the plant will ultimately process 16,000 hogs per day, and the ultimate target is 4 million hogs per year.

To secure this plant, Guymon's leaders placed competitive bids against Dodge City, Liberal, and Garden City, Kansas; and Dalhart and Amarillo, Texas. Incentives included $8 million "up front," to be repaid from a one-cent sales tax, to be collected over 15 years. In return, Seaboard pledged $175,000 per year to the Guymon school system, payable over 25 years. Seaboard will also be granted a five-year tax holiday by the state of Oklahoma (MacDonald 1993).

The industry is puzzled over Seaboard's expected source of "materials," that is, slaughter hogs. By April 1993, however, 140 applications had been filed by persons interested in engaging in contract hog production. Terms are as follows: Seaboard will supply pigs, feed, medication, and transportation. Farmers will provide buildings, land, labor, management, utilities, maintenance, insurance, and taxes. A contractor must construct a minimum of three buildings at a cost of $135,000 each, together with a well, lagoons, and site preparation (Wilson 1993). Close to half a million dollars per contractor will be needed.

These details have been provided in order to frame a troublesome question. Under the conditions imposed by corporations on poultry and hog producers, and the credit liabilities that contractors have assumed, how much political independence can a small community retain?

Environmental Protection. Persons other than fanatical environmentalists are concerned over the consequences of the scale on which beef, pork, and poultry producers are operating. On March 21, 1994, a thought-provoking article appeared in the *New York Times* concerning Hennessy, Oklahoma (pop. 1,800). It has been selected by the Pig Improvement

Corporation, a British company, as the site on which it proposes to produce 100,000 hogs:

> European companies are taking advantage of America's less stringent pollution standards. And the General Agreement on Tariffs and Trade will dramatically increase the amount of pork the US can export to Europe—624,000 metric tons in 1999, up from less than 100,000 tons in 1991. This will make the US the center of global pork production, and companies are rushing to raise hogs in new places. One Danish company plans to raise 600,000 hogs in Alaska.
>
> The trouble with huge hog farms is the manure they produce. . . . If the Pig Improvement Company brings 100,000 hogs to Hennessy, the result will be the sewage equivalent of 170,000 people. (Casey and Hobbs 1994)

Let us return for a moment to Seaboard Corporation's operation in the Oklahoma Panhandle. With an anticipated slaughter capacity of 16,000 hogs per day, and all the company's contract growers within a radius of 50 miles, the pollution problem could be massive. But the community has been assured by Rob McCulloch, Seaboard's farm manager, that "the open hog units do not smell" (Wilson 1993). He informed a gathering of concerned citizens that the dry weather, porous soil, and management practice of rotating herds around plots of at least 160 acres would prevent contamination. Many citizens were unconvinced.

The point of this section is not to echo environmentalist mantras. The risk of toxicity is one more cost that the industry has externalized. It should be added to the other "externalities" imposed on small communities by the uncompensated needs of minority workers, including the costs of health and welfare, housing and security, language teaching and skills training.

The asymmetrical relationship between the corporation and the community places the latter in a position analogous to that of minority workers. Can communities and minorities identify common causes? Can either or both of them combine with others to form multicommunity interest groups? In short, to bring this essay to full circle, can they organize?

The Spirit of Joe Hill

I dreamed I saw Joe Hill last night, alive as you and me, Says I, "But Joe your ten years dead," "I never died," says he.

And standing there as big as life and smiling with his eyes Joe says, "What they forgot to kill went on to organize."

From San Diego up to Maine in every mine and mill Where workers strike and organize, says he, "You'll find Joe Hill." (Hayes 1925, in Smith 1969, pp. 194–95)

Regaining Control of Our Borders: The El Paso Model

The stream of immigrant labor entering the United States is not exclusively Hispanic, nor does it derive entirely from Mexico. But whatever its origin, Stanly Lieberson's point remains unchallenged. An unlimited supply of unskilled labor will continue to drive wages down, and eventually the native-born will display resentment and discriminate against the newcomers. This point has already been reached in southern California. It becomes necessary to block or greatly reduce the volume of immigration in the interest of recent arrivals if we wish to increase their earnings by requiring employers to bid against each other for their services.

The consensus of two of the best-informed writers on migration issues, Wayne Cornelius (1993) and Saskia Sassen (1992), is that entry of Mexicans into the United States will be increased by NAFTA. The primary reason is the predicted removal of traditional agriculturists from *ejidos* (communal farms established by President Cardenas) under the privatization law pronounced by President Salinas in 1992.

The secondary determinant is the anticipated displacement of additional thousands of farm operators whose income depends upon producing the heavily subsidized Mexican corn crop. NAFTA requires the elimination of the subsidy, which raises the price of Mexican corn to twice that of imported corn from the United States. The internal Mexican corn market will collapse, and heavy migration will occur from the central states.

Is this an admission of defeat? Not quite. Contrary to the conventional wisdom, illegal border crossings in the vicinity of El Paso have been reduced by 85 to 95 percent, beginning in September 1993 and continuing to the present. It was the fear of many observers that militaristic and repressive measures, including wholesale violations of human rights, would be employed in the effort to "regain control of our borders" (Jimenez 1992).

In fact, the El Paso experiment demonstrates that increased surveillance alone, in the conspicuous absence of intimidation, will get the job done. The secret weapon was redeployment:

> The reform was a sharp de-emphasis of the hot pursuit of illegal immigrants after they cross the border. The redeployment was a new concentration of agents along the borderline itself. Of 650 agents in the district, 400 were now deployed along the border. . . . Apprehensions for illegal entry have dropped to about 150 from an average daily level of 800 to 1,000. . . . The new approach will continue indefinitely, without new funding, as Operation Hold the Line. (Miles 1994:34)

El Paso citizens, 75 percent of Hispanic ancestry, have supported the program, and merchants report that business is back to 85 to 90 percent of its preoperation volume. Thefts and shoplifting have sharply declined.

The report on the El Paso experience concludes:

> The normal rate of legal border crossings at El Paso is estimated by the INS at 120,000 per day, or well over 35 million a year. If Operation Hold the Line has reduced the number of apprehensions of illegals . . . by more than 85 percent while keeping the border open to ordinary traffic, staying within the existing budget and lowering the level of violence and citizens' complaints, then this approach merits serious consideration as a border control model. (Miles 1994:42)

The focus of Miles's essay is California, the most frequent point for illegal Hispanic entry. He argues that if the Immigration and Naturalization Service at San Diego could replicate the El Paso experience, then a proposal that would initiate immigrant political activism might be attempted. Jorge Castaneda argues that illegal Mexican immigrants in California should not just be legalized but also be given the vote!

California is the most explosive pressure point on the issue of the costs and consequences of its swelling Hispanic minority. Castaneda's argument (presented in Miles 1994) is as follows:

1. Reorganize the Immigration and Naturalization Service to effectively eliminate further illegal entry. Both Hispanics and Anglos in California favor this.

2. Once this has been accomplished and recognized, authorize amnesty and legalize the status of present illegal residents.
3. Enfranchise them to vote in state and local (but not national) elections.

Castaneda admonishes that continued refusal to permit several million state residents to vote essentially de-democratizes the political process across the state.

His example drawn from the present situation in Los Angeles is disturbing; it could probably be replicated in the factory towns we have examined: "Sixty-three percent of the students in the Los Angeles Unified School District are Latinos, many of whose parents are legally ineligible to vote, but . . . 88 percent of those who actually vote have no children in school" (Miles 1994:33). In a healthy democracy, the self-interest of the parents would be seen to coincide with the long-term self-interest of the society. Detachment of parents from the system fosters disinterest in education and increases dropout rates and gang membership, and so on down the slippery slope to urban riots.

Castaneda observes that the Scandinavian countries, Ireland, the Netherlands, and Switzerland already permit immigrants to vote in state and local elections. The proposal parallels earlier observations concerning the potential benefits to be secured both from closing the border and from worker activism. In California's present political climate the Wilson administration would find it unthinkable—even outrageous. However, as in the case of school desegregation, local enfranchisement may be only one Supreme Court decision away.

But the European and black migrant experiences in Chicago were contrasted by a generation of sociologists (Bonacich 1976; Lieberson 1981; Sullivan 1986) to make a critical point. The *right* to vote is necessary but not sufficient. It's the strategic *use* of the vote that confers empowerment. And so we come full circle with the admonition with which we began: organize.

The Spirit of Joe Hill: Trade Union Revival in the Meat Industries

The background of social change is often more important than the foreground. The anthropologist develops a holistic perspective on the issues of concern to minority workers in the meat, poultry, and fish industries. From this point of view, interlocking determinants such as closing the border and progress toward political activism may generate more basic lifestyle improvements than a frontal assault on one or more specific economic issues.

But the minority worker and the Hispanic household do not share this view. Their concerns are specifically related to the substance of industry employment and related factors of family life. They want changes in line speeds, production quotas, tools and equipment, workers' compensation, injury rates, medical evaluations, insurance coverage, rehabilitation arrangements, and, of course, periodic upgrades in job classification with appropriate salary increments and recognition of seniority.

In the words of an older generation of union shop stewards, these are "pork chop" issues, and the reference is appropriate to the industries at hand. These concerns were the substance of bargaining agreements negotiated by union representatives with management in order to conclude the terms of the annual or biennial contract. At least that's the way it was back in the years of the union shop. Could it happen again?

Without any special legislation, favorable court decisions, or massive increases in demand for meat products, it *is* happening. And the mechanism is the organizing election under the watchful eye of the National Labor Relations Board (NLRB). In 1993, for the first time in two decades, union membership increased. Numbers declined from 22 million in 1975 to 16.4 million in 1992. But in the following year there was a net growth of 200,000 recruits (Judis 1994:25).

A significant part of that increment was added at the Monfort beef plant in Greeley, Colorado. In a successful organizing election on April 29, 1993, the United Food and Commercial Workers Union (UFCW) overcame substantial opposition, and narrowly reversed a loss in 1983. The UFCW representative affirmed that the Monfort vote is likely to be one of the largest union victories of the year.

The union plans to petition NRLB for organizing elections in two other Monfort plants in Greeley and Grand Island, Nebraska. The outcome was even more surprising since Monfort intimated that it would reconsider a profit-sharing plan that would provide a benefit of $1,500 per year to each worker should the UFCW be the winner (Leib 1993a).

The Monfort experience is not an isolated case. Substantial organizing success is being reported among white-collar, service, and government workers. And the union of most importance to meat and poultry workers, the UFCW, has reported the largest gains: "Since 1988, the UFCW has increased the number of unionized workers in retail grocery stores from 67 percent to 72 percent and in meat packing from 50 percent to 65 percent. The UFCW, which added 100,000 workers during the entire 1980s, added the same amount in 1993 alone" (Judis 1994:25). Judis attributes labor's awakening from a long sleep to new and younger leadership, more interested in recruitment and expansion than in cutting deals with corporate management to favor older, contract-protected members of the "rank and file."

The new spirit has been captured by an older observer with a long memory. Nat Hentoff writes as follows:

> There still are, to be sure, some organizers with the fire of Joe Hill of the Industrial Workers of the World [who are inspired by his final admonition]: "Don't waste time in mourning: Organize."
>
> That's what the Organizing Institute—formed by a dozen awakening unions and based in Washington—has been doing. The 700 new organizers it has trained are not mourning labor's defeat over NAFTA. They're going into the shops that have never seen a union organizer.
>
> On National Public Radio, Bob Lawson of the Organizing Institute noted that the emphasis in the new organizing is on "the changing nature of the work force. The influx of women, people of color, of new immigrants . . . those are the people who are being most exploited."
>
> The other priority in the new organizing drives is the realization, Lawson says, that "union organizers who come from those backgrounds—and relate to those people—are going to be the backbone of rebuilding the labor movement in this country." (Hentoff 1994)

An example of a young and effective union organizer, a minority member who has risen to a prominent position in a major union is 37-year-old Ernest Duran, Jr., a 1981 law school graduate of the University of Colorado. The union is Local 7 (Colorado) of the United Food and Commercial Workers:

> This year, Duran emerged as Colorado's most charismatic labor leader as he led grocery workers in negotiations with the state's leading grocery chains. . . .
>
> As Colorado's largest union, Local 7 represents more than 20,000 employees in the grocery, meatpacking and health care industries in Colorado. . . .

Ernie Duran's ancestors have inhabited southern Colorado for five or six generations. His heritage is richly varied. There are Mexican, French and Native American branches of the family tree. . . .

Local 7, UFCW, represents many Hispanic workers in Colorado's meatpacking industry, and Duran's greatest bargaining challenge may come when he sits at the negotiating table with representatives from Monfort, Inc. (Leib 1993b)

Corporate management is aware of the revival of organized labor and is exerting every effort to contest, intimidate, and reverse the process:

Corporate management has aggressively fought unionization and has even attempted to decertify existing unions. They have used the threat of moving jobs overseas to intimidate workers . . . they have hired anti-union consultants to contest representative elections; and they have sometimes refused to sign contracts . . . when they have lost union elections. Many of their tactics violate existing labor law. In 1957 the NRLB ordered reinstatement of 922 workers fired illegally for organizing a union; *in 1980 more than 10,000 workers were reinstated.* (Judis 1994:29)

Both the successful elections in Colorado in which Ernest Duran and the UFCW were involved are being contested. A bill to outlaw management's use of strikebreakers ("replacement workers") and another to strengthen health and safety rules are presently being fought out in Congress. Secretary of Labor Robert Reich and Secretary of Commerce Ron Brown have appointed a Commission for the Future of Worker-Management Relations, which is charged with proposing changes in labor law.

Labor-management relations are conflict-ridden, and labor is making gains against the odds. Militancy could result from escalation. Open conflict was the major mistake of the Industrial Workers of the World, whose organizers followed Haywood's commandment to "fan the flames of discontent." Some of us drive past Ludlow, Colorado, on I-25, the highway from Denver to the south and west. It was the scene of a massacre of immigrant miners on strike in 1914. Neither the labor movement nor minority workers need any more martyrs.

From the writer's vantage point, informed by the Aspen Institute conference on "New Factory Workers in Old Farming Communities," the substance of which appears in this book, several options are indicated. The path outlined by Lieberson (1981) and Sullivan (1986) toward improved socioeconomic status may be pursued, with effective border closing, largely on the initiative of minority members themselves.

Institutional assistance in attaining empowerment may be provided by government intervention to raise wages and benefits, regulate the workplace, and strengthen the bargaining position of organized labor. But there is a real fear, as Bonacich (1976) predicted 20 years ago, that inflicting these costs on industry will drive factories overseas.

There is a third option, not discussed in this essay. It is the "human capital" option now openly advocated by Labor Secretary Robert Reich and a number of other representatives of management and labor, such as Charles Cerami (1994). Reich foresees an era of "flexible system" enterprises in which management must shift its product design almost continuously and workers must have the aptitudes to both follow and facilitate the process:

> Unlike high-volume production, where most of a firm's value is represented by physical assets, the principal store of value in flexible system enterprises is human assets. Specialized machines and unskilled workers cannot adapt easily to new situations. Flexible machines and teams of skilled workers can. Only people can recognize and solve novel problems. The future prosperity of America . . . will depend on our citizens' ability to recognize and solve new problems, for the simple reason that processes which make routine the solutions to older problems are . . . the special province of the developing nations. . . .
>
> Unless America moves quickly into the new era in which upgrading and using our human capital become central concerns, however, our future wealth will come primarily from extracting coal, timber, and grain from our lands, from assembling advanced components that have been designed elsewhere, and from distributing the resulting products to our own citizens. We will become a nation of extractors, assemblers and retailers—poor by the standards of the rest of the world. (Reich 1983:234–38)

So there is still hope. Reich's formula, written a decade before his ascent to the president's cabinet, is now government policy. Results are awaited.

Action, improperly conceived or poorly executed, may have adverse consequences. But, as the contributors to this volume point out, inaction will have consequences also. The lifestyle and socioeconomic status of many minority-worker households described in these pages is in decline. Their fertility rate alone determines that the numbers sharing their fate will multiply. The specter of an expanding underclass looms before us.

The "Latin Americanization" of our secondary labor force—referring to a permanent lower tier of our society—has been used repeatedly as a term of reference. In a now-classic study, Janice Perlman labeled a similar group in Rio de Janeiro the *marginal class* and offered an often-quoted characterization of marginality: "Specifically, [marginals] are mostly visible and identifiable as living in peripheral, sub-standard housing settlements, they are predominantly of migrant origin, and they are generally employed in the most unstable and least remunerative jobs" (1976:96). In a diagnostic table, Perlman (1976:130–31) adds the characteristics of internal social disorganization, isolation from the dominant community, political apathy, and potential radicalism.

The goodness of fit between the concept of marginality and the minority labor force we have described needs no emphasis here. But there is another aspect of Perlman's assessment that is also troubling: the acceptance of a marginal class, and passive exploitation of it, as a permanent feature of the social system by a nation's middle and upper classes. Except among the practitioners of liberation theology, moral indignation seems to have burned out in Brazil. In the United States also, it seems to be the exclusive property of certain churches.

Robert Reich heralds the arrival of a new industrial order, with a prominent place reserved for an upgraded labor force. Janice Perlman warns against the permanent damage that accommodation to a marginal class of impoverished industrial nomads could inflict on our society.

Perhaps, through no fault of our own, we can still choose.

References

Auletta, K. 1983. *The Underclass.* New York: Random House.

Barnet, R., and R. Muller. 1974. *Global Reach.* New York: Simon and Schuster.

Beatty, J. 1994. Who Speaks for the Middle Class? *Atlantic Monthly* 273(5):65–79.

Beck, E. M., P. Horan, and C. Tolbert. 1978. Stratification in a Dual Economy. *American Sociological Review* 43:704–20.

Bluestone, B., and B. Harrison. 1982. *The Deindustrialization of America.* New York: Basic Books.

Bluestone, B., W. Murphy, and M. Stevenson. 1973. *Low Wages and the Working Poor.* Ann Arbor: Institute of Industrial and Labor Relations, University of Michigan.

Bonacich, E. 1976. Advanced Capitalism and Black/White Relations in the United States: A Split Labor Market Interpretation. *American Sociological Review* 41:34–51.

Burawoy, M. 1976. The Functions and Reproduction of Migrant Labor: Comparative Material from South Africa and the United States. *American Journal of Sociology* 81:1050–87.

———. 1983. Factory Regimes Under Advanced Capitalism. *American Sociological Review* 48:587–605.

Casey, J. A., and C. Hobbs. 1994. Look What the GATT Dragged In. *New York Times,* March 21.

Cerami, C. 1994. Three New Ways to Create Jobs. *Atlantic Monthly* 273(3):102–8.

Chavez, L. R. 1988. Sojourners and Settlers: The Case of Mexicans in the United States. *Human Organization* 47:95–108.

Chavez, L. R., E. Flores, and M. Lopez-Garza. 1990. Here Today, Gone Tomorrow? Undocumented Settlers and Immigration Reform. *Human Organization* 49:193–205.

Copeland, P. 1994. Economic Impact of Immigrants. *Rocky Mountain News,* May 25.

Cornelius, W. 1993. The Uncertain Connection: Free Trade and Rural Mexican Migration to the United States. *International Migration Review* 27:484–512.

Dos Passos, J. 1930. *Nineteen Nineteen.* New York: Random House, pp. 422–23.

Eaton, W. 1994. Path to Nowhere: Many Americans Working Longer, Getting Less. *Denver Post,* June 3.

Erickson, K. C. 1994. Guys in White Hats: Short-Term Participant Observation Among Beef-Processing Workers and Managers. In *Newcomers in the Workplace: Immigrants and the Restructuring of the U.S. Economy,* edited by L. Lamphere, A. Stepick, and G. Grenier. Philadelphia: Temple University Press, pp. 78–98.

Hackenberg, R., D. Griffith, D. Stull, and L. Gouveia. 1993. Creating a Disposable Labor Force. *Aspen Institute Quarterly* 5(2):78–101.

Heffernan, W. 1984. Constraints in the U.S. Poultry Industry. *Research in Rural Sociology and Development* 1:237–60.

Hodson, R., and R. Kaufman. 1982. Economic Dualism: A Critical Review. *American Sociological Review* 47:727–39.

Hentoff, N. 1994. New Drives Revive Organized Labor. *Rocky Mountain News,* May 15.

James, B., and M. Ludwig. 1994. Funding Latin America. *U.S./Latin Trade* 2(4):52–62.

Jimenez, M. 1992. War in the Borderlands. *Report on the Americas* 26:29–33.

Johnson, H. 1994. *Divided We Fall.* New York: Norton.

Jones, D. 1993. The Culture of Achievement Among the Poor. *Critique of Anthropology* 13:247–66.

Judis, J. 1994. Can Labor Come Back? *New Republic* 140(4):25–29.

Kay, S. 1992. Globe-Trotters: American Meat Companies Increase Their Foreign Presence as Exports Rise. *Beef Today,* February:37–38.

Knox, D. 1994. 109 Nations Sign World Trade Pact. *Rocky Mountain News,* April 16.

Kornbluh, J. 1969. The Industrial Workers of the World. In G. M. Smith, *Joe Hill,* Salt Lake City: University of Utah Press, pp. 1–14.

Leib, J. 1993a. Union Wins Close Monfort Plant Vote. *Denver Post,* April 30.

———. 1993b. In Labor's Corner. *Denver Post Magazine,* September 5:10–14.

Lenin, V. I. 1939. *Imperialism.* New York: International Publishers. [First published in 1917.]

Lieberson, S. 1981. *A Piece of the Pie: Blacks and White Immigrants Since 1880.* Berkeley: University of California Press.

Loth, R. 1994. Tales of Despair: Disunity Across U.S. *Rocky Mountain News,* May 17.

MacDonald, D. 1993. High Plains Revival: Oklahoma Panhandle Welcomes Seaboard Corporation's Expansion. *Hogs Today,* March:12–13.

MacLeod, J. 1987. *Ain't No Makin' It: Leveled Aspirations in a Low-Income Neighborhood.* Boulder: Westview.

Marx, K., and F. Engels. 1932. *The Communist Manifesto.* New York: International Press. [First published in 1848.]

Massey, D. 1987. Understanding Mexican Migration to the U.S. *American Journal of Sociology* 92:1372–403.

Massey, D. S., R. Alarcon, J. Durand, and H. Gonzalez. 1988. *Return to Aztlan: The Social Process of International Migration from Western Mexico.* Berkeley: University of California Press.

Mead, W. 1994. Agreement Is Changing Many Mexicans' Way of Life. *Denver Post,* May 9.

Meillassoux, C. 1981. *Maidens, Meals and Money.* Cambridge: Cambridge University Press.

Miles, J. 1994. A Bold Proposal on Immigration. *Atlantic Monthly* 273(6):32–45.

Mills, C. W. 1963. The Labor Leaders and the Power Elite. In *Power, Politics and People.* New York: Ballantine, pp. 97–109.

Mines, R., B. Boccalandro, and S. Gabbard. 1992. The Latinization of U.S. Farm Labor. *Report on the Americas* 26:42–46.

Newman, K. 1988. *Falling from Grace: The Experience of Downward Mobility in the American Middle Class.* New York: Free Press.

Novek, J. 1989. Peripheralizing Core Labor Markets? The Case of Canadian Meat Packing Work. *Employment and Society* 3:157–77.

Papademetriou, D., and R. Bach. 1989. *The Effects of Immigration on the U.S. Economy and Labor Market.* Bureau of International Labor Affairs. U.S. Department of Labor. Washington, D.C.: U.S. Government Printing Office.

Perlman, J. 1976. *The Myth of Marginality: Urban Poverty and Politics in Rio de Janeiro.* Berkeley: University of California Press.

Portes, A., and A. Stepick. 1985. Unwelcome Immigrants. *American Sociological Review* 50:493–514.

Reich, R. 1983. *The Next American Frontier: A Provocative Program for Economic Renewal.* New York: Times Books.

Rhodes, V. J. 1993. *Cooperatives' Role in Hog Contract Production.* Agricultural Cooperative Service. ACS Research Report no. 116. Washington, D.C.: U.S. Department of Agriculture.

Robinson, R. 1994. Agriculture Finds Pact Dual-Edged. *Denver Post,* May 9.

Sassen, S. 1992. Why Migration? *Report on the Americas* 26:14–19.

Schumpeter, J. 1955. *Two Essays by Joseph Schumpeter: Imperialism and Social Classes.* New York: Meridian Books.

Smith, G. M. 1969. *Joe Hill.* Salt Lake City: University of Utah Press.

Stull, D. D. 1994. Knock 'em Dead: Work on the Killfloor of a Modern Beefpacking Plant. In *Newcomers in the Workplace: Immigrants and the Restructuring of the U.S. Economy,* edited by L. Lamphere, A. Stepick, and G. Grenier. Philadelphia: Temple University Press, pp. 44–77.

Stull, D. D., M. J. Broadway, and K. C. Erickson. 1992. The Price of a Good Steak: Beef Packing and Its Consequences for Garden City, Kansas. In *Structuring Diversity: Ethnographic Perspectives on the New Immigration,* edited by L. Lamphere. Chicago: University of Chicago Press, pp. 35–64.

Sullivan, T. 1985. Review Essay: A Supply Side View of the Melting Pot. *American Journal of Sociology* 88:590–95.

———. 1986. Stratification of the Chicano Labor Market under Conditions of Continuing Mexican Immigration. In *Mexican Immigrants and Mexican Americans,* edited by H. Browning and R. de la Garza. Austin: University of Texas Press, pp. 55–73.

Tolbert, C., P. Horan, and E. M. Beck. 1980. The Structure of Economic Segmentation. *American Journal of Sociology* 85:1095–116.

Unruh, T. 1994. Plans Eye U.S. 83. *Garden City Telegram,* January 13.

Wilson, L. 1993. Residents Protest Hogs, First Animals Arrive. *Guymon Daily Herald,* April 7.

Wilson, W. J. 1987. *The Truly Disadvantaged: The Inner City, the Underclass, and Public Policy.* Chicago: University of Chicago Press.

Index